Sisyphus No More

Sisyphus No More

The Case for Prison Education

Roger C. Byrd and Harvey McCloud

ROWMAN & LITTLEFIELD
Lanham • Boulder • New York • London

Published by Rowman & Littlefield
An imprint of The Rowman & Littlefield Publishing Group, Inc.
4501 Forbes Boulevard, Suite 200, Lanham, Maryland 20706
www.rowman.com

6 Tinworth Street, London SE11 5AL, United Kingdom

British Library Cataloguing in Publication Information Available

Library of Congress Cataloging-in-Publication Data

Library of Congress Control Number: 2020946484
ISBN 978-1-5381-3660-7 (cloth)
ISBN 978-1-5381-8380-9 (pbk)
ISBN 978-1-5381-3661-4 (electronic)

This book is dedicated, with love, to each of our wives, April and Teresa. Thank you both for your constant loving support throughout this project.

Contents

Preface

For most Americans, the human side of incarceration is hidden behind the razor-wired walls of state and federal prisons typically built in relatively isolated areas. There, nearly 1.5 million prisoners pass lives of extreme regimentation in brutally unforgiving prison environments. Some of these people have committed heinous crimes for which they will never again wake to a free day. The great majority, however, after at least a year of dreary sameness and often many more, finally will finish serving their sentence or be released on parole. They then will walk away from the walls and razor wire to try to make their way in society. Though impending release is a reason for a prisoner to celebrate, it also can be a source of anxiety and fear. How will he be able to handle merging into the world outside? How will he earn a living? Where will she live? How will he be able to pay the restitution fees or child support that may be demanded as a condition of parole?

The prisoners about to be released who are most troubled by such questions may be those who are educationally unprepared for reintegration into society. These are the multitude of incarcerated men and women whose education before and within prison was grievously inadequate. This vast group includes hundreds of thousands who have no postsecondary education or even a high school degree or GED certificate, individuals who often have no marketable skills and may even lack the ability to read and complete a job application. For these people especially, release to the outside world can present an enormous challenge.

What makes the challenge even more formidable is that as they make their entrance into the world outside, released prisoners already have one big strike against them—being a convicted felon. That fact alone is enough to close many doors that could lead to gainful employment and decent housing. Add lack of education to the mix, and the challenge becomes huge. In an increasingly technological society, obtaining a good job requires proficiency in verbal, math, and reasoning skills. Job seekers lacking such competencies typically are condemned to the lowest-paying, most humble employment, offering nothing more than subsistence pay with minimal chance of advancement. Yet, poorly educated former prisoners are unlikely to have funds or opportunity to pursue additional education that might enable them to attain a higher-paying job.

The dismal result for those released from confinement with deficient education is that their dream of freedom may quickly become a realization that they have been sentenced to a new type of confinement. They observe fellow citizens enjoying nice homes, new cars, and money to spend on entertainment and vacations and conclude that these are rewards they will never have if they stay within legal boundaries. Therefore, it is not surprising for many released prisoners to open themselves to illegitimate ways to increase their income, whether through theft, drug trafficking, or some other criminal enterprise. And, not surprising, many soon find their way back to the razor-wired walls.

Recidivism—defined in this book as the reincarceration of released prisoners—is alarmingly high in the U.S. justice system. The five-year recidivism rate for individuals released from state prisons—the percent rearrested and sent back to confinement within five years of their release—was found by the U.S. Bureau of Justice to be more than 55 percent.[1] This excessive rate of reincarceration adds greatly to overcrowded prison populations and the cost of housing them, a per-prisoner average of more than $33,000 annually in state prisons in 2015[2] and more than $36,000 per year in federal prisons in 2017.[3]

The phenomenon of recidivism is a reminder of the story of Sisyphus, a mythological Greek king. When Sisyphus violated the rules of the Greek gods, they punished him by forcing him to push a large boulder up a tall hill. When he reached the top, he had to let the boulder roll back down; he was then forced to push it back up again. He was required to undergo this punishment for eternity. The similarity of the fate of Sisyphus to the situation of today's prisoners is that their punishment does not end when they have completed their mandated time in prison. After release, they typically face onerous challenges in their efforts to reintegrate into a largely unwelcoming society. Their ongoing punishment, in the form of social and employment constraints, financial obligations, collateral consequences, and lost opportunities, is for a lifetime. And a grievous consequence of society's continuing sanctions of released prisoners is an increased likelihood of making their way back to prison walls.

Of course, multiple factors determine whether a released prisoner does or does not recidivate. Notwithstanding, it is our contention that one of the main factors affecting the likelihood of returning to prison is the individual's educational level. While providing some education to prisoners is a virtually universal activity in both public and private U.S. correctional institutions, these programs typically are seriously limited in their range and effectiveness, largely due to lack of funds. As a result, many prisoners discharged into the larger society have meager intellectual tools with which to make their way.

In this book, we make the case for federal and state governments to invest substantially increased funds in prison education programs. We present our argument on psychological, sociological, ethical, and financial grounds. Admittedly, increasing prison-based education will not, on its own, empty our prisons; but we hold that it will reduce prison populations significantly and thereby benefit society in important ways. Today, many government bodies and much of our society are waking to the necessity of reducing a bloated prison population that has grown immensely in the past several decades. We hold that one of the most effective ways to promote that reduction is to increase targeted prison education programs substantially, providing former prisoners tools to help them overcome obstacles and find success as they rejoin law-abiding society.

The necessity for more and better prison education goes hand in hand with the need for a new sensibility in the nation's attitude toward those who have been caught up in the criminal justice system and sent to prison. The first part of this new sensibility is to realize that what we should hope for and work toward is not the social exclusion of former prisoners that they typically encounter today. That does no good for anyone. And for that reason, it makes no sense. What does make sense—not only for the individuals themselves, but also for their families and communities and for society as a whole—is the full reintegration of former prisoners into free society. As we suggested above and will detail in later chapters, in many ways these people are given the cold shoulder and made into second-class citizens after their release. This is a major factor that sets many of them on the road to becoming a modern-day Sisyphus, while promoting recidivism.

A second part of the new sensibility is the need to humanize those who are incarcerated. They are almost 1.5 million strong, but because they are out of sight behind prison walls, it is all too easy for their individuality to become lost in the eyes of society. However, former Supreme Court Justice Anthony Kennedy had eyes to see. In his 2003 address to the American Bar Association, after citing some justifications for criminal punishment, he added the words, "Still, the prisoner is a person; still, he or she is part of the family of humankind."[4] He then spoke of ways to increase the humanity and actual justice in the criminal justice system.

We wholly agree with Justice Kennedy's words. Each of the hundreds of thousands of people in our prisons today is a unique individual. And despite past mistakes, each should be respected as an individual. What is more, great numbers of these people have abundant untapped potential to become out-standing citizens who will benefit society through their endeavors. Education is the quintessential way to unlock that potential. It is right not only for them but for our entire society. In subsequent chapters, we will do our best to uphold that claim in a number of ways.

The book is divided into two main parts.

In part I, we describe the situation we are currently in—the prisons, the prisoners, the egregious prices paid for incarceration by prisoners, their fami-lies, and communities, and the state of prison education today.

In part II, we present a four-pronged argument for providing much-ex-panded educational opportunities to our prisoners. These are powerful psychological, sociological, ethical, and financial reasons for delivering more and better education to the vast number of people who today are housed behind razored walls, hoping that when they are released, they will be able to reunite successfully with free society.

In part II, we also describe some innovative ways that governments and nongovernment organizations, especially academic ones, are providing edu-cation to our prisoners. Our main message, however, is that it is time for the federal and state governments to put much more thought, planning, and mon-ey into prison education than currently is allocated. As you will learn here, the clear sense is that coming up with the money should be the easiest part, given a main argument that runs throughout the book:

- Educating prisoners reduces recidivism.
- Reduced recidivism means fewer prisoners in our prisons and a barrel of money saved.
- The money saved is much more than the added money spent on prison education.
- This excess money then can be used better for important things such as infrastructure projects and reduced taxes.

In this book, we will do our best to put some big teeth into that overall argument.

NOTES

1. U.S. Department of Justice, Bureau of Justice Statistics, *Recidivism of Prisoners Re-leased in 30 States in 2005: Patterns from 2005 to 2010*, by Matthew R. Durose, Alexia D. Cooper, and Howard N. Snyder, Special Report NCJ244205 (Washington, DC, April 2014), 1, https://www.bjs.gov/content/pub/pdf/rprts05p0510.pdf.

2. Chris Mai and Ram Subramanian, *The Price of Prisons: Examining State Spending Trends, 2010–2015* (New York: Vera Institute of Justice, May 2017), 7, https://www.vera.org/downloads/publications/the-price-of-prisons-2015-state-spending-trends.pdf.

3. U.S. Federal Bureau of Prisons, Notice, "Annual Determination of Average Cost of Incarceration," *Federal Register* 83, no. 83 (April 30, 2018): 18863, https://www.govinfo.gov/content/pkg/FR-2018-04-30/pdf/2018-09062.pdf.

4. Anthony M. Kennedy, "Speech Delivered by Justice Anthony M. Kennedy at the American Bar Association Annual Meeting, August 9, 2003," *Federal Sentencing Reporter* 16, no. 2 (December 2003): 127, https://doi.org/10.1525/fsr.2003.16.2.126.

Part I

Understanding the Situation

Chapter One

Getting Our Bearings

The degree of civilization in a society can be judged by entering its prisons.
—Fyodor Dostoevsky

OVERVIEW OF CORRECTIONS IN THE UNITED STATES

The U.S. corrections system is immense. Its chief divisions are local jails; federal, state, and private prisons; and parole and probation operations. The system also includes various other holding facilities, including juvenile jails, territorial prisons, Indian country jails, and military holding installations. Adult jails, one of the primary means of incarceration, generally are operated by local governments to confine individuals for relatively short terms. These include men and women accused of a crime and awaiting trial, offenders convicted of a crime but not yet sentenced, individuals accused of immigration violations, and detained juveniles. In some states, jails also may house people who have been sentenced to incarceration for less than a year.

In this book, we do not focus on jails but, rather, on the largest segment of the U.S. incarceration system—state, federal, and private prisons—and on the current status of prison education and how education can and should be a key part of an overall strategy designed to reduce prison populations. We deal only minimally with jails, though the fact that we restrict ourselves mainly to prisons and prison education should not be seen as our believing that educating the adults and juveniles held in our nation's jails is not an important matter in itself. How could it not be important, given that jails are the main pipeline that feeds our prisons and that, according to the U.S. Bureau of Justice Statistics for 2017, more than 745,200 individuals were being held in local jails at midyear?[1]

In fact, issues we mention and suggestions we make regarding prison education may apply with only minimal or no changes to the education of people held in jails. However, for the sake of a unified treatment and to avoid an explosion of our page count, we focus on prisons, those incarcerated there, and prison education. (Note that when we speak of *prison education*, we are referring to both academic education and career technical education—CTE. The former includes basic education, classes at the secondary level such as GED preparation, and postsecondary education. The latter comprises what often is called vocational or occupational education or training.)

The U.S. prison system is where the great majority of offenders sentenced to more than one year of incarceration are confined. Most U.S. prisons are of two main types: federal and state. The federal system is managed, naturally, by the federal government and consists of 122 prisons located in a number of states, including one in Puerto Rico. The purpose of federal prisons is to incarcerate offenders convicted of a wide range of violations of federal statutes. Examples include white-collar crime, cybercrime, terrorist acts, mail fraud, immigration violations, child pornography, kidnapping, aircraft hijacking, drug crimes involving the distribution of illegal drugs across state or national borders, and RICO racketeering laws. Federal prisons hold approximately 10 to 11 percent of the total prison population in the United States, with another 2 to 3 percent of the total being federal violators held in privately managed prisons and community-based confinement facilities.

Federal institutions occur at five security levels, ranging from minimum (federal prison camps), through low, medium, and maximum security, as well as administrative security institutions with special missions such as housing seriously physically or mentally ill prisoners, arrested individuals pretrial, or offenders considered to be extremely dangerous or violent. Administrative security prisons usually are capable of housing those who are incarcerated at any of the other security levels.[2] Department of Justice data for 2016 show that in federal institutions, the most prevalent reason for incarceration was a drug offense (especially drug trafficking), at 47.5 percent. Public order (including immigration and weapons violations), violent, and property crimes (including fraud) totaled 38.2, 7.7, and 6.1 percent, respectively.[3]

Most U.S. prisoners are incarcerated in more than seventeen hundred state prisons, which confine offenders sentenced for violating state or local laws. Residents include those convicted of violent crimes (mainly murder and nonnegligent homicide, rape, robbery, and aggravated assault); property crimes (including burglary, larceny, and motor vehicle theft); public order crimes (such as driving under the influence of alcohol or drugs, weapons violations, prostitution, and disorderly conduct); and possession, distribution, or manufacture of illegal substances. In 2017, the state prison population in the fifty states ranged from fewer than 2,000 individuals each in North Dakota and Vermont to more than 160,000 in Texas.[4] Like the federal government, states generally classify prisoners as needing different levels of security and may include minimum, medium, and maximum security institutions. For state prisons in 2016, the predominant type of offense committed was violent crimes (54.5 percent); property crimes, drug offenses, and public order crimes were at 18.0, 15.2, and 11.6 percent, respectively.[5]

Private prisons are a third type of correctional institution. Both the federal and some state governments contract with private corporations that confine federal and state violators in for-profit institutions for a fee. The number of prisoners[6] incarcerated in private prisons has been declining in recent years from its peak of 137,200 in 2012. As of 2017, nearly 122,000 prisoners, approximately 8.2 percent of the total prison population, were held in private prisons, including individuals from twenty-eight states and the federal system. Of the states that contracted with private corporations to manage prisoners, New Mexico and Montana housed 50 and 38 percent, respectively, of their incarcerated population in private facilities; fifteen states confined 10 percent or fewer of their prisoners in privately controlled prisons.[7]

THE DISMAL FIGURES

More important than the various types of prisons are who and how many are confined in these institutions. To start addressing these questions, we can consider the following sum: the total of all of the men, women, and children who resided within the city limits of Atlanta, Pittsburgh, Minneapolis, and St. Louis at the time of the last nationwide census. Together, these American cities contain hundreds of thousands of homes and businesses large and small, with people everywhere you go. So, the number we're thinking of likely is a big one. And it is, for the combined adult population of those four cities in 2010 was more than 1,420,000 people.

Now consider that the number of residents in those cities in 2010 was less than the number of people locked up in our nation's prisons today, in early 2020, when nearly 1.5 million individuals are living behind the razor wire. It is an enormous sum. And, as if the figure itself weren't disconcerting enough, it becomes even more so when we realize that in 1978, just a little more than forty years ago, the number of state and federal prisoners sentenced to more than one year of incarceration was under 300,000, about one-fifth of today's prison population.

It was at about that time, in the late 1970s, that the number of prisoners in U.S. state and federal correctional institutions began to grow at an alarming pace. In the 1980s and 1990s, the prison population burgeoned at tremendous annual rates until it began to slow in the early 2000s. Finally, in 2009, the number incarcerated peaked at 1,615,487.[8] This constituted an increase in people sentenced to prison of more than 500 percent in thirty years. Census Bureau figures show the U.S. population rose by only 36 percent during the same period; the increase in prisoners outstripped the growth in the overall population fourteenfold.

What caused such a drastic explosion in the U.S. prison population? A crime spree of gargantuan proportions? Not as evidenced by the figures. Though the 1980s saw an uptick in violent crimes, the violent crime rate began to decrease in 1992 until it fell below the 1978 level in 2002, and it has fallen substantially further in years since then. A similar pattern in rates occurred for property crimes. Since 1993, the property crime rate has been on a downward trend, and from 1995 onward it has been below 1977 levels. [9] Clearly, an increase in violent and property crime rates does not explain the huge increase in the prison population since 1978.

THE TOUGH-ON-CRIME MENTALITY

But how about drug offenses, the violation of laws against the manufacture, distribution, and possession of illegal substances? Here we have at least part of an explanation for the meteoric rise in prison incarceration rates over the past few decades. In regard to drug trafficking and possession, the data show that drug arrests almost doubled from 1980 to 1990, rose another 45 percent in the next decade, and continued to grow until they reached a peak of almost 1.9 million in 2006. [10] These increases in drug arrests largely have been the upshot of the famed "War on Drugs," a term Richard Nixon first used in the early 1970s and given teeth by later administrations as Congress passed several acts meant to deal harshly with what was seen as a drug culture out of control.

The so-called War on Drugs went hand in hand with a new national "tough-on-crime" approach to criminality that resulted in the passage of a slew of new laws increasing the severity and inflexibility of sentencing, including the introduction of three-strikes laws in many states and longer mandatory prison sentences. Arguably facilitated and encouraged by the media, a kind of fever against criminality gripped a wide swath of the electorate, marked by a heightened fear of crime and criminals and an inclination toward severe retribution—making lawbreakers pay a stiff price for their activities—perspectives that continued even after violent and property crime rates began to fall.

This change in the public's attitude was reflected in the results of two polls, taken thirteen years apart, asking about the primary purpose of prison. The first poll, administered by the Roper Center for Public Opinion Research from March 29 to April 5, 1980, found that more than half (53 percent) of respondents believed that the primary purpose of prison was to rehabilitate, whereas fewer than one-third (32 percent) believed that the primary purpose was to punish. By 1993, a poll taken by the *Los Angeles Times* found that only a quarter (25 percent) of respondents believed the primary purpose of prisons was to rehabilitate, whereas well over half (61 percent) believed the main purpose of prisons was to punish offenders.[11]

A LITTLE LIGHT, BUT STILL DISMAL

In recent years, the public gradually has returned to less severe views about the purpose of prisons and less harsh attitudes toward punishing prisoners.[12] At the same time, after 2009, the number of state and federal prisoners slowly began to decline. This occurred in large part because in the late 1990s and the early years of the new century, leaders in the federal and some state governments began to realize that the high rate of incarceration was untenable. Correctional costs exceeding $80 billion annually and severe overcrowding in prisons had pushed these governments to find ways to reduce the number of incarcerated people. The result was several sentencing reforms and programs that led to a gradual slowing of the overall incarceration rate. In time, other states followed suit, though still others did little to change their policies and practices regarding incarceration. The overall result is that during the past decade, the rapid increase in prison populations has stalled, even reversed to some degree.

And yet, the number of incarcerated individuals in the United States remains extremely high in comparison to other countries. The latest figures show that the U.S. prison incarceration rate for 2018 is about 450 per one hundred thousand population,[13] a figure much higher than for any other industrialized nation. For instance, the 2019 rates per one hundred thousand for England and Wales and for Germany were 140 and 77, respectively.[14] Comparing these numbers is even more telling when we learn that the U.S. rate of 450 included only sentenced prison occupants, while the rates for the UK and Germany included both sentenced prisoners and individuals who were held prior to being tried in a court of law. In other comparisons with industrialized nations, the U.S. comes out as a solid number one in the very dubious statistic of incarceration rates.

RECIDIVISM

Two obvious purposes of incarcerating individuals are to punish them for having broken the law and to incapacitate them—that is, to prevent them from committing further crimes out in the public world. Both the punishment and incapacitation purposes are clearly well fulfilled as long as the person is behind prison walls. When he is released from confinement, the incapacitation stops cold, but not the punishment. The purpose of punishing the person for having broken the law continues to be fulfilled to a substantial extent, as released prisoners must drag the millstone of having "done time" throughout their lives. This is the Sisyphus effect: for people who have been incarcerated in the past, their penalty to society never finally is paid.

A third reason given for incarcerating individuals is to deter them from committing future crimes. In prison, supposedly they learn what will happen to them if they get caught committing crimes in the future and are found guilty—more years of spending every day in a tiny cell, being ordered what to do by corrections officers, trying to protect their backs from other prisoners, and being unable to spend time with their family and friends on the outside. Who would want that? Nobody, right? So, it may seem reasonable that being sent to prison for a first crime should serve as a superb deterrent to committing any future crimes.

But it is not so. As we will report in some detail in a later chapter, research suggests that spending time in prison has little or no future deterrent effect. In fact, imprisonment for some may exert a contrary outcome as they live and converse with other prisoners, learn new methods and techniques for committing crimes with less chance for apprehension, or become aware of criminal elements in the world outside prison and how to contact them upon release. In a 2016 report, the National Institute of Justice (NIJ), an arm of the U.S. Department of Justice, noted that research evidence indicates that "sending an individual convicted of a crime to prison isn't a very effective way to deter crime."[15]

Nor is the severity of the punishment effective in reducing future crime, a conclusion that calls into question the efficacy of three-strikes laws and the imposition of severe minimum sentences. According to the NIJ, which summarizes the conclusions of a scholarly paper by Daniel Nagin[16] that appeared in the journal *Crime and Justice*, the most effective deterrent to crime is the potential offender's perception of the probability of being caught, which has a much greater preventive effect than having been previously punished or the severity of that punishment. Consequently, increasing police patrols and other police presence in an area, which raises the likelihood that an offender will be apprehended, is a much better deterrent to a former prisoner engaging in new criminal activity than the fact that she previously was incarcerated.

Statistics on recidivism appear to support the conclusion that in itself, incarceration does little to prevent future criminal activity. A study by the Bureau of Justice Statistics that examined more than four hundred thousand individuals in thirty states after their release from prison in 2005 found that of twenty-three states reporting, 49.7 percent of released prisoners were returned to incarceration within three years for a new crime or a parole violation, and 55.1 percent were returned within five years.[17]

These figures about recidivism rates are sobering. With more than 650,000 prisoners released from our correctional system every year,[18] the cited statistics suggest that more than 320,000 of them will be sent back to incarceration within three years, and 35,000 more within another two years. These returned offenders add greatly to the overcrowding that plagues our nation's prisons, as well as to the very substantial direct and indirect financial costs of incarceration, the topic of chapter 3.

AT A CROSSROADS

As we mentioned above, since the turn of the new century, various governmental authorities have begun to make promising changes in incarceration policies. Innovative programs include drug courts that involve mandatory substance abuse treatment and provide alternatives to incarceration. Mental health courts offer opportunities for mental health treatment in lieu of being sent to prison. Increased use of community corrections programs, usually overseen by a probation department, restrict the activities of offenders while keeping them outside prison walls. Various changes in laws, to some extent, reverse the tough-on-crime approach that helped lead to the glut in the prison population. These include modifications of three-strikes laws and support by the Supreme Court of judges' use of discretion in imposing sentences that deviate from federal sentencing guidelines if the judge determines that a lighter sentence is more appropriate.[19]

The mood of the public also has changed significantly, from the rigid tough-on-crime mentality to a growing appreciation that the U.S. correctional system needs reform. These changes are reflected in the results of a random telephone survey of 1,003 individuals of various political leanings that the Benenson Strategy Group conducted in October 2017. To the question of whether the goal of preventing released prisoners from committing further crimes would be reached more effectively by making prison as hard and unpleasant as possible so releasees are afraid of going back or by providing rehabilitation services and training so released individuals can reenter society and become productive citizens, 72 percent of the respondents indicated that the latter strategy would be more effective. When asked whether they agreed that more incarcerated people, including those convicted of serious crimes who show they can be rehabilitated, should be eligible for reduced sentences if they complete education, job training, drug treatment, or rehabilitation programs, 67 percent agreed, and only 29 percent disagreed.[20] The survey results reveal a notable change in public attitude in the twenty-four years that have passed since the 1993 survey whose results we previously reported.

Textbox 1.1: President George W. Bush, State of the Union Address, 2004

This year, some 600,000 inmates will be released from prison back into society. We know from long experience that if they can't find work, or a home, or help, they are much more likely to commit more crimes and return to prison. . . . America is the land of the second chance, and when the gates of the prison open, the path ahead should lead to a better life.

These changes strongly suggest that we are at an important crossroads with regard to the U.S. correctional system. The realization is growing that the course we have been on, resulting in mass incarceration, is untenable. A few steps already taken are leading us in a new direction that is not only smarter and more practical, but also more humane and more in line with American values of justice. It is certain that we all treasure safety for our families and ourselves and want secure homes and safe streets. At the same time, it is becoming clear that we also want a system of justice that is not only fair and judicious, but that also realizes the humanity of those who are confined in our prisons. The idea of incarceration as an opportunity for rehabilitation has resurfaced in our society and is becoming stronger. Being smart about corrections means doing our best to prepare prisoners for reentry into society, as President George W. Bush noted in his 2004 State of the Union address (see textbox 1.1).[21]

Among the various means for performing that function, providing education to those who are incarcerated is, we believe, one of the most promising. As we will show in the following pages, it is also a method that offers a great deal of bang for the buck, not only for the incarcerated person, but for the society he eventually will reenter.

NOTES

1. U.S. Department of Justice, Bureau of Justice Statistics, *Jail Inmates in 2017*, by Zhen Zeng, Bulletin NCJ 251774 (Washington, DC, April 2019), table 1, https://www.bjs.gov/content/pub/pdf/ji17.pdf.

2. Federal Bureau of Prisons, *Sleep Soundly. We'll Be up All Night*, accessed February 21, 2020, https://www.bop.gov/about/facilities/federal_prisons.jsp.

3. U.S. Department of Justice, Bureau of Justice Statistics, *Prisoners in 2016*, by E. Ann Carson, Bulletin NCJ 251149 (August 7, 2018), table 14, https://www.bjs.gov/content/pub/pdf/p16.pdf.

4. Jacob Kang-Brown, Eital Schattner-Elmaleh, and Oliver Hines, *People in Prison in 2018* (New York: Vera Institute of Justice, April 2019), Prison Population, https://www.vera.org/downloads/publications/people-in-prison-in-2018-updated.pdf.

5. *Prisoners in 2016*, table 12.

6. Several terms are commonly used to refer to incarcerated people. Two of these, "convict" and "inmate," may be viewed as having unwanted connotations that go beyond the idea of being incarcerated. In our view, the term "prisoner" carries a minimum of extra linguistic baggage and so is a primary term we use to refer to incarcerated people. We also use "individuals," "people," and "returning citizens," because they are all of these.

7. The Sentencing Project, *Private Prisons in the United States* (October 2019), table 1, https://www.sentencingproject.org/wp-content/uploads/2017/08/Private-Prisons-in-the-United-States.pdf.

8. *Prisoners in 2016*, table 1.

9. Federal Bureau of Investigation Uniform Crime Reporting Program, UCR Tool, years 1997–2014, accessed January 27, 2020, https://www.ucrdatatool.gov/; also *2016 Crime in the United States*, table 1, accessed January 28, 2020, https://ucr.fbi.gov/crime-in-the-u.s/2016/crime-in-the-u.s.-2016/topic-pages/tables/table-1.

10. U.S. Department of Justice, Bureau of Justice Statistics, *Drugs and Crime Facts*, Drug abuse violation arrests, 1982–2007, accessed February 23, 2020, https://www.bjs.gov/content/dcf/enforce.cfm.

11. Arit John, "A Timeline of the Rise and Fall of 'Tough on Crime' Drug Sentencing," *The Atlantic*, April 22, 2014, https://www.theatlantic.com/politics/archive/2014/04/a-timeline-of-the-rise-and-fall-of-tough-on-crime-drug-sentencing/360983/.

12. American Civil Liberties Union, *91 Percent of Americans Support Criminal Justice Reform, ACLU Polling Finds*, November 16, 2017, https://www.aclu.org/news/91-percent-americans-support-criminal-justice-reform-aclu-polling-finds.

13. Kang-Brown, Schattner-Elmaleh, and Hines, *People in Prison in 2018*, prison incarceration rate.

14. World Prison Brief, *Data: Europe* (London: World Prison Brief, 2020), accessed February 23, 2020, http://www.prisonstudies.org/world-prison-brief-data.

15. National Institute of Justice, *Five Things about Justice* (June 5, 2016), https://nij.gov/five-things/pages/deterrence.aspx#addenda.

16. Daniel S. Nagin, "Deterrence in the Twenty-first Century," *Crime and Justice* 42, no. 1 (2013): 199–263, doi: 10.1086/670398.

17. U.S. Department of Justice, Bureau of Justice Statistics, *Recidivism of Prisoners Released in 30 States in 2005: Patterns from 2005 to 2010*, by Matthew R. Durose, Alexia D. Cooper, and Howard N. Snyder, Special Report NCJ244205 (April 2014), 1, February 23, 2020, https://www.bjs.gov/content/pub/pdf/rprts05p0510.pdf.

18. U.S. Department of Justice, *Prisoners and Prisoner Re-entry*, introduction, accessed May 25, 2020, https://www.justice.gov/archive/fbci/progmenu_reentry.html.

19. Mona Lynch, "Legal Change and Sentencing Norms in Federal Court: An Examination of the Impact of the *Booker, Gall,* and *Kimbrough* Decisions," paper presented to the American Society of Criminology Annual Meeting, Washington, DC, November 16–19, 2011.

20. American Civil Liberties Union, *Smart Justice Campaign Polling on Americans' Attitudes on Criminal Justice*, accessed February 23, 2020, https://www.aclu.org/report/smart-justice-campaign-polling-americans-attitudes-criminal-justice.

21. George W. Bush, State of the Union Address, January 20, 2004, *Washington Post*, accessed May 25, 2020, https://www.washingtonpost.com/wp-srv/politics/transcripts/bush-text_012004.html.

Chapter Two

Who's in Prison?

Who are the people who experience, firsthand, the force of the criminal justice system by being incarcerated? An overall demographic description of individuals being held in state and federal prisons can help us comprehend where we are today in our criminal justice system and may nurture insights about where we should be in the future.

Before detailing these demographics, we want to emphasize strongly that though it is valuable to obtain a bird's-eye view of the prison population, we should not allow that view to obscure the fundamental reality that each prisoner is an individual human being with a singular personality, history, weaknesses, strengths, and outlooks. We profess that we never really begin to understand who any prisoner is without sitting down and talking at length with him. Each one is a unique person whose humanity and individuality always should be acknowledged and respected. Never forgetting that, let us focus on some of the broad characteristics of this large assembly of people who are forced into confinement, often for years.

LIFE BEFORE PRISON

The prison population represents the full range of socioeconomic levels, as well as educational and professional achievements. However, the majority of prisoners emerge from the lower echelons of the socioeconomic and educational spectrum. These individuals include many men and women of color who grew up in poverty in largely segregated urban areas. They also include many people of all ethnicities who come from other economically deprived areas, such as those who grew up in poorer rural areas and Native Americans who spent their childhood on impoverished reservations. What is common to all such environments is that jobs typically are scarce, and those that exist

13

usually pay low wages. In urban areas, manufacturing jobs that once were common have disappeared and numerous other employers long since have relocated to the suburbs, while in many rural areas and reservations, jobs always have been scarce. The result is that these areas embody a lack of economic opportunity that keeps many families in poverty, with limited money to pay for advantages and opportunities for their children. Benefits that many other families enjoy, such as healthy (and often more costly) diets, educational toys, computers, musical instruments, and vacations to allow children to visit new locales and have novel experiences are outside the monetary grasp of these families. As the children become young people entering adulthood, the dearth of jobs available in the area continues to exact a heavy economic toll and finally creates a relative vacuum of activity and opportunity that promotes the rise and proliferation of criminal activity.

As a consequence of lack of economic opportunity, the preincarceration income of prisoners tends to be very low, as shown by comparing the average annual earnings of incarcerated men and women before they were sent to prison to the earnings of nonincarcerated men and women of the same age. Based on 2004 Department of Justice survey data (the most recent government statistics available on preincarceration earnings), the average annual income of men and women prisoners ages twenty-seven to forty-two before they entered prison was 41 percent less than for nonprisoners in the same age range, $19,650 versus $32,505 (both amounts in 2014 dollars). The discrepancy was greatest for imprisoned men, whose preincarceration annual income was 52 percent less than that of nonincarcerated men, and especially for white males in prison, who had 54 percent less income than nonincarcerated white males. Among imprisoned females, African American women fared the worst comparatively, with 47 percent less preincarceration income relative to nonimprisoned African American women.[1]

A more recent study of prisoner earnings suggests that preincarceration income of prisoners may have deteriorated further in recent years. Using Internal Revenue Service data, the researchers found that among prisoners eighteen to sixty-four years of age who were in prison for at least one year from 2009 to 2013, at most only about 50 percent had reported earnings in any of the eight years before incarceration, with their greatest annual income in any one year being less than $14,500. Postincarceration annual income decreased even further, with median annual earnings two years after release being less than $11,000.[2]

According to the same study, the differences in incarceration rates at discrete income levels indicate that the majority of the prison population consists of people who come from low-income and often single-parent families. The researchers found that approximately 15 percent of the individuals sent to prison at around age thirty came from families in the bottom 5 percent of income distribution, while almost half (47 percent) came from families in the bottom 20 percent.

They also found that family structure was a predictor of incarceration. In particular, about 46 percent of all prisoners in 2012 were men who grew up in single-parent families that had $33,000 or less annual income, although this demographic comprises less than 19 percent of the US male population. In comparison, men who grew up in a two-parent household in the top 50 percent of income accounted for only 14 percent of imprisoned men, though they represented 46 percent of the population.[3]

Lack of education is a prominent factor that adds to the poor employment prospects of many inner city and other youth. Both male and female prisoners have lower levels of educational achievement than the same genders in the nonincarcerated population. Based on the findings of the 2009 American Community Survey, approximately 40 percent of male prisoners did not complete high school, whereas the rate in the general population was only 15 percent; and 56 percent of men in the general population had attended some postsecondary institution, whereas only 23 percent of male prisoners had any education past high school. These differences in educational attainment were more marked for younger prisoners than for older. Of prisoners ages eighteen to twenty-four, 58 percent of African American males and 41 percent of white males did not complete high school. Among female prisoners, 37 percent had not completed high school in 2009, whereas only 14 percent of women in the general population did not graduate. Only 31 percent of female prisoners had any postsecondary education, whereas 57 percent of women in the general population had some college or higher education.[4]

GENDER MAKEUP IN PRISONS

It will likely come as no surprise that men outnumber women in U.S. prisons by a wide margin. What may not be so widely known is that the proportion of female to male prisoners has grown considerably over the past few decades. In 2016, more than 111,000 prisoners (7.4 percent) under the jurisdiction of federal and state authorities were women.[5] The number of incarcerated women has grown substantially over the past several decades. In 1980, fewer than 15 out of 100,000 female residents were incarcerated in the prisons of the fifty states, but by 2015 that statistic had grown by four times to approximately 60 female prisoners per 100,000 women.[6] Main factors contributing to the increase of women prisoners were the War on Drugs and the attendant proactive policing that made it more likely to apprehend women who were involved in low-level drug crimes. Also, the tough-on-crime mentality made the option of sentencing women to a community-based sanction such as probation, community service, or halfway houses less likely to be considered. In 1979 approximately one in ten imprisoned women was there for a drug-related offense, whereas twenty years later the number had grown to one in three.[7]

As with male prisoners, the number of women in prisons varies widely by state. In Arizona, more than 100 women per 100,000 were in prison in 2015; and in Oklahoma, the state with the highest proportion of incarcerated women, the number was more than 150 out of 100,000. In Maine, on the other hand, only about 20 women per 100,000 female residents were prisoners in 2015. In some states over the past decade, such as Idaho, Texas, and Wisconsin, the number of women in prison has grown while the number of imprisoned men has decreased. In various other states, such as New York, Vermont, and Massachusetts, the number of women prisoners has declined somewhat along with the count of imprisoned men.[8]

A special concern regarding the increasing proportion of women in prison is the adverse effect that women's imprisonment often has on family structure and integrity. In the next chapter, we will examine more closely the detrimental effects on children of having an incarcerated mother.

THE AGING PRISON POPULATION

Prisoners vary in ages from under 18 to well over 65 years, with the largest age group (31.5 percent) being 30 to 39 years of age and the second largest (25.8 percent) ranging from 20 to 29. The total number of prisoners ages 18 to 49 approaches 80 percent. However, the prison population is aging. During the seventeen-year period from 1999 to 2016, the number of prisoners under age 55 grew by only 3 percent, while the number of those 55 or older grew almost fourfold. This trend has continued recently. Whereas 8.2 percent of prisoners were over 55 years of age in 2010,[9] approximately 11.3 percent were older than 55 as of 2016.[10] The increase in the number of older prisoners is the result of several factors, including a rise in the arrest and conviction of older individuals even while the number for younger offenders has stayed flat or declined. A second factor is the lengthening of prison sentences, which has resulted in more prisoners growing old while incarcerated.[11]

The aging of the prison population has resulted in rising costs as the rates of disabilities and chronic illnesses among older prisoners increase. These health and medical issues may be exacerbated by poor health management, inadequate diet, and the stress caused by the threat of violence that living in a prison environment can engender. Aging and increasingly infirm prisoners include those who are elderly, chronically ill, or terminally ill. Each of these populations, which often overlap, may be in need of special accommodations, facilities, and programs, and special housing may be required for those who are seriously ill and otherwise debilitated. A major challenge for prison authorities is to finance these special services, which may add considerably to the expense of incarceration. [12]

JUVENILES IN PRISON

Despite the aging of the overall prison population, some very young prisoners have not even reached the age of majority. The incarceration of individuals as young as sixteen in adult facilities has been a reality in our correctional system for decades. Most of these youths are held in adult jails, but some are in our prisons. The numbers for both types of incarceration have declined since 1999, though juveniles still comprised about 3,500 people held in adult jails and almost 1,000 confined in prisons as of 2016. [13]

Federal laws, including the Prison Rape Elimination Act (PREA) of 2003, mandate that youths under eighteen cannot be incarcerated alongside adults in federal prisons but must be housed separately. The PREA requires that in cases where juveniles must be placed in the same facility as adults, the two contingents must be housed apart, with separate showers and public spaces. However, though the federal government has sought state compliance with the laws prohibiting youths from being incarcerated with adults, a number of states continue to place juveniles assigned to their prison facilities with the adult population. One factor complicating the situation is diverse state definitions of what constitutes being a minor and differing state laws regarding under what conditions a juvenile may be prosecuted as an adult. [14] Another factor is that even if a correctional institution attempts to comply with the PREA, a condition for doing so may be to place a juvenile in solitary confinement for all but one or two hours per day. [15]

Prison placements of juveniles with adult prisoners can result in serious harm to the youth. One detrimental consequence is that placing juveniles in isolated confinement to comply with the PREA may exacerbate preexisting mental disorders or cause new and potentially lasting mental distress. Even aside from possible adverse psychological consequences of solitary detention, the condition alone of being incarcerated with adults has been found to increase the likelihood of youthful prisoners committing suicide. [16] Another harm is that juveniles in prison have a greater likelihood than other prisoners of being raped or otherwise sexually abused, eventualities that the PREA was intended to prevent. A report by the National Prison Rape Elimination Commission noted that the percentage of juveniles who were victims of substantiated sexual violence in state prisons in 2005 was four and one-half times the percentage of state prisoners under eighteen. [17] Factors other than age that may increase juveniles' risk of being sexually victimized are being new to a facility, having a small body structure compared to other prisoners, and the alertness exercised by prison authorities.

Other harmful results of incarcerating juveniles with adults include their coming of age in a pitiless environment where the art of survival may be honed down to its basic elements: at all times be watchful of everyone, be ready to defend yourself, and make efforts to appear strong to others. The young person also has an increased probability of assimilating antisocial viewpoints and attitudes from some of the older prisoners, as well as learning lessons on how to be a more successful criminal. All of this comes at a time when the youth's brain and mind are barely developed and too easily susceptible to lessons we should not want her to learn—not only for the sake of the individual, but for the welfare of the society to which she probably will return eventually.

Efforts to reduce the number of juveniles held with adults in U.S. prisons and jails have resulted in a 60 percent reduction over the past two decades. A number of factors have helped this decline. These include scientific evidence indicating that confining youth in the typically harsh conditions of adult prisons and jails leads to damaging consequences for not only the juveniles but also for the society to which they return, widespread publication of deplorable conditions in some facilities, determined activities by youth advocates, and the passage of federal protective legislation for confined juveniles.[18]

RACIAL MAKEUP

The racial makeup of prisoners in 2016 differed considerably between sexes. African American male prisoners sentenced to more than one year in a state or federal jurisdiction prison numbered 467,000 (34.5 percent) of all male prisoners, whereas non-Latino white males totaled 391,300 (28.9 percent) and Latino males accounted for 320,300 (23.7 percent). For women, the largest racial category was non-Latino white females, who numbered 49,000 (46.4 percent) of female prisoners. African American women totaled 20,400 (19.3 percent), and Latino women accounted for 19,300 (18.3 percent) of the total. Other racial and ethnic groups, accounting for 12.9 percent of male prisoners and 16.1 percent of female prisoners, included American Indians and Alaska Natives, Asian Americans, Native Hawaiians, other Pacific Islanders, and prisoners of two or more races.[19]

Both African American and Latino prisoners are overrepresented in U.S. prisons. In 2016, African Americans totaled only 12 percent of the nation's adults but represented 33 percent of the prison population; and Latino Americans comprised 16 percent of the U.S. population, yet totaled 23 percent of prisoners. In contrast, white non–Latino Americans numbered 64 percent of the U.S. adult population, but this ethnic demographic comprised 30 percent of prisoners.[20]

PHYSICAL HEALTH OF PRISONERS

Prisoners are at higher risk of physical health problems than the general population. This often is due partly to their having unhealthy lifestyles and poor health practices before they were incarcerated. In the socioeconomically disadvantaged groups from which prisoners often come, health-damaging drug, alcohol, and smoking addictions are common, and other unhealthy factors such as limited exercise and deficient diets are widespread. Such destructive practices tend to weaken general health and make individuals more susceptible to communicable diseases such as hepatitis, HIV, and tuberculosis. Yet, personal and family resources to pay for preventive and needed health care may be limited, making visits to doctors and dentists hostage to a meager pocketbook. As a result, many prisoners have had little contact with their community's health services before entering a jail.[21]

Upon being incarcerated, such prisoners move from one unhealthy environment to another. Prisons typically are poorly ventilated, overcrowded, and frequently stressful, which may exacerbate preexisting health conditions such as asthma and contribute to the spread of communicable diseases. We already have pointed out how the aging of the prison population leads to an increased rate of disability and chronic disease, but younger prisoners are also at higher risk of contracting various chronic illnesses when compared to nonprisoners of similar ages. Research findings suggest that even prisoners in the eighteen to thirty-three age group have higher rates of chronic hypertension and asthma than those outside prison. In addition, prisoners with physical or developmental disabilities such as hearing loss or ambulatory impairment, conditions that might not seriously impair their activities outside prison, may have difficulty performing daily tasks such as hearing and obeying the orders of correctional officers, showering, or climbing into an upper bunk in the more demanding prison environment.[22]

Another health issue that plagues correctional institutions is injury to prisoners. This includes self-injury and, because prisons are environments where violence is not uncommon, injury as a result of physical or sexual assault. A study of 6,964 adult male prisoners in twelve prisons in one state found that 2,207 (31.7 percent) reported having experienced at least one incident of physical assault while incarcerated, and 201 (2.9 percent) reported experiencing sexual assault. The most common physical assaults were being threatened with a weapon and being hit. The most common sexual assaults were attempted or completed forced oral or anal sex and forced sexual acts to prevent future harm to the victim. The prisoners reported that physical and sexual assaults were perpetrated both by other prisoners and prison staff. Of 2,781 physical assault incidents reported, the largest number, 1,466 (52.7 percent), was alleged to have been perpetrated by staff. Of 244 sexual assaults reported, 138 (56.6 percent) were reported to have been committed by staff.[23]

The health of the female incarcerated population may be at even greater risk than that of male prisoners, with rates of multiple health concerns exceeding those for imprisoned men and for women outside of prison. These concerns include chronic health issues such as hepatitis C, cardiovascular disease, and HIV/AIDS. Yet, female prisoners have lower rates of treatment than both incarcerated men and nonincarcerated women.[24] Female prisoners have unique healthcare needs related to their reproductive health. Women are in need of gynecological care, yet they often do not receive the necessary screening to detect health issues specific to women or to obtain appropriate treatment. According to the Committee on Health Care for Underserved Women, health services specific to women's needs may be especially limited for women incarcerated in facilities with predominantly male populations. Consequently, women prisoners are often at risk of having undetected diseases such as breast and ovarian cancer.[25] Also, it is not uncommon for women to learn after they enter prison that they are pregnant. These women tend to have complex and higher-risk pregnancies than nonincarcerated women due to having a high rate of substance use disorders and other medical issues, yet they often do not receive adequate prenatal care in prison.[26]

More than three-quarters of incarcerated women have been physically or sexually abused, or both, before their stay in prison,[27] and the sexual victimization of women may continue in prison. The U.S. Justice Department reports that between 2009 and 2011, of 824 substantiated allegations by state and federal prisoners of being victimized by other prisoners with nonconsensual sexual acts or abusive sexual contacts, about 22 percent of the victims were women. Also, during the same period, of 895 substantiated victims of sexual misconduct or sexual harassment by prison staff, 32.6 percent were women. These figures are especially notable because only about 7 percent of the prison population at the time were women,[28] suggesting that women are three to more than four times more likely than men to be a victim of sexual abuse while incarcerated.

NOVEL CORONAVIRUS AND COVID-19 IN PRISONS

At the time of this writing, late May 2020, the coronavirus pandemic is still in full force in the United States and throughout the world. By the time you read this, the fast-moving coronavirus and COVID-19 story is likely to have advanced far beyond today's news. However, we feel it appropriate to report what currently is known about the potentially deadly COVID-19 illness that results from the novel coronavirus as it is affecting the nation's correctional institutions. Prisoners generally are considered to be more susceptible to the virus than most of the outside population due to the confined environment in which they must live. Their required proximity to one another strongly suggests that the protective social distancing measures that have been advised, and in some cases mandated, for the rest of the U.S. population may be difficult to practice in the prison environment. Evidence also points to prison staff members, including guards, nurses, and other workers, being more susceptible to contracting the virus due to the setting in which they work and the duties they perform.

Our most up-to-date comprehensive state-by-state information at present appears to be from the Marshall Project, located in New York City, which compiles weekly information from state and federal prisons about the internal occurrence of COVID-19. According to the organization's website, as of May 22, 2020, 29,251 state and federal prisoners had been diagnosed with the coronavirus. Testing of prisoners for the virus has varied greatly among states. Ohio, Michigan, Tennessee, and Texas, along with the Federal Bureau of Prisons, all have reported more than two thousand COVID-19 cases in their prisons so far. As of the May 22 date, many other states have reported fewer than one hundred cases, with these lower number possibly being the result of a lack of testing prisoners. Authorities have reported at least 415 deaths from COVID-19 among prisoners throughout the nation.[29] The novel coronavirus also has affected prison staff, but the numbers regarding staff members are patchy. As of May 22, 7,435 cases have been reported among prison staff. However, during the previous week, only sixteen states had provided information on how many prison workers had been diagnosed as infected by the virus. By May 22, thirty-three deaths among staff members from COVID-19 had been reported publicly.[30]

Various other reports indicate that sizable outbreaks of COVID-19 have occurred in several prisons. At Parnall Correctional Facility in Michigan, 162 prisoners, almost 10 percent of the population, have been diagnosed with the disease, and 4 have died. Twenty-one percent of staff members, a total of 64 workers, also have been diagnosed.[31] At the California Institution for Men in Chino, 635 prisoners have tested positive for coronavirus and 9 have died as of May 26. At this point, the facility accounts for about half of prisoners who have been diagnosed with COVID-19 in the California correctional system and all who have died. Staff members at Chino who have tested positive number 58.[32]

Correctional systems are dealing with the pandemic in various ways. Federal and most state systems temporarily have suspended or severely restricted in-prison visitations, and a number of systems have lowered or eliminated phone call charges so prisoners can keep in phone contact with family and others. Several states are allowing the release of some nonviolent offenders with preexisting medical conditions. Others have reduced new admissions to their prisons.[33] Much is unknown and yet to be determined regarding how the coronavirus pandemic is affecting and will affect the U.S. prison population. It seems likely at this point that the adverse consequences will be extensive.

MENTAL HEALTH OF PRISONERS

Based on interviews with prisoners and symptom criteria set out in the *Diagnostic and Statistical Manual of Mental Disorders*, fourth edition, research by the U.S. Department of Justice suggests that more than half of state and federal prisoners have at least one mental health condition. The most common mental health problems diagnosed for prisoners in the 2006 study were depression and mania. This rate of mental disorders among incarcerated people was far beyond that of the general population, which is estimated to be about 11 percent.[34] Other mental health conditions prisoners experienced include post-traumatic stress disorder, personality disorders, schizophrenia, bipolar disorder, and anxiety disorder.[35]

The high rate of mental disorders among prisoners may be tied to two main factors. One is the deinstitutionalization of state hospitals for the mentally ill that began in the 1960s. Although it was believed that community care options for individuals with psychological disorders would compensate for the loss of what amounted to 95 percent of hospital beds over time, this expectation went largely unfulfilled due to the costs involved. One result is that jails and prisons became sites for housing many psychologically challenged individuals who otherwise would be able to occupy a bed at a facility equipped to treat their disorder.[36]

A second factor that likely adds to prisoners' mental health problems is their being forced to live in the prison environment. Not only are prisoners more likely than the nonincarcerated population to have had a prior mental health challenge, but the condition of living in a prison, with its lack of autonomy and privacy, severe restrictions, and potential for violence, may exacerbate old psychological disorders. The prison setting also may engender a new mental health problem. This is suggested by the finding that fewer than half of state prisoners and fewer than one-third of federal prisoners diagnosed with a mental health condition reported having a recent history of a mental health problem in the year before arrest or since admission.[37] It also is suggested by the list of symptoms that resulted in the two psychological diagnoses of depression and mania. These symptoms included reports of persistent sad, numb, or empty mood; loss of interest or pleasure in activities; insomnia or hypersomnia; feelings of worthlessness or excessive guilt; diminished ability to concentrate or think; and persistent anger or irritability.[38] It is not difficult to believe that any or all of these symptoms could be induced by being compelled to live in the prison environment.

Imprisoned women have a higher rate of mental health issues than incarcerated men. Almost three-quarters of women in state prisons have symptoms of a mental health disorder, including depression, anxiety, and posttraumatic stress disorder, and almost two-thirds have a history of a mental health problem. In many cases, such an issue is related to a woman's abusive experiences outside prison that occurred in her childhood or youth.[39] These experiences often adversely affect both physical and mental health, leading to persistent psychological problems.

SUBSTANCE ABUSE AND DEPENDENCE

Drug and alcohol dependence characterize a large percentage of both state and federal prisoners. Statistics for 2004 indicate that 53 percent of state prisoners and 45 percent of federal prisoners met the criteria for drug dependence or abuse in the twelve months preceding their incarceration. Younger prisoners were more likely to report drug dependence or abuse than older prisoners; white prisoners were the ethnicity with the highest percentage of drug problems in both state and federal facilities.[40]

Researchers at the National Center on Addiction and Substance Abuse at Columbia University (CASA), combining statistics for U.S. prisons and jails, found that alcohol use was involved in 56.6 percent, and illicit drug use in 75.9 percent of the offenses for which individuals were convicted and sent to prisons or jails. The study found that 65.2 percent of state and 54.8 percent of federal prisoners had a substance use disorder in the form of substance abuse, substance dependence, or both.[41]

Both men and women prisoners have high rates of substance abuse and dependence. Figures for 2010 show that in federal institutions, men had the higher rate of substance abuse disorder, 55.2 versus 49.4 percent. However, women incarcerated in state prisons had a higher rate than men; whereas 65.0 percent of men in state prisons had a substance abuse disorder, the rate for women was 67.6 percent.[42] For many women, drug use at the time of imprisonment may have been furthered by a need to deal with a history of traumatic events, victimization, and poverty.

A TROUBLED POPULATION

Our overview of some main characteristics of prisoners makes clear that in this population many individuals were distressed in various ways for years before they were imprisoned. According to numerous researchers and commentators—and we agree—a main culprit that has added greatly to prison rosters is poverty. A wide swath of the prison population arose out of an impoverished childhood and youth. For some who emerge out of poor communities, criminal activity may seem to offer an escape from their situation. For others, a poverty-infused environment may tempt them to believe early that acceptance by their peers and even survival require them to embrace antisocial attitudes and behaviors.

This is not to say that there are not millions of others who escape lean beginnings to become productive, successful, and law-abiding citizens. Which factors help promote that success, whether personal, familial, or situational, is a subject worthy of much investigation. But many others who come from such settings enter into unlawful activities and soon find themselves imprisoned in an environment a good deal more limiting and unforgiving than the one they left.

What policies might reduce incarceration rates and recidivism by helping families and individuals drowning in poverty is a perennial major issue in our nation. It is not for us, in this book, to argue for what those policies should be. But it is for us to point out that for whatever reasons, a huge number of incarcerated individuals in our prisons are living miserable lives and have limited hope for a successful future. And it is for us to argue strongly, as we do in part II, that for compelling reasons it would be wise for us, as a society, to provide effective educational tools that many of these individuals can carry with them out of prison—tools that will give them hope while they are incarcerated and a leg up when they are released, and that will significantly reduce the likelihood that they ever will return to prison.

Before moving to the next chapter, we want to address a query that may be on the minds of some of our readers. It is this: by reporting on the problems that beset many who are incarcerated in our prisons, have we not been invalidating our own argument that greatly increased educational opportunities are needed in our prisons? After all, with so many of those who are incarcerated experiencing psychological troubles, substance abuse challenges, age-related medical problems, or other issues, who is left to educate?

Our answer is: *Plenty.* We acknowledge that surely many imprisoned individuals may benefit little or not at all from increased prison education. These include prisoners who have significant learning deficits, strong antisocial attitudes, or serious psychological or physical problems. However, the majority of prisoners are not heavily burdened by any of those challenges, and even some who are would welcome and respond well to more and better prison education programs. With almost 1.5 million individuals incarcerated in our state and federal prisons, we maintain that many hundreds of thousands can gain from educational programs. To identify those prisoners who will benefit from different types of education should be one of the main functions of improved prison education initiatives. Our view, as you will see throughout this book, is that hundreds of thousands of incarcerated individuals in need of education are a largely untapped resource that we can harness, not only for their sake but also for that of their families and communities.

Our entire society will benefit from more and better prison education by enjoying less crime, reduced recidivism, and hundreds of millions or even billions of tax dollars saved from lower incarceration costs. We can do that simply by deciding to invest in the education of prisoners to prepare them for their reentry into society. By doing so, we also will take huge steps toward humanizing our correctional system, which, in itself, is a goal greatly to be desired.

Textbox 2.1: Prisoner who has served twenty-four years of a life sentence

Prison is a depressing environment filled with hopelessness and despair. For most, it becomes simply a warehouse. Few jobs or details are available, and opportunities for improvement are almost nonexistent. A large percent of inmates have had trials too tragic to share and losses too great to describe. Their lives seem hopeless, with nothing before them but darkness. The consequences of wrong choices have left them scarred for life.

For some reason, society tends to forget that 95 percent of prisoners return to society. Upon their return, most are no better off than when they were incarcerated. Some, with nothing better to do, honed their talent as criminals by networking with fellow inmates.

This does not need to be the case. Into this dreary environment can come education, opening doors long since closed to opportunities and bringing hope for a life as a productive, taxpaying citizen and not a drain on the economy.

Education takes on many different forms. The primary forms are academic and vocational. Education provides the prisoner with not just the knowledge gained from books, but also a better self-image, hope for the future, and a positive direction for his life. He develops improved decision-making abilities, which in turn should reduce recidivism. Earning a GED while incarcerated reduces recidivism dramatically. Continuing to learn a trade or to go to college further helps to give the inmate a sense of worth and provides a means of income previously unavailable. It is a win-win situation for the inmate and society.

NOTES

1. Bernadette Rabury and Daniel Kopf, *Prisons of Poverty: Uncovering the Pre-Incarceration Incomes of the Imprisoned* (Northampton, MA: Prison Policy Initiative, July 9, 2015), Findings, https://www.prisonpolicy.org/reports/income.html.

2. Adam Looney and Nicholas Turner, *Work and Opportunity Before and After Incarceration* (Washington, DC: Brookings Institution, 2018), table 1, https://www.brookings.edu/wp-content/uploads/2018/03/es_20180314_looneyincarceration_final.pdf.

3. Looney and Turner, *Work and Opportunity*, 13.

4. Stephanie Ewert and Tara Wildhagen, *Educational Characteristics of Prisoners: Data from the ACS*, working paper no. SEHSD-WP2011-08 (Washington, DC: U.S. Census Bureau, April 2011), tables 4 and 6, https://www.census.gov/library/working-papers/2011/demo/SEHSD-WP2011-08.html.

5. U.S. Department of Justice, Bureau of Justice Statistics, *Prisoners in 2016*, by E. Ann Carson, Bulletin NCJ 251149 (August 7, 2018), Table 1, https://www.bjs.gov/content/pub/pdf/p16.pdf.

6. Wendy Sawyer, *The Gender Divide: Tracking Women's State Prison Growth* (Northampton, MA: Prison Policy Initiative, January 9, 2018), State level trends, https://www.prisonpolicy.org/reports/women_overtime.html.

7. Gina Fedock, "Number of Women in Jails and Prisons Soars," *University of Chicago School of Social Service Administration Magazine* 25, no. 1 (Spring 2018), https://www.ssa.uchicago.edu/ssa_magazine/number-women-jails-and-prisons-soars.

8. Sawyer, *Gender Divide*, state graphs.

9. U.S. Department of Justice, Bureau of Justice Statistics, *Prisoners in 2010*, by Paul Guerino, Paige M. Harrison, and William J. Sabol, Bulletin NCJ 236096 (modified February 9, 2012), table 13, https://www.bjs.gov/content/pub/pdf/p10.pdf.

10. *Prisoners in 2016*, table 9.

11. Matt McKillop and Alex Boucher, "Aging Prison Populations Drive up Costs" (Philadelphia: Pew Charitable Trusts, February 20, 2018), Why State Prison Populations Are Aging, https://www.pewtrusts.org/en/research-and-analysis/articles/2018/02/20/aging-prison-populations-drive-up-costs.

12. U.S. Department of Justice, National Institute of Corrections, *Correctional Health Care: Addressing the Needs of Elderly, Chronically Ill, and Terminally Ill Inmates*, by B. Jaye Anno et al. (Accession Number 018735, 2004), https://nicic.gov/correctional-health-care-addressing-needs-elderly-chronically-ill-and-terminally-ill-inmates.

13. Maddy Troilo, *Locking up Youth with Adults: An Update* (Northampton, MA: Prison Policy Initiative, February 27, 2018), table, https://www.prisonpolicy.org/blog/2018/02/27/youth/.

14. Jessica Lahey, "The Steep Costs of Keeping Juveniles in Adult Prisons," *The Atlantic*, January 8, 2016, https://www.theatlantic.com/education/archive/2016/01/the-cost-of-keeping-juveniles-in-adult-prisons/423201/.

15. "Let's Get Children out of Adult Courts, Jails, and Prisons," Campaign for Youth Justice, last modified December 10, 2018, http://www.campaignforyouthjustice.org/images/factsheets/Basic_Facts_FINAL.pdf.

16. Campaign for Youth Justice, *Jailing Juveniles: The Dangers of Incarcerating Youth in Adult Jails in America* (November 2007), 4, http://www.campaignforyouthjustice.org/Downloads/NationalReportsArticles/CFYJ-Jailing_Juveniles_Report_2007-11-15.pdf.

17. National Prison Rape Elimination Commission, *National Prison Rape Elimination Report* (June 2009), https://www.ncjrs.gov/pdffiles1/226680.pdf.

18. Wendy Sawyer, *Youth Confinement: The Whole Pie 2019* (Northampton, MA: Prison Policy Initiative, December 19, 2019), https://www.prisonpolicy.org/reports/youth2019.html#facilities.

19. *Prisoners in 2016*, table 9.

20. John Gramlich, "The Gap between the Number of Blacks and Whites in Prison Is Shrinking," *Fact Tank* (Philadelphia: Pew Research Center, April 30, 2019), https://

www.pewresearch.org/fact-tank/2018/01/12/shrinking-gap-between-number-of-blacks-and-whites-in-prison/.

21. Brenda J. van den Bergh et al., "Imprisonment and Women's Health: Concerns About Gender Sensitivity, Human Rights and Public Health," *Bulletin of the World Health Organization* 89 (2011): 689–94, doi: 10.2471/BLT.10.082842.

22. Jeremy Travis, Bruce Western, and F. Stevens Redburn, eds., *The Growth of Incarceration in the United States: Exploring Causes and Consequences* (Washington, DC: National Academies Press, 2014), 211.

23. Nancy Wolff and Jing Shi, "Contextualization of Physical and Sexual Assault in Male Prisons: Incidents and Their Aftermath," *Journal of Correctional Health Care* 15, no. 4 (2009): tables 2 and 3, https://doi.org/10.1177/1078345808326622.

24. Fedock, "Number of Women."

25. Committee on Health Care for Underserved Women, American College of Obstetricians and Gynecologists, *Reproductive Health Care for Incarcerated Women and Adolescent Females*, Committee Opinion no. 535, August 2012, reaffirmed 2019, 1–2, https://www.acog.org/clinical/clinical-guidance/committee-opinion/articles/2012/08/reproductive-health-care-for-in carcerated-women-and-adolescent-females.

26. *Women's Health Care in Correctional Settings*, National Commission on Correctional Health Care, position statement reaffirmed with revision May 3, 2020, Pregnancy, https://www.ncchc.org/womens-health-care.

27. Fedock, "Number of Women."

28. U.S. Department of Justice, Bureau of Justice Statistics, *Sexual Victimization Reported by Adult Correctional Authorities, 2009–11*, by Allen J. Beck, Ramona R. Rantala, and Jessica Rexroat, Special Report NCJ 243904 (Washington, DC, January 2014), tables 4, 8, and 10, https://www.prearesourcecenter.org/sites/default/files/library/sexualvictimizationreportedby-correctionalauthorities2009-2011.pdf.

29. Marshall Project, *A State-by-State Look at Coronavirus in Prisons*, updated May 22, 2020, https://www.themarshallproject.org/2020/05/01/a-state-by-state-look-at-coronavirus-in-prisons.

30. Marshall Project, *State-by-State Look*.

31. Angie Jackson and Kristi Tanner, "Infection Rate at Michigan Prison Exceeds New York, Chicago Jail Hot Spots," *Detroit Free Press*, updated April 16, 2020, https://www.freep.com/story/news/local/michigan/2020/04/16/infection-rate-michigan-prison-ex ceeds-new-york-chicago-jail-hotspots/2987935001/.

32. Richard Winton, "As Inmate Deaths and Infections Rise, Chino, Avenal Prisons Will Test All Employees for Coronavirus," *Los Angeles Times*, May 26, 2020, https://www.latimes.com/california/story/2020-05-26/with-nine-inmates-at-chino-prison-dead-after-getting-covid-19-it-and-avenal-prison-require-all-staff-testing.

33. *Responses to the COVID-19 Pandemic*, Prison Policy Initiative, updated May 27, 2020, https://www.prisonpolicy.org/virus/virusresponse.html; also *BOP Implementing Modified Operations*, Federal Bureau of Prisons, accessed May 28, 2020, https://www.bop.gov/coronavirus/covid19_status.jsp.

34. U.S. Department of Justice, Bureau of Justice Statistics, *Mental Health Problems of Prison and Jail Inmates*, by Doris J. James and Lauren E. Glaze, Special Report NCJ 213600 (Washington, DC, September 2006), 3, https://www.bjs.gov/content/pub/pdf/mhppji.pdf.

35. Jennifer M. Reingle Gonzalez and Nadine M. Connell, "Mental Health of Prisoners: Identifying Barriers to Mental Health Treatment and Medication Continuity," *American Journal of Public Health* 104, no. 12 (2014), table 1, doi: 10.2105/AJPH.2014.302043.

36. Daniel Yohanna, "Deinstitutionalization of People with Mental Illness: Causes and Consequences," *AMA Journal of Ethics* 15, no. 1 (2013): 886–87, doi: 10.1001/virtualmentor.2013.15.10.mhst1-1310.

37. James and Glaze, *Mental Health Problems*, Bureau of Justice Statistics, table 1.

38. James and Glaze, *Mental Health Problems*, Bureau of Justice Statistics, 2.

39. Fedock, "Number of Women."

40. U.S. Department of Justice, Bureau of Justice Statistics, *Drug Use and Dependence, State and Federal Prisoners, 2004*, by Christopher J. Mumola and Jennifer C. Karberg, Special

Report NCJ 213530 (Washington DC, October 2006), 1, table 6, https://www.bjs.gov/content/pub/pdf/dudsfp04.pdf.

41. *Behind Bars II: Substance Abuse and America's Prison Population*, CASA (National Center on Addiction and Substance Abuse at Columbia University), (February 2010), 2, table 4.3, https://www.centeronaddiction.org/addiction-research/reports/behind-bars-ii-substance-ab use-and-america%E2%80%99s-prison-population.

42. *Behind Bars II*, CASA, table 4.10.

Chapter Three

The Many Costs of Incarceration

The costs to our nation of a correctional system glutted with more than two million people in our prisons and jails are enormous. When we think about those expenses, we may be tempted to dwell on only the direct financial costs to taxpayers of locking up almost 1.5 million people in our prisons and 700,000 more in our jails (many of whom will matriculate from jail to prison). And those direct costs, as we will soon see, are plenty. But there are other major costs, some hidden. These include the *indirect* financial costs of imprisonment, which amount to another hefty burden taxpayers must carry. They also cover a slew of sizable financial hits that plague the relatives of prisoners, expenditures that very often help keep poverty-stricken families in the grips of privation. This is not to mention the appalling emotional toll families pay with a member in prison. Or one of the biggest expenses of incarceration, the lost opportunity costs—opportunities for a better life that are missed forever by the prisoner and his family. And finally, consider the troubling costs paid by the communities into which prisoners are released and, by extension, the entire society.

Let us look closer at these grievous costs.

DIRECT COSTS OF INCARCERATION

Incarceration creates a flood of direct financial expenses. First is the capital outlay for constructing a secure facility—a sprawling structure often covering thousands of acres, with thick, impenetrable walls topped with miles of razor wire, tiered cell blocks, and tall guardhouses to oversee the walls, yard, and entire structure—and the monies required for its ongoing upkeep and maintenance. Next is the cost of furnishing the prison: beds, blankets, tables, chairs, stoves, pots, pans, laundry facilities, medical facilities, uniforms for prisoners and those who monitor them, and much more. Daily operations require heavy recurring costs, such as for electricity, water, and refuse disposal. Large influxes of food and other supplies are needed constantly, and every delivery must be paid for. Caring for prisoners' physical and mental health is another ongoing expense, and a big one, representing as much as 20 percent or more of the total prison budget for some states.[1] And, of course, the largest and most burdensome category of expenses consists of the salaries paid to employees working at the prison—the corrections officers and the medical, administrative, and other staff. Besides their salaries, prison employees also typically earn benefits, including health insurance, retirement plans, and retirement healthcare allowances, all of which add millions to state and federal budgets annually.

These and other direct costs of incarceration add up to an enormous amount of money required to sustain the nation's prisons and jails. The total direct financial cost of all corrections operations in the United States, including federal and state prisons, jails, and parole and probation programs, is estimated to be $81 billion annually.[2] Considering just the direct costs for prison confinement, the annual amount for federal correctional facilities in 2017 was $36,299 per prisoner.[3] Based on this figure, the total annual cost for holding the 169,080 people incarcerated in federal prisons on May 7, 2020,[4] was approximately $6.14 billion. For state prisons, which confine seven times more prisoners than federal facilities, the cost in forty-five reporting states in 2015 (all but Maine, Mississippi, New Hampshire, Nebraska, and Wyoming) was almost $43 billion annually. The average annual costs for individual states ranged from more than $65 million in North Dakota to $8.6 billion in California. Annual costs per prisoner ranged from $14,780 in Alabama to $69,355 in New York State.[5]

INDIRECT CRIMINAL JUSTICE SYSTEM COSTS

Direct expenses for prison incarceration are far from all of the costs taxpayers bear for a correctional system with seven times more people incarcerated today than in 1970. To the massive direct expenses of housing the country's nearly 1.5 million prisoners, we can add the cost—estimated to be $63.2 billion annually—for the criminal policing required to deter, identify, and arrest the offenders who, if not exonerated for the alleged crime, likely will be jailed or imprisoned. Once arrested, the accused person enters the judicial and legal system. Insofar as that system deals with criminal law proceedings, it accounts for an additional $29 billion spent per year, with an estimated $10.3 billion of that amount expended for prosecution of criminal cases and indigent defense.[6] Add these costs of criminal policing and criminal law proceedings to the $81 billion direct incarceration costs, and the result is an enormous $173 billion per year. Based on an estimate of 156.4 million tax-payers filing individual returns in 2018,[7] each taxpayer pays $1,106 annually for the criminal justice system in the United States to apprehend, adjudicate, and incarcerate offenders.

COSTS TO FAMILIES

In addition to the direct costs for incarceration and associated criminal justice system costs, expenses borne almost wholly by taxpayers, families of those who are imprisoned pay a multitude of costs. These are the spouses, parents, children, and others who care about the well-being of individuals who have been sentenced to one or more years behind prison walls. These family members are innocent of any crime. Yet they pay a terrible price for their loved one's incarceration. That price can be separated into two main catego-ries: the financial expenses and the emotional costs resulting from a spouse, parent, or child being imprisoned.

The financial costs to the family can amount to a hefty percentage of resources that in many cases are meager, especially if the imprisoned offend-er was a main breadwinner for the family. The costs include sending money to the incarcerated family member's account for commissary purchases such as soap, deodorant, and envelopes and paying for phone calls to or from home. These funds typically are necessary because, though the prisoner may receive money for the work she performs in or for the facility, the amount is likely to be only a few dollars a day or less. In some states (e.g., Arkansas and Georgia), the person earns nothing for her daily work, even if it is done for the sake of state-owned correctional industries.[8] Commissary costs paid by families of prisoners are thought to be $1.6 billion annually, and phone call costs are estimated to be $1.3 billion each year.[9] These expenses may be especially burdensome if the prisoner's income has been lost to the family. One study found that after a father was incarcerated, family income dropped 22 percent compared to the year before the father's imprisonment. After he was released, family income rose, but remained 15 percent less than the year before imprisonment.[10]

For the multitude of prisoners' families whose incomes already place them at or below the poverty line, the extra expenses to support a prisoner can ensure that the family remains cemented in an impoverished financial condition. The choices such families must make often are brutal. What is it to be? Set aside twenty dollars so the imprisoned family member can make a collect call home on Saturday to receive a dose of encouragement and a few warm minutes in a dismal week? Or put that money toward a used laptop a daughter needs for school? Send ten dollars to the prisoner's account so he can purchase coffee and a few precious packages of ramen noodles and thereby get a bit of culinary freedom from the unpalatable food in the chow hall? Or buy fresh fruit and maybe the fixings for a pie the kids can enjoy on Sunday after church? These can be difficult choices for a family that cares about and realizes the bleak situation of their loved one in prison but also needs to care for those at home.

We realize that some might maintain that the financial punishment a prisoner's family undergoes is part of the price an imprisoned offender pays for committing a crime. That certainly is true. But if that observation is put forth as a moral justification for the price that families pay, we totally reject that viewpoint. First, for her transgression, whatever it may be, the offender already is paying a very heavy price. More important, the prisoner's family is innocent and undeserving of being punished; yet it finds itself caught between the criminal justice system and the prisoner. Most families do not entertain the possibility of not extending their best efforts to support their imprisoned one. But the financial cost of that support, given the resources available, can be dear.

The emotional cost to the family when a member is imprisoned may be even more exorbitant. Consider the parents of an offspring caught up in the judicial system and eventually put behind the razor wire. It is natural for those parents to spend a good deal of time wondering what they did wrong, and worrying about what is happening to and what will become of their child in prison. It is to be expected that parents are beside themselves with recrimination and anxiety for the well-being of a child they brought into the world.

Spouses and other partners of prisoners may undergo even greater emotional turmoil than parents. The partner cast her lot with the imprisoned person, for better or for worse, and now the worse has come to pass. Keeping the household together by one's self, spending nights alone, planning alone, with no partner there to be with, eat with, bounce ideas off, and just share the day and the daily load with can feel like a lonely, thankless life. The hope and aspirations with which the partners began their life together have now devolved into letters, a few phone calls, and visits to the facility if it is near enough. For a partner waiting for a prisoner whose sentence stretches into a decade or more, visiting him may be deeply unsatisfying, perhaps not totally unlike going to a cemetery on Sunday to visit the grave of a loved one. Holidays such as Christmas may be bittersweet: not only is the partner absent, but he is spending the holiday in a joyless environment.

Perhaps the family members who experience the most enduring and potentially damaging emotional distress are a prisoner's children. Due to the upsurge in imprisonment in the late 1980s and 1990s, having a parent in prison has become a childhood risk in America that is particularly prevalent among black children and children of parents with low education.[11] The enforced relegation of a parent to prison confinement leaves children lacking the daily emotional support from their incarcerated parent that is critical to their healthy growth and maturation. Such loving support can come in many forms—simple displays of affection, words of praise, tucking the child in at night, and other actions that promote a sense of family togetherness and the security and warmth of home. The lack of affective support from an imprisoned parent loads the child with an emotional burden that friends may not have to carry.

The son who is shooting baskets alone on the corner playground imagines what it would be like if his father were there to admire his hook shot or play a game of one-on-one. The daughter in the school play yearns deeply for her incarcerated mother to be in the audience with her father, taking photographs and applauding her performance, in the same way both parents are there for her classmates' performances. But she knows it will not happen tonight, and it may add to her disappointment as she realizes it will never happen during all of her young years in school.

Textbox 3.1: A daughter

Do you know how it feels to have a parent who's incarcerated? If not, then I'll tell you about it.

My dad has been in prison for almost ten years. Children such as me are forever impacted by our parents who broke the law. Parents who are incarcerated are removed from day-to-day activities and most importantly the lives of their children. Having a family member in prison is very hard to deal with. Communicating with that family member is also hard to deal with, whether by letters, telephone (whenever they are allowed a phone call), or visitation.

When my dad went to prison, I did not know how to feel at first. I was very lonely even though I had my mom. I always wanted my dad here with me. Over the years I would get very angry and sad and wonder why did my dad do the stuff that he did.

Throughout high school I never had my dad in my life. All my other classmates would talk about their dads, and their parents would come to their sporting events. I never really talked about my dad's incarceration because I did not want anyone to find out. So, I basically kept it a secret. I still do not tell anyone about my dad being incarcerated unless it's someone I really trust.

The emotional distress children pay with an incarcerated parent is closely related to another expense arising from the parent's extended absence. This is the cost to their chances of successfully weathering the numerous challenges they must overcome as they move toward adulthood. In many cases single parents do an admirable job of raising one or more children alone, but it remains true that children with two engaged parents at home have a better chance of successfully negotiating the risky obstacle course to adulthood. Parents provide a stabilizing force that helps children resist the many other unsettling forces that impinge on their lives. These influences may take the form of peers who bully or coerce or who tempt the child to follow a path leading to academic apathy, drug experimentation, or antisocial behaviors that eventually may result in criminal activity. The incarcerated parent is not there to offer the guidance the child may need desperately when facing trials at school or in the neighborhood.

The inimical effects on children of having a parent in prison are not restricted to families in any socioeconomic class. However, lack of a parent in the home due to incarceration may especially be problematic for children living in economically limited families. It is no secret that for children from families with scarce resources, residing in neighborhoods shot through with privation, the challenges and risks of growing up often are multiplied. Unfortunately, as we have seen, that is precisely the financial state that characterizes the families from which a preponderance of incarcerated individuals come. For such children, both parents are sorely needed if the child is to have the best chance of making his way successfully through the obstacle course. This may most notably be true during children's teen years, when the dreadful attractions of drugs and gangs may start to gain their attention.

Because the missing incarcerated parent is, in most cases, a father, it is significant that research results support the positive importance to children of having an involved father in the home. In particular, a 2008 review of twenty-four studies examining the relationship of paternal involvement to children's well-being found that a father's or father figure's engagement with his child in various ways, such as playing with, reading to, taking outings with, or providing care for the child, was positively associated with a number of favorable outcomes, including reducing the incidence of behavioral problems in boys and lessening the occurrence of psychological problems in young women. Particular studies that were reviewed found that involvement of the father protected against adolescent smoking, was positively related to educational outcomes, and predicted better social and relational functioning in children and after the child had reached adulthood. [12]

Research found that among poorer families, father involvement improved the cognitive development of young children and decreased the rate of delinquency in older children. The clear implication is that when a father is unable to interact with his child due to being imprisoned, the child's cognitive development may suffer, while the chances of delinquency increase. These results provide strong research support for the idea that a child's well-being is enhanced by a father who is at home and engages with the child on a daily basis—an impossible task for a father living in a cell block.

An ironic and ugly phenomenon that may occur in regard to an imprisoned father is that a son who has felt shame for years at his father's absence may discover, upon entering his teens, that some of his peers actually approve of his parent's situation. Perversely, they may view the father's status as being a badge of honor. The child, sensing his friends' approval of his parent's situation, may begin to view his father as an antisocial hero. This may be an attractive thought for a young boy who has long desired to feel pride in his father. Most unfortunately, it may be a thought that, eventually, will send him on his own course to prison as he begins to model some of his actions on his father's.

The adverse impact on children of a mother being incarcerated may be even greater than that of a father being imprisoned. A mother's imprisonment may have a devastating effect on family structure and integrity. The detrimental impact that women's imprisonment has on families is especially troubling given the fact that more than 60 percent of incarcerated women have at least one minor child, many of them under the age of nine. Nearly 50 percent of these female prisoners were the primary caretakers of their children prior to their incarceration. [13]

In a review of studies about how parental imprisonment is related to one or more children's outcomes, including antisocial behavior and mental health, researchers found evidence that the adverse effects on a child of parental imprisonment may be greater when the parent is a mother rather than a father. [14] The investigators suggested several reasons why that might be so, one of which is that children more likely live with their mother than their father before parental imprisonment and thus may form stronger attachments to the mother. Also, it is less likely for a child to be placed with the other parent after a mother is imprisoned and more likely for the child to be placed in foster care. A third possibility is that because fewer women's prisons exist, a mother is more likely to be placed in an institution at a considerable distance from home, which makes it difficult for children to visit her. Given the importance for young children to have a secure attachment to their primary caregivers, [15] there is ample reason to conclude that having a mother in prison tends to have long-term adverse effects on children left behind. One of the worst of these effects is that such children eventually may find themselves subject to the criminal justice system. [16]

THE COST OF LOST OPPORTUNITIES

There may be no greater cost of imprisonment than the opportunities for life and living that could have been but will not be. We already have touched on some lost opportunities in talking about the financial cost to a prisoner's family, especially one with very limited resources. Impoverished families who understandably choose to use a portion of their funds to support an incarcerated member may be required to forfeit activities and pleasures that could provide definition and richness to their lives. Money for school supplies, clothing, family outings, entertainment, and even sufficient nutritious food—money already in short supply—may be even more inadequate with an incarcerated family member who not only adds nothing to the coffers but also requires some minimal financial support.

The most obvious payers of the opportunity costs of incarceration are the prisoners. One such cost is loss of the richness of life. Every year prisoners spend incarcerated is a year lost in which they could have enjoyed many days and evenings being together with family or friends. For those with a family, the multitude of missed opportunities include enjoying an after-dinner walk with a spouse, taking the children to the zoo and buying peanuts for the elephants, and attending the school open house to see a daughter's face light up when she shows her art work or talk to the teacher about how a son is doing. Whatever their family status, incarcerated people miss out on scores of opportunities to do things most others take for granted, such as inviting a few friends over for a Saturday barbecue. These and countless other possibilities for living a full life go unrealized.

Left is the opportunity to go to the toilet in a tiny cell in view of corrections officers and other prisoners, to hear the constant clanging of metal doors opening and closing and the cursing and screaming of other prisoners, passively to endure the frequent scheduled cavity searches, and always to watch your back, 24/7, 365, maybe for years.

Prisoners also bear the lost opportunities to develop a career or at least to secure employment that could provide advancement—the chance to lay down a financial foundation that eventually would enable a degree of economic freedom. This cost is incurred both during incarceration and after release. They spend precious time at first locked away from opportunities for economic progress and then, after release, they typically are relegated to the most basic employment with little chance of advancement. In the next chapter, we will detail the difficult challenges and limitations that released prisoners face, including poor prospects for gaining living-wage employment. We define living-wage employment as being a job that allows the prisoner to purchase reasonable shelter, put food on the table, pay any fees and obligations, afford basic medical care, purchase other necessities, buy a few pleasures, and gradually set aside a little money for the future.

COSTS TO COMMUNITIES

Incarceration levies substantial costs to communities. We will say a lot more about the seriously adverse effects of incarceration on communities in a later chapter, but here we briefly highlight some of those effects. First is the social cost of the productivity that could have occurred if individuals had not been imprisoned. Lost wages, as a measure of missing productivity, have been estimated at $70.5 billion for all prisoners during the average 2.25 years they are incarcerated.[17] After being earned, those wages would have been subject to taxes, with billions of dollars returned to communities to help fund education, roads, and other public services. Lost lifetime earnings of former prisoners due to restrictions on their occupational choices, discriminatory hiring practices, weakened social networks, and reduced human capital are an estimated $230 billion.[18] This compounded measure of the cost of lost productivity represents an even greater reduction in the tax dollars that could have benefited communities.

A second major cost of incarceration to the community is the breakdown of community bonds and social networks, resulting in social disorganization. Much of this breakdown arises from various other adverse outcomes of incarceration we outlined earlier. These include removal of a member of the community and his productivity if employed. They include weakening families financially, loosening of family bonds, and harmful effects on children that frustrate the transmission of parental norms and knowledge and increase the likelihood of school dropouts and juvenile crime.

Incarceration of young people is socially harmful by obstructing the otherwise natural progression from school to employment, resulting in greater difficulty in obtaining living-wage employment after prison. This, in turn, adds to the prevalence of poverty, homelessness, and other unfavorable social conditions within the community. By impinging on the community's organization, all of these results weaken its ability to exert social norms on residents, which adds further to social breakdown. Incarceration of community members also undermines networks that create social capital—the connections between individuals and groups that promote employment, social activities, and neighbors uniting to achieve common goals such as cleaning a lot to establish a neighborhood playground.

These community costs are borne most heavily by inner-city African American communities, which contribute an inordinate percentage of young men and women to prison rosters. These neighborhoods typically already are torn by economic disadvantage, and the high numbers of residents who are incarcerated leave many families deeper in poverty. The high recidivism rate suggests that when former prisoners return to the community, their stay before being reincarcerated may be short. It is questionable whether, during their time outside prison, they have added to or detracted from the social stability of the community. This bidirectional pipeline between prison and the community then confounds the efforts of families and groups such as churches and neighborhood associations to impose informal social controls.[19]

A third cost communities incur is the price they pay for new crimes committed by former prisoners. Determining the cost of incarceration to the community and its members is a matter of assigning a dollar amount to the probabilities and various adverse effects of such crimes. The annual cost of incarceration has been estimated at an enormous $285 billion.[20] This amount is impacted greatly by so-called intangible results of crime for community members, including the pain, suffering, and reduced quality of life associated with being a victim or potential victim of crime. Psychological effects of crime or its threat may include fear, anxiety, and changed behavior such as not walking on neighborhood streets. These "intangibles" have a powerful adverse financial effect on the community. Fear of crime may prompt neighborhood residents to spend their money on protection such as security alarms, locks, and weapons. Also, fewer visitors and reduced retail sales may stem from a perception that criminal activity is more likely to occur in part or all of a community than in other places. Such impressions may result in businesses leaving the area and house values dropping precipitously. Perceived high crime potential may further impede economic development by leading potential businesses and employers to decide against locating in a community.

It is evident from the preceding catalog that the costs of incarceration are many and enormous. That is why it is vital to determine strategies for reducing the likelihood of released prisoners committing new crimes and being returned to confinement. However, in the next chapter, we will see that a number of legal and social factors interfere with reducing recidivism by seriously impeding the reintegration of released prisoners. Perhaps the most problematic issue former prisoners face is their need to secure a job that pays a living wage. Partaking in prison education could make this key challenge much less formidable, thereby substantially increasing the likelihood of their successful reintegration with society.

NOTES

1. Chris Mai and Ram Subramanian, *The Price of Prisons: Examining State Spending Trends, 2010–2015* (New York: Vera Institute of Justice, May 2017), Prison Spending in 2015, https://www.vera.org/downloads/publications/the-price-of-prisons-2015-state-spending-trends .pdf.

2. Peter Wagner and Bernadette Rabury, *Following the Money of Mass Incarceration* (Northampton, MA: Prison Policy Initiative, January 25, 2017), methodology and data sources, https://www.prisonpolicy.org/reports/money.html.

3. Federal Bureau of Prisons, Notice, "Annual Determination of Average Cost of Incarceration," *Federal Register* 83, no. 83 (April 30, 2018), 18863, https://www.govinfo.gov/content/ pkg/FR-2018-04-30/pdf/2018-09062.pdf.

4. Federal Bureau of Prisons, *Population Statistics*, accessed May 7, 2020, https:// www.bop.gov/about/statistics/population_statistics.jsp.

5. Mai and Subramanian, *Price of Prisons*, table 1.

6. Wagner and Rabury, "Following the Money."

7. Brett Collins, "Projections of Federal Tax Return Filings: Calendar Years 2011–2018," U.S. Internal Revenue Service, *Statistics of Income Bulletin*, Winter 2012, https://www.irs.gov/pub/irs-soi/12rswinbulreturnfilings.pdf.

8. Wendy Sawyer, "How Much Do Incarcerated People Earn in Each State?" *Prison Policy Initiative Blog*, April 10, 2017, https://www.prisonpolicy.org/blog/2017/04/10/wages/.

9. Wagner and Rabury, "Following the Money."

10. Rucker C. Johnson, "Ever-Increasing Levels of Parental Incarceration and the Consequences for Children," in *Do Prisons Make Us Safer? The Benefits and Costs of the Prison Boom*, edited by Steven Raphael and Michael S. Stoll (New York: Russell Sage Foundation, 2009), 151–76.

11. Christopher Wildeman, "Parent Imprisonment, the Prison Boom, and the Concentration of Childhood Disadvantage," *Demography* 46, no. 2 (2009): 265–80, doi: 10.1353/dem.0.0052.

12. Anna Sarkadi et al., "Fathers' Involvement and Children's Developmental Outcomes: A Systematic Review of Longitudinal Studies," *Acta Paediatrica* 97 (2008): 153–58, doi: 10.1111/j.1651-2227.2007.00572.x.

13. Gina Fedock, "Number of Women in Jails and Prisons Soars," *University of Chicago School of Social Service Administration Magazine* 25, no. 1 (Spring 2018), https://www.ssa.uchicago.edu/ssa_magazine/number-women-jails-and-prisons-soar.

14. Joseph Murray and Davis P. Farrington, "The Effects of Parental Imprisonment on Children," in *Crime and Justice: A Review of Research*, vol. 37, edited by Michael Tonry, 133–206 (Chicago: University of Chicago Press, 2008).

15. John Bowlby, *A Secure Base* (New York: Basic Books, 1988).

16. Fedock, "Number of Women."

17. Michael McLaughlin et al., "The Economic Burden of Incarceration in the U.S.," working paper no. #AJI072016 (St. Louis: Concordance Institute for Advancing Justice, George Warren Brown School of Social Work, Washington University, October 2016), 7, https://joinnia.com/wp-content/uploads/2017/02/The-Economic-Burden-of-Incarceration-in-the-US-2016.pdf.

18. McLaughlin et al., "Economic Burden," 7.

19. Dorothy E. Roberts, "The Social and Moral Cost of Mass Incarceration in African American Communities," Faculty Scholarship Paper 583 (Philadelphia: University of Pennsylvania Law School, 2004), https://scholarship.law.upenn.edu/cgi/viewcontent.cgi?article=1582&context=faculty_scholarship.

20. McLaughlin et al., "Economic Burden," 16.

Chapter Four

The Tolls of Reentering Society

BRINGING PRISON HOME

The day a prisoner is released to community supervision is understandably happy. Liberated at last from confinement, debt to society seeming on the cusp of being paid after many months or years of imprisonment, all that seems left is having to jump through what hopefully will be the relatively minor hoops of parole. Otherwise, the former prisoner is likely to feel born anew upon entering society, finally free of prison walls, rules, stress, and dreariness. It is plainly cause for joyful celebration with friends and family.

But in the days following release, a joyless truth becomes increasingly evident to newly released prisoners—the relative freedom gained has many provisos, their release setting in motion numerous substantive qualifications, obligations, and constraints. They quickly find that the debt for their transgression is not yet close to being paid in full—not according to the society they have reentered.

Returning citizens' debt is ongoing because the criminal justice system and the society supporting it do not consider removal from free society through imprisonment sufficient payment for stepping outside the law. Upon release, paroled former prisoners encounter a morass of demands codified in the criminal justice system, set out in state statutes assigning various civil penalties, and thrust on them by a less than welcoming public. Together, these mandates, limitations, and social attitudes create an enormous set of challenges former prisoners must overcome as they attempt to meld successfully with society. But these demands raise a contradiction. The conflict—some would say the absurdity—is that on the one hand, the criminal justice system and the larger society supposedly espouse the value of socially reintegrating those who have been imprisoned; on the other hand, they construct a plethora of obstacles undermining that ideal. As released prisoners continue to encounter legal sanctions and others' unreceptive attitudes, many come to realize that even if they obey all laws religiously and are not again incarcerated, their debt, like that of Sisyphus, will never be fully paid.

Limitations on former prisoners' freedom are of two main types. One type consists of legal restrictions placed on them as conditions of community supervision or demanded by laws specific to people convicted of a felony. The other type comprises limitations that are not codified into law but are the result of society's perception of and attitude toward former prisoners. In this chapter, we will go into some detail about these two types of constraint on the lives of former prisoners, with an eye to their implications for recidivism rates.

LEGAL CONSTRAINTS

We first focus on the legal restrictions brought to bear on former prisoners' lives. These are mainly of three kinds: parole conditions, monetary fines and fees, and collateral sanctions.

Community Supervision Restrictions

Community supervision of those convicted of a crime is a complex subject due to the multitude of laws and regulations that characterize the many criminal justice systems in different states and the federal government. Most offenders subject to community supervision have been sentenced to a period of probation or released from incarceration to serve part of their sentence on parole. They also include those who have been placed on mandatory community supervision after serving their sentence.[1]

Almost all prisoners put on parole have been convicted of violating state laws, as parole for individuals convicted of federal crimes was all but eliminated under the Sentencing Reform Act of 1984. Yet federal courts may— and often do—require a prisoner in the federal system to spend a set period of time on community-supervised release after completing his sentence. Those who are convicted of federal crimes may also be sentenced to a probationary period instead of incarceration, in which case they, too, are subject to supervision by federal community supervision officers.[2] Our focus in this chapter is on state-held prisoners who have been imprisoned and then released on parole—almost 756,000 people as of January 2016.[3] However, many of the points we make about community supervision for parolees released from state prisons also apply to both state and federal violators assigned to community supervision after their sentence is completed.

Parole

Parole is considered part of the offender's sentence—the nonincarceration portion. Some prisoners sentenced by state courts do not have the opportunity for early release because they have been sentenced to a lifetime of incarceration without the possibility of parole. Other prisoners who might be eligible for parole decide to forgo that possibility and to voluntarily "max out" their sentence by remaining incarcerated until their prison term has ended; those people may exit state prisons with no supervision.[4] However, the majority of state-held prisoners who at some point are eligible to leave prison and spend the rest of their sentence under community supervision choose to do so.

Eligibility for parole results from prisoners having served a minimum amount of time of their sentence in a correctional facility. The decision to grant parole typically is decided by a state's parole authority, usually a parole board. In most states, the decision to release a prisoner to parole is contingent on a number of factors, including the nature and severity of the offense for which incarcerated, prior adult and juvenile criminal record, disciplinary record while incarcerated, and risk assessments. Also considered may be inputs from any victims of the prisoner's crime, the prisoner's family, the prosecutor, and the sentencing judge, as well as the prisoner's case plan as prepared by prison staff and his testimony and demeanor at the parole hearing.[5]

Conditions of Parole

Prisoners granted parole are given specific conditions they must adhere to after release. They then are discharged from incarceration and placed under the supervision of parole officers charged with seeing that they abide by the terms of release. Parole conditions generally place a number of substantial restrictions on the parolee's activities. In every case, one condition is that the individual abide by all local, state, and federal laws. Being arrested for a crime may result in revocation of parole even before trial, whether or not the parolee is convicted.

Conditions of release also generally include parolees having to meet with their parole officer within a few days of having been released, having scheduled meetings with the officer as instructed, and answering all reasonable inquiries. Parolees must keep their officer apprised of their current address and of any intention to move, and they are not to leave the jurisdiction without the officer's permission. They must allow the parole officer to visit and enter their home, enabling the officer to observe any indications that the parolee may be violating release conditions, such as signs of drug or alcohol use. Parolees typically are expected to search for steady employment and to maintain employment when found, though they may be relieved of this requirement if they are attending an education institution. If they have difficulty finding work, which many parolees do, they are expected to keep their parole officer apprised of efforts they have made to secure employment.

Parolees are not to associate with any person with a criminal record, which may mean they are forbidden to keep company with a sibling or other relative with a criminal conviction. They must refrain from drug use and submit to drug testing at the demand of their parole officer. They are to pay all fines that are part of their sentencing including any court-ordered restitution, and they must develop and adhere to a payment plan approved by their parole officer. They may be required to attend a substance abuse or mental health counseling program.[6] Other conditions may be placed on the released prisoner depending on the type of crime for which she was incarcerated.

Parole can be revoked not only for being arrested for a crime but also for what is termed a *technical* or *administrative* violation, which amounts to failure to adhere to parole terms. Parole officers generally have considerable discretion concerning how to deal with a technical violation. The response may range in severity from giving a verbal admonition, to instructing the parolee to attend counseling, to revoking parole and returning the parolee to incarceration either in jail or prison. A recent study showed that in forty-two states in early 2017, more than sixty-one thousand prisoners previously released had been reincarcerated in prison, not for being arrested or committing a new crime, but for one or more technical violations while on parole. This number constitutes an estimated 5 percent of the prison population in the states surveyed. It is believed that thousands more technical parole violators have been reincarcerated in jails or halfway houses; however, we have no reliable statistics on the number.[7]

Criticisms of Parole Practices

Several arguments are put forward to help justify the demands that parole conditions make on the activities of released prisoners. One contention is that a parole period constitutes part of the parolee's sentence, and its attendant requirements are justified to ensure that a released prisoner completes the sentence. A second argument holds that parole restrictions are designed to protect community safety and foster the parolee's reintegration by helping prevent her from engaging in any criminal activity. A third consideration is that parole allows the individual to strengthen ties to family, work, and community while undergoing rehabilitation.[8]

However, although released prisoners may consider adhering to parole terms to be less of a hardship than they endured while incarcerated, terms of parole typically substantively restrict the activities of parolees in a number of ways—including their use of time, travel possibilities, and social activities— that are outside the experience of other citizens. Questions have been raised whether parole restrictions often are more numerous than necessary and may work against reintegrating the parolee into society. A report by the Vera Institute of Justice calls into question the practices of many community supervision agencies, holding that research indicates that instead of being helpful, the number and severity of restrictions on parolees detract from the goal of reintegration.

The report cites the practice of requiring a parolee to submit to drug testing or participate in a drug treatment program when substance abuse was not a factor in his criminal conviction. In addition, restrictions may frustrate the requirement to find and maintain steady employment because they make it more difficult to schedule work hours. Work impediments may include curfews, appointments with parole officers, driving restrictions, and mandatory attendance at treatment programs. Individually, each requirement may seem worthwhile; but taken together, they may substantially reduce already-meager employment opportunities. The longer the parole period, the more difficult it may be to live by all of the restrictions, increasing the probability that the parolee will commit a technical violation that may result in being returned to incarceration, erasing whatever credit was earned by living in the community violation-free.[9]

Critics also argue that parole conditions may inhibit reintegration by significantly reducing parolees' autonomy and privacy and that constantly being at risk of failure and reincarceration may further reduce parolees' sense of being a self-controlling agent.[10] Reduction in autonomy may adversely affect the parolee's self-motivation to negotiate the challenges of parole and successfully merge with society (a topic to which we will return in a later chapter). Evidence also indicates that the circumstance of parole being revoked due to not meeting requirements may erode parolees' respect for the criminal justice system. A study of 294 people who had been incarcerated found that revocation of parole was significantly associated with participants' reduced perceptions of the fairness and legitimacy of the criminal justice system.[11] Such altered perceptions, which may be due to believing that revocation often seems arbitrary, are not likely to advance respect for law, a crucial attitude to instill among released prisoners.

Sending a parolee back to prison for a technical violation also is unlikely to add to public safety. Research indicates that returning parolees to incarceration for violating a condition of parole—which could include anything from failing a drug test to not showing up for a scheduled meeting with the parole officer—may increase crime rates due to the criminogenic effect of being incarcerated. Criminogenic effects comprise offenders' personal characteristics and the situations they experience that make future criminal activity more likely. Examples of criminogenic personal characteristics are antisocial attitudes, poor stress management skills, and lack of empathy for others; instances of criminogenic situations include having marital problems and association with other criminals. In the case of revocation of parole due to a technical violation, research indicates that the simple fact of being reimprisoned constitutes a criminogenic situational factor that increases the likelihood that the person will commit a future crime. [12]

Evidence shows that often it is difficult for released prisoners to negotiate parole successfully. For example, in 2016, of the 379,914 individuals under state jurisdiction who exited their parole, only 213,248 (56 percent) did so successfully. Another 105,541 (28 percent) were reincarcerated, and most of the returns to imprisonment were for 58,579 parole revocations. [13] Figures for different states vary widely, with more than 80 percent of former prisoners completing their parole in Kansas and almost 90 percent in South Carolina. However, in Arkansas only 37 percent (3,665 of 9,902 parolees) successfully completed parole, and another 5,741 (58 percent) had their parole revoked. [14]

According to the Vera Institute of Justice study we mentioned above, one problem with community supervision programs that leads to unsuccessful outcomes is applying the same set of core conditions to all parolees, no matter their level of risk. Many parole boards have a standardized list of as many as thirty conditions that they apply to all people on community supervision, both low- and high-risk parolees. Applying conditions that may be appropriate for high-risk parolees to those who pose little risk is held to waste the time and efforts of understaffed community supervision offices. Intensive supervision of low-risk parolees also increases their chances of being found to have violated a parole condition, resulting in parole being revoked and their being returned to incarceration though they pose little risk to the community and are almost certain to lose any job they may have, the ability to spend time with their family if they have one in the locale, other ties they have established in the community, and whatever progress they have made toward reintegration. Critics argue that supervision strategies and plans should fit an individual parolee's risk assessment and needs in order to maximize effectiveness. [15]

Fines and Fees

Another type of legal condition typically placed on prisoners released on parole consists of financial obligations. These assessments begin with court-ordered fines for the crime that led to imprisonment, with the amounts levied depending on the type of crime committed. Financial obligations the offender incurred also may include court fees, public defender fees, and restitution. Payment for losses that victims of the crime endured may be included in restitution fees. These court-ordered assessments may vary from a few hundred to hundreds of thousands of dollars, with the released offender generally having to agree to pay the fees over a set period of time.

Supervision and Program Fees

A second kind of monetary payment required of prisoners released on parole consists of supervision and program fees, which many states charge. Supervision fees consist of a designated amount demanded from the parolee for the cost of supervision. These assessments usually are due monthly and typically range from fifteen to fifty dollars, but they may be more. How nonpayment of supervision fees is handled varies by jurisdiction, parole office, and parole officer. In some cases, if the parolee is deemed to have no resources for payment or to be making substantial efforts to pay, failure to pay supervision fees may be treated leniently. In other cases, not paying the supervision fee may be considered a technical violation of parole and lead to an increase in parole length, imposition of additional parole conditions, or revocation. Jurisdictions also may require program fees from the parolee for drug testing or participation in substance abuse or other programs that are conditions of parole.[16]

Supervision and program fees are considered a type of "user fee" intended to provide budgetary support to the parole system. Sold to the public as a way to keep down taxes for a rapidly growing correctional system by insisting that those convicted of a crime should pay for the system, they are another offshoot of the tough-on-crime mentality. The assessment of such fees has grown rapidly until they have become an extensive aspect of much of the criminal justice system. They may even include, early in the criminal justice process, charges for public defenders and jail stays. The fees are not fines levied as a form of punishment, and they are not restitution assessments meant to compensate victims. Their purpose is simply to raise revenue for jurisdictions.[17] Such fees, along with fines and court-ordered restitution, follow former prisoners when they are released on parole, often creating a substantial financial burden and increasing the weight of the boulder they must push uphill.

Criticisms of Parole and Program Fees

Arguments in favor of levying supervision and program fees on parolees begin with the claim that such fees bring in funds that help defray the cost of supervision, and because parolees are the ones who committed a crime, it is more appropriate that they, rather than taxpayers, bear the cost of their supervision. A second argument defending the imposition of such fees is that being on supervision is an advantage over being incarcerated, so it is only fair that the parolee should be the one to pay for that benefit. Some also argue that by having to pay the fees, parolees will be more invested in the success of any programs to which they are assigned and more dedicated to successfully negotiating their parole.[18]

In response to such arguments, critics of the practice of assessing parole fees argue that efforts to collect the fees may incur greater costs than what is collected, thereby canceling any financial advantage of the fee system. These opponents point out that states generally do not gather and save systematic information about what fees are owed by people on parole or probation and how much is collected. Jurisdictions that do gather information on fees collected typically fail to track the costs of collection, including the salaries and time spent by office clerks and parole and probation officers, as well as attorneys and judges. Costs also are associated with penalties for nonpayment, which can include time preparing and executing arrest warrants and the expenses involved in jailing a parolee for nonpayment.[19] In addition, if the person is sent back to incarceration for failure to pay fees, the attendant court and reincarceration expenditures may cost considerably more than the fees that would have been collected.

Critics of parole fees also argue that requiring released prisoners to pay supervision fees represents a conflict of interest—jurisdictions have an incentive to levy higher fees and extend parole periods to bring in increased revenue. In addition, opponents claim that emphasis on raising income through collecting fees obscures the intended focus of the parole system. As an integral part of the criminal justice system, parole systems should target public safety and ensuring that parolees successfully rejoin society. Dedicating time and effort to collecting money from parolees confounds the parole system's natural purpose. Parole officers, with their very high caseloads, may need substantial time to develop payment plans, monitor payments, bill parolees, and instigate punitive actions when parolees fall behind. Such efforts may sidetrack officers from protecting public safety, which requires that they closely monitor parolees and help ensure that those at risk of reoffending do not do so.[20] Many would argue that another main goal for parole officers should be to help the parolee make the transition from prison to free society, and that time spent collecting and enforcing the payment of fees operates against that purpose.

Accordingly, the strongest argument against charging supervision and program fees to released prisoners may be that it creates a substantial roadblock to the parolees' reintegration into society and thereby promotes recidivism. Having to pay the fees creates an additional obstacle for released prisoners who already must address a number of other challenges to postrelease success. Paying fees is especially onerous for the majority of former prisoners who are financially poor. Consequences include lost income needed by the returning citizen and possibly his family for basic living expenses such as housing and food, as well as for transportation to jobs. These effects may promote housing and food insecurity and undermine the parolee's efforts to locate and travel to work.[21]

We do not have the data to perform a cost-benefit analysis to show whether parole systems generally benefit financially from collecting supervision and program fees. However, we concur with the arguments that levying such fees blurs what should be the main goals of parole systems and increases the likelihood that parolees fail to complete parole successfully.

Collateral Consequences

Collateral consequences—often termed *collateral sanctions*—are legal and regulatory constraints on people sentenced for criminal behavior that diminish their rights and privileges as American citizens. Collateral consequences are not part of the penal code or the sentencing process but rather are civil regulations that apply to people convicted of a crime. In that sense, they are *collateral* to the sentencing process. Collateral consequences are encoded in federal, state, and local laws and statutes and limit the activities of released prisoners in substantive ways, not only while they are on parole, but even after they successfully complete parole and often for a lifetime.

Another type of collateral consequences follow from being convicted of a crime but are not encoded in state or federal laws or statutes. In effect, they are punitive measures that society places on individuals who have been convicted of a crime after they have served their sentence. We term these *societal sanctions*, and we will focus on them in the next section. Here we attend to collateral consequences reflected in various laws and statutes and how these affect individuals convicted of a felony after they have been released from incarceration.

Most courts in the United States must warn an individual on trial of the sentencing consequences of a guilty plea, but they are not required to warn her of collateral consequences that may accompany a guilty verdict. Also, though the Constitution guarantees an accused individual capable defense, most courts have held that a defense attorney need not advise a client of the collateral consequences of a guilty verdict.[22] Today, most collateral sanctions are determined by particular states and may include canceled voting rights, inability to qualify for public funds including education loans and public housing, reduced parental rights, loss of a professional license, and revocation of driving privileges.

In his 2005 book *But They All Come Back: Facing the Challenges of Prisoner Reentry*, Jeremy Travis points out that promoting the imposition of collateral consequences on prisoners and former prisoners is attractive to politicians because they can demonstrate to the public that they are "tough on crime" while also emphasizing that such sanctions do not require raising taxes. Yet these consequences, though significant, remain effectively invisible to the public, which has limited understanding of what they are and their effects. Because such sanctions are not part of the criminal justice sentencing system, they also may be overlooked in legislatures debating sentencing policies. Because they are somewhat unseen and unnoticed, their effects can be difficult to measure. [23]

Imposition of collateral consequences can make a former prisoner into something less than a full citizen by taking away rights and privileges that other Americans enjoy. Among the most fundamental is the right to vote. State voting restrictions vary; two states—Maine and Vermont—have no restrictions, fourteen states remove voting rights only for prisoners, and twenty-two also disenfranchise parolees or both parolees and probationers. Several states eliminate voting rights for life for those convicted of particular felonies or having multiple convictions. It is estimated that in the 2016 elections, more than six million Americans who had become involved in the criminal justice system were denied the right to vote. [24]

A number of states also prohibit former prisoners from serving on juries for a period; for several states, the prohibition is for life. Those convicted of a felony also typically are prevented from holding public office or working in certain municipal positions. School districts may prevent parents with a criminal conviction from volunteering at a child's school, even if the conviction was not for anything related to children and occurred years ago; parents also may be banned from activities outside of school involving youth, such as coaching. [25]

Some rights and privileges ruled out for convicted felons pertain to the social support system established by federal, state, and local governments through various statutes. According to U.S. law, released prisoners with certain types of criminal convictions are strictly forbidden from public housing; and local public housing authorities can choose to deny housing to those with any criminal convictions. If a released prisoner's spouse or family lives in publicly supported housing, the sanction against residing in public housing bars parolees from living with them. Families may be required to sign an agreement that a returning former prisoner will not live with them or even visit them at their home. In some jurisdictions, an entire household can be evicted from public housing if one household member has been arrested. [26] If the parolee's spouse or family wants to move from public to private housing in order to be with the parolee, the added expense may place that move financially out of reach. Clearly, this sanction can adversely affect the structure of a parolee's family. For many parolees, it may decrease the likelihood of successfully completing parole by putting at a distance their main social support after their release at a time when they especially need it. At the same time, because the vast majority of former prisoners are poor and come from poverty-stricken families and communities, this sanction helps sustain their state of poverty.

In a majority of states, released prisoners with felony drug-related convictions also have a lifetime prohibition from accessing other forms of public assistance, such as food stamps. The American Bar Association reports that in the dozen states with the most severe policies, about 180,000 formerly incarcerated women were banned from receiving such assistance in 2013, adding to their and many of their families' food insecurity, and reinforcing the poverty they may be experiencing.[27] State prohibitions on felons receiving public assistance also may include restricting them from entering into public-funded programs focusing on mental health and substance abuse, services they may urgently need as they attempt to rejoin society.

In various states, some or all former prisoners face other collateral consequences. They may lose or be unable to obtain a professional license. Depending on the state, professional licenses for cosmetologists, barbers, accountants, nurses, real estate brokers, architects, and others may be revoked or denied, restricting the type of job the released prisoner can obtain and preventing former prisoners from performing the work they may have trained for. Released prisoners may be prohibited from certain kinds of employment, including in law enforcement, the healthcare and pharmaceutical industries, and any job that requires a security clearance. In addition, individuals with criminal convictions are in jeopardy of losing parental rights; some states consider incarceration itself sufficient cause to terminate those rights, and other states hold that incarceration is a relevant factor in assessing parental rights. In parental custody cases, a prior criminal conviction may become a main consideration, even if it was many years prior and did not involve engaging in any activity directly related to care or welfare of a child.[28]

Former prisoners, even those who have completed parole successfully, often have statutory restrictions on where they can live and travel. Those who have been convicted of a sex-related crime are not allowed to live within a certain distance of schools or where children gather; those who have been convicted of a drug-related crime may be restricted in what part of a community they can live. Foreign travel is limited for former prisoners; several nations do not allow convicted felons to enter.

Another type of collateral consequence can be exercised against immigrants who are not U.S. citizens. According to U.S. immigration law, these individuals are subject to deportation if it is discovered that they have a criminal record, even if the conviction was for a single nonviolent, relatively insignificant act that occurred years previously. The Immigration and Customs Enforcement agency can apply this consequence to immigrants who are permanent residents with green cards as well as to others. Even those who have lived in the United States for many years and have established families and lives here may be subject to deportation.[29]

Over the past several decades, laws restricting the activities of those with criminal records have increased. The result is to impede former prisoners' efforts at rehabilitation and alienate them from society, making them outcasts of a sort. These consequences likely increase the probability of recidivism for many former prisoners. Thus, insisting on legal consequences for those who in many cases are harmless to society jeopardizes public safety. Insofar as such consequences are intended as ongoing punishment for breaking the law, they do not help former prisoners reintegrate into society. Evidence suggests that released prisoners may consider some collateral consequences a form of unfairly "piling on," analogous to piling on in football, which is illegal because it is unnecessary, may result in serious injury, and does not further the goals of the game. To the degree that released prisoners consider collateral consequences a form of piling on, they may impede them from successfully graduating from community supervision, thereby reducing, instead of increasing, public safety.[30]

SOCIETAL SANCTIONS

Added to the numerous legal restraints and consequences of having been incarcerated, former prisoners must face the stigma placed on them by a mostly unreceptive, even disdainful society. It is true that the strictly legal consequences of criminality reflect society's displeasure with those who have been convicted of a crime and sent to prison. But aside from the purely legal effects of having been incarcerated—time in prison, parole restrictions, fines, fees, and collateral consequences—a large residue of antipathy remains that is expressed by many people's attitudes toward those who have been incarcerated. This enmity finds its expression not in legal consequences but in extralegal practices that serve as very real hindrances to the successful return to society of prisoners who have served their sentence. The words of a former prisoner, spoken years after his release from prison, describe the results of facing such ill-feeling.

Textbox 4.1: Former prisoner

Despite being home from prison for twenty-one years, being granted a pardon, and having my rights restored by the State Board of Pardons and Paroles, almost daily I am subjected to obstacles with employment, closed doors to civic and social opportunities, and attitudes of supposed superiority leveled towards me.

Many of those attitudes and closed doors come from people whose transgressions, whether violations of man's laws or God's, simply have not been brought to light. They have not been caught; their little secret hasn't been exposed. Until their "errors in judgment" are found out, they feel within their right to assume superiority. Still others have been caught, but they escape disapproval and dismissal because of their social standing, financial status, or influence within the community.

People will remember the negative parts of your life forever but forget the positive quickly. From childhood to early adulthood, I was in preparation to be a leader in my community but made bad choices later in life. I paid for those choices dearly; but should I be punished for them the rest of my life? I've found that the only pardon you get in life is when you accept Jesus Christ as your savior, your sins are forgiven. Man, however, never forgives or forgets.

Anybody who really knows my character and my heart doesn't think any less of me. My crime was nonviolent, growing marijuana, which thirty-four states, as of this writing, have legalized to be used and grown for medical purposes and ten for recreational use. People don't realize how quickly and easily someone in their own family could end up on the wrong side of the law. I wonder what their thoughts and attitudes would be then?

Employment Limitations

Of the societal sanctions that burden released prisoners, the most far-reaching and relevant for their day-to-day life and future outlook may be social attitudes and practices that reduce their employment opportunities. In the previous section, we saw that legal collateral consequences of having been imprisoned often include restrictions on the types of job former prisoners can take and their ability to attain and keep a license in various fields, both of which adversely affect employment prospects. Societal sanctions go beyond the legal limitations, creating additional difficulties in former prisoners' efforts to secure and maintain employment, especially living-wage employment.

The social penalties that diminish employment options begin during parole. These penalties are among the most serious of parolees' challenges, as evidenced by research on the opinions of a group whose views on the issue are very credible: parole officers. For instance, in a study seeking opinions of a focus group of Massachusetts parole officers about problems parolees encounter, they reported that one of the greatest challenges was securing and maintaining employment. The officers estimated that as many as 90 percent of the parolees they dealt with had a difficult time locating gainful employment, and the jobs they did manage to find often paid wages so low that it was difficult to support themselves and their family.[31] Research indicates that during the first full year after release, only 55 percent of former prisoners reported earnings. The median earnings of those who work is just above $10,000 annually, with only 20 percent earning more than $15,000 per year.

Even after released prisoners have successfully negotiated parole, difficulties in finding meaningful employment generally persist. Three years after exiting incarceration, only 52 percent of released prisoners reported any employment earnings.[32]

A main reason securing employment is so difficult for former prisoners is that as a matter of policy, many companies and other organizations will not hire individuals who have been convicted of a felony. The greatly increased availability of online databases that provide information about individuals' criminal history, along with the ease of accessing that information, makes it easy for organizations to perform background checks on potential employees and reject applications of those who are found to have a criminal history. Applications, many of which ask job seekers to report any prior criminal history, may be rejected no matter the nature of the conviction or how many years in the past. These widespread practices close many avenues of employment to returning citizens. Some organizations now are willing to accept at least some employees who formerly were incarcerated, a sign of gradual change, but the practice of denying employment to former prisoners remains common.

Homelessness

Another consequence of society's distaste for released prisoners is housing insecurity. Homelessness, or having to live in transient housing such as motels or rooming houses, is rife among those released from prison. Results of a study on homelessness among former prisoners indicate that even after several years, they are about four times more likely to be homeless than others in the population. The percentage of homelessness is greatest among women, individuals who have been recently released, people of color, and those who have been incarcerated more than once. A little less than half of these citizens reside in homeless shelters; the remainder are unsheltered.[33]

The problem of housing insecurity released prisoners face is exacerbated by the difficulty of obtaining a rental unit in residences overseen by property management companies, including apartment complexes, as well as by others who refuse to rent to former prisoners. This exclusion may be due to insurance issues, biases about the risk of renting to an individual who has been incarcerated, or both. These restrictions can add greatly to the difficulty of locating adequate housing.

Another reason for the high rate of homelessness is closely related to the problem of finding employment. Without adequate funds, locating a place to call home can become almost impossible. Even if a potential renter can locate a rental unit that will accept a former prisoner, it may be beyond the person's monetary capacity. These two problems feed on one another. Lacking a home address to supply on a job application creates another roadblock to gaining employment, and lacking employment income results in inability to pay for housing.

Being homeless also is a risk factor for being rearrested and sent to jail or returned to prison, as homelessness has been criminalized in a number of jurisdictions. Criminalization of homelessness results in a kind of revolving door, which amounts to prisoners being released, rearrested for a minor offense such as sleeping in a public place, and then returned to incarceration, a pattern to be repeated following the next release.[34] This revolving door obviously adds to the former prisoner's instability and failure to merge successfully with society and to the problem of recidivism.

What Social Attitudes Show

It is difficult not to conclude that our nation does not yet support the full integration of former prisoners. Numerous legal sanctions and widespread pejorative attitudes proclaim that, at most, society endorses limited reintegration. Employment and housing restrictions may be the most materially harmful impacts of unfavorable social attitudes directed at former prisoners, but negative attitudes can make themselves known in other ways. Overall, they reveal that though released prisoners may be well received by family and friends, they are not welcomed by the larger society.

Society's inhospitable sentiment and attendant behavior leave returning citizens a contingent of millions who are stigmatized and thereby hobbled for life. Because this widespread unwelcoming attitude contributes greatly to former prisoners' difficulties in obtaining living-wage employment, it is a way our society shoots itself in the foot. This is evident given the abundant research showing that employment reduces recidivism, thereby decreasing the tremendous financial and human costs that attend reincarceration—money and lives that could best be spent otherwise.

As a society, we could make significant steps to improve this situation by first recognizing that the human beings who are paying their debt to society by being incarcerated should not be made to pay—like Sisyphus—forever. We also could acknowledge the substantial difficulties former prisoners face after release that put their reintegration at risk—including that very formidable obstacle of securing living-wage employment. We then could make up our minds to provide these individuals, while incarcerated, with tools to substantially expand their prospects of gaining a job that pays living wages once they reenter society. By doing so, not only would we strengthen a large group of our citizens upon their return to society, but we would strengthen society in a number of important ways, the most obvious being by reducing the recidivism rate that demands billions of dollars annually and decimates our communities. This book, of course, is one long argument that those are exactly the steps we should be taking.

Education and training are the preeminent tools we should provide our incarcerated population. As we reported in chapter 2, many individuals enter prison with little formal education—about 40 percent have less than a high school diploma. Serving prison time with no additional education or training, and exiting at the same level where they were when they entered, has a great impact on the types of work they may qualify for and results in an increased likelihood of unemployment after release. By furnishing expanded and improved education and training opportunities to those eager to prepare themselves for the world they eventually will reenter, we could help them overcome that most troublesome obstacle of finding a decent job after release.

THE LINK BETWEEN EDUCATION AND EMPLOYMENT

Considered together, three premises—that securing living-wage employment is a major problem as returning prisoners try to integrate into society, that education level is related positively to the likelihood of finding such employment, and that many prisoners have low educational achievement—make a powerful argument for providing education to prisoners while they are incarcerated. That is, they provide a powerful argument if we recognize that for the sake of public safety, reducing recidivism, and justice, our goal should be to support these returning citizens in their attempts to merge successfully with society.

Research clearly reveals an association between released prisoners' level of formal education and their employment options. Community supervision officers agree that having at least a secondary education is an important factor in securing employment and in the types of jobs former prisoners can obtain. In a recent study soliciting the views of ten Georgia community supervision officers, nine agreed that a secondary education opens job prospects that otherwise would remain closed and eases the individual's efforts to reenter the community.[35]

Abundant research also shows that post-release employment decreases the likelihood of former prisoners returning to criminal activity and thereby serves as a positive factor reducing recidivism. Here, we cite the results of three studies.

First, researchers in a five-year follow-up study of offenders released from prison found that among 6,561 offenders released from the Indiana Department of Corrections in 2005, "post-release employment was the major [negative] predictor of recidivism."[36] These findings were true of the full range of offenders who had been imprisoned for different types of crimes—violent, nonviolent, sex, and drug offense.

And the result apparently was not affected by the released prisoner's race or ethnicity, given the results of a second study that examined a subsample of

3,927 offenders who were released from the Indiana Department of Corrections and returned to urban Indianapolis. Based on findings of that study, the researchers concluded, "This study's results clearly indicated that post-release employment was the most influential factor on [reducing] recidivism, regardless of the offender's ethnicity."[37] These research findings agree with those of a third study, in which the researchers found that "post-release employment had a significant, negative influence on recidivism, indicating that men who secured jobs following release from prison are less likely to fail on parole and fail less quickly than unemployed men."[38]

What makes the findings of these three studies even more notable is that they did not take into account the quality of job or the wages earned by former prisoners who were able to secure employment following their release. Quality of employment is a variable often overlooked in research that attempts to determine the relationship between post-release employment and recidivism, and the three studies found that employment after release reduced recidivism without taking into account whether or not it was living-wage employment. The results of the three studies thus suggest that *any* employment reduces the likelihood of recidivism. How much better if we were to educate and train prisoners to the degree that they could qualify for obtaining *living-wage* employment.

NOTES

1. Peggy McGarry et al., *The Potential of Community Corrections to Improve Safety and Reduce Incarceration* (New York: Vera Institute of Justice, 2013), https://www.vera.org/publications/the-potential-of-community-corrections-to-improve-safety-and-reduce-incarceration-configure.

2. William Rhodes et al., *Recidivism of Offenders on Federal Community Supervision* (Cambridge, MA: ABT Associates Inc., 2013), https://www.ncjrs.gov/pdffiles1/bjs/grants/241018.pdf.

3. U.S. Department of Justice, Bureau of Justice Statistics, *Probation and Parole in the United States, 2016*, by Danielle Kaeble, Bulletin NCJ 251148 (Washington, DC, April 2018), https://www.bjs.gov/content/pub/pdf/ppus16.pdf.

4. In efforts to advance public safety and reduce recidivism, an increasing number of states are requiring some form of post-release supervision even for those who have served all of their sentence, according Adam Gelb et al., *Max Out: The Rise in Prison Inmates Released Without Supervision* (Philadelphia: Pew Charitable Trusts, June 2014), https://www.pewtrusts.org/-/media/assets/2014/06/04/maxout_report.pdf.

5. Ebony Ruhland et al., *The Continuing Leverage of Releasing Authorities: Findings from a National Survey* (Minneapolis: University of Minnesota, Robina Institute of Criminal Law and Criminal Justice, 2016), chapter 4, https://robinainstitute.umn.edu/sites/robinainstitute.umn.edu/files/final_national_parole_survey_2017.pdf.

6. Ruhland et al., *Continuing Leverage*, 36.

7. Eli Hager, *At Least 61,000 Nationwide Are in Prison for Minor Parole Violations* (New York: Marshal Project, April 23, 2017), accessed February 29, 2020, https://www.themarshallproject.org/2017/04/23/at-least-61-000-nationwide-are-in-prison-for-minor-parole-violations.

8. Linh Vuong et al., *The Extravagance of Imprisonment Revisited* (Berkeley: University of California Faculty Publications, 2010), 18, https://www.nccdglobal.org/sites/default/files/publication_pdf/specialreport-extravagance.pdf.

9. McGarry et al., *Potential of Community Corrections*, 12.

10. Ioan Durnescu, "Pains of Probation: Effective Practice and Human Rights," *International Journal of Offender Therapy and Comparative Criminology* 55, no. 4 (2011): 534–36, https://doi.org/10.1177/0306624X10369489.

11. Amy B. Smoyer, Trace S. Kershaw, and Kim M. Blankenship, "Confining Legitimacy: The Impact of Prison Experiences on Perceptions of Criminal Justice Legitimacy," *Journal of Forensic Social Work* 5, nos. 1–3 (2015): Results, https://doi.org/10.1080%2F193692 8X.2015.1092905.

12. Lynne M. Vieraitis, Tomislav V. Kovandzic, and Thomas B. Marvell, "The Criminogenic Effects of Imprisonment: Evidence from State Panel Data, 1974–2002," *Criminology and Public Policy* 6, no. 3 (2007): 589–622, https://doi.org/10.1111/j.1745-9133.2007.00456.x.

13. Other reasons for exiting parole include the parolee's death, being moved to a different state, and absconding.

14. U.S. Department of Justice, *Probation and Parole, 2016*, appendix, table 7.

15. McGarry et al., *Potential of Community Corrections*, 11–12.

16. Alicia Bannon, Mitali Nagrecha, and Rebekah Diller, *Criminal Justice Debt: A Barrier to Reentry* (New York: Brennan Center for Justice at New York University School of Law, 2010), https://www.criminallegalnews.org/media/publications/brennan_center_for_justice_re entry_report_2010.pdf.

17. Bannon, Nagrecha, and Diller, *Criminal Justice Debt*, 4.

18. Ebony Ruhland, "The Impact of Fees and Fines for Individuals on Probation and Parole," *Robina Institute of Criminal Law and Criminal Justice Blog*, May 23, 2016, https://robinainstitute.umn.edu/news-views/impact-fees-and-fines-individuals-probation-and-parole.

19. Bannon, Nagrecha, and Diller, *Criminal Justice Debt*, 10–11.

20. Bannon, Nagrecha, and Diller, *Criminal Justice Debt*, 31.

21. Katherine Beckett and Alexes Harris, "On Cash and Conviction: Monetary Sanctions as Misguided Policy," *Criminology & Public Policy* 10, no. 3 (2011): 505–7, https://doi.org/10.1111/j.1745-9133.2011.00727.x.

22. Gabriel J. Chin, "Collateral Consequences of Criminal Conviction," *Criminology, Criminal Justice, Law & Society* 18, no. 3 (2017): 4.

23. Jeremy Travis, *But They All Come Back: Facing the Challenges of Prisoner Reentry* (Washington, DC: Urban Institute Press, 2005).

24. Christopher Uggen, Ryan Larson, and Sarah Shannon, *6 Million Lost Voters: State-level Estimates of Felony Disenfranchisement, 2016* (Washington, DC: Sentencing Project, October 6, 2016), https://www.sentencingproject.org/publications/6-million-lost-voters-state-level-esti mates-felony-disenfranchisement-2016/.

25. Christopher Uggen and Robert Stewart, "Piling On: Collateral Consequences and Community Supervision," *Minnesota Law Review* 99 (2015): 1871–1910.

26. American Bar Association, Criminal Justice Division, *Collateral Consequences of Criminal Convictions Judicial Bench Book*, NCJRS no. 251583 (Chicago: American Bar Association, March 2018), 5, https://www.ncjrs.gov/pdffiles1/nij/grants/251583.pdf.

27. American Bar Association, *Collateral Consequences*, 5.

28. Uggen and Stewart, "Piling On," 1892.

29. Uggen and Stewart, "Piling On," 1898–99.

30. Uggen and Stewart, "Piling On," 1872.

31. Lisa E. Brooks et al., *Reincarcerated: The Experiences of Men Returning to Massachusetts Prisons* (Washington, DC: Urban Institute, 2008), 32, https://www.prisonlegalnews.org/media/publications/uijpc_report_reincarcerated_men_returning_to_ma_prisons_apr_2008.pdf.

32. Adam Looney and Nicholas Turner, *Work and Opportunity Before and After Incarceration* (Washington, DC: Brookings Institution, 2018), 1, table 1, https://www.brookings.edu/wp-content/uploads/2018/03/es_20180314_looneyincarceration_final.pdf.

33. Lucius Couloute, *Nowhere to Go: Homelessness among Formerly Incarcerated People* (Northampton, MA: Prison Policy Initiative, August 2018), https://www.prisonpolicy.org/reports/housing.html.

34. Couloute, *Nowhere to Go*, The Revolving Door.

35. Roger C. Byrd, "Secondary Education and Offender Recidivism in Middle Georgia: An Analysis of Perspectives of Community Supervision Officers" (PhD diss., Valdosta State University, 2018).

36. John M. Nally et al., "Post-Release Recidivism and Employment Among Different Types of Released Offenders: A 5-Year Follow-up Study in the United States," *International Journal of Criminal Justice Sciences* 9, no. 1 (2014): 16–34, accessed May 11, 2020, http://www.ijcjs.com/pdfs/nallyetalijcjs2014vol9issue1.pdf.

37. Susan Klinker Lockwood, John Nally, and Taiping Ho, "Race, Education, Employment, and Recidivism among Offenders in the United States: An Exploration of Complex Issues in the Indianapolis Metropolitan Area," *International Journal of Criminal Justice Sciences* 11, no. 1 (2016): 57–74, https://www.sascv.org/ijcjs/pdfs/lockwoodetalijcjs2016vol11issue1.pdf.

38. Mark T. Berg and Beth M. Huebner, "Reentry and the Ties That Bind: An Examination of Social Ties, Employment, and Recidivism," *Justice Quarterly* 28, no. 1 (2011): 382–410, https://doi.org/10.1080/07418825.2010.498383.

Chapter Five

Prison Education in the United States

To realize both the need and the promise of making prisoners' education a priority for the nation's correctional institutions, it is important to understand the state of prison education today. To do that, it helps to see where we have been and how we got here. In this chapter, we first present a brief history of prisons and prison education in America and then explain the different forms, purposes, and availability of education provided today to at least some prisoners.

A SHORT HISTORY OF PRISON EDUCATION IN AMERICA

Although imprisonment in some form or other has been known since antiquity, prisons in early colonial America mostly were reserved for political and religious offenders and debtors. The use of prisons to incarcerate and punish lawbreakers was all but unknown in colonial times. Crimes were punished through levying fines, corporal punishment such as flogging or cutting off an ear, shaming (e.g., branding the offender with a visible letter or placing him in stocks to be viewed by the public), or death. Following the practice in England, the death penalty was used widely and could be imposed for numerous crimes, even some that today would be considered misdemeanors.[1]

On religious and philosophical grounds, would-be reformers of the criminal justice system at the time objected to the rampant use of the death penalty to punish lawbreakers. In opposition to the Calvinist and Puritan belief that humans basically were sinful and incapable of change, Pennsylvania Quakers put forward a more optimistic view. They believed that criminals could be rehabilitated and redeemed and that the death penalty abruptly and, for the most part unjustifiably, cut short the possibility of redemption. These opposing views marked an early instance of a theme that has played out repeatedly concerning the issue of how best to deal with offenders. The central question has been: what principle should guide the hand of the community and the state in responding to criminality? Should we seek retribution from offenders by punishing them for past deeds? Or should we emphasize rehabilitating the wrongdoer so he will not commit further offenses in the future? And if the answer is that we should seek both punishment and rehabilitation, with an eye on both the past and the future, then in what mixture?

In colonial America, Quakers and their more merciful approach found a powerful ally in William Penn, the founder and first governor of Pennsylvania. Penn, strongly influenced by the principles of the Quaker religion, believed that the English laws mandating the death penalty for a wide variety of transgressions were too harsh. As governor, he decreed that the penalty of death be applied only to those found guilty of murder or treason. The Quakers also argued that rather than sentencing offenders to death or even physical punishment for their transgressions, a more humanitarian option, according better with Christian theology, would be to imprison them and require them to work. Penn agreed that confinement and prison labor for lesser crimes than murder or treason was the appropriate penalty for lawbreakers. Thus was born in the United States the concept of incarceration as punishment for committing a crime. What followed was reequipping older structures and building new ones to serve as prisons for punishing criminal offenders, the first real prison system in America.

After Penn's death in 1718, forces dedicated to maximum retribution for offenders sought to demolish his efforts based on Quaker principles. As a result, Pennsylvania prisons, like those in other states, became dreadful places. Prisoners—who may have been incarcerated for anything from violent crimes to being unable to pay their debts—were held in crowded, poorly lit, unhealthy buildings, badly ventilated and filled with stench and vermin. Cells, some underground, often were no more than dungeons. Prisoners young and old, first-time petty offenders as well as confirmed felonious criminals, typically were held in common cages.

Yet, throughout the late 1700s and 1800s, the prison reform movement continued and gradually gained strength, with a more charitable view of criminals guiding the thoughts and actions of those who believed that the contemporary incarceration conditions amounted to cruelty. Eventually, the movement resulted in the founding, in 1783, of the Philadelphia Society for Alleviating the Miseries of Public Prisons by Benjamin Franklin and other prominent Philadelphia citizens. Formation of this organization marked a growing realization of the terrible conditions in correctional institutions and spurred reformers to press for building prisons that allowed for more humane treatment. One key improvement sought was to insist that prisoners be housed in separate cells instead of holding, in the same large room, adults and young people, violent and nonviolent offenders, and both genders, a practice that still was common in some prisons. This resulted in the construction of Western State Penitentiary near Pittsburgh and then, a few years later, in 1829, Eastern State Penitentiary, also known as the Cherry Hill prison, in Philadelphia.

The thought guiding the construction of Eastern State Penitentiary (as it had been for the Western State facility) was that prisoners should be confined in solitary cells and not be allowed to mix with others. It was believed that spending all of their time alone would provide abundant opportunity to contemplate the actions that had resulted in incarceration and decide not to make such choices again. That would reduce recidivism and save money in the long run. The result of this thinking was an imposing structure where prisoners were assigned cells in which they lived, ate, and worked at some manual trade such as weaving or woodworking, always alone. Each cell was updated with some of the latest conveniences, including running water and a flush toilet, and each had a tiny yard attached. A few years after opening, Eastern State Penitentiary began to incarcerate women, who were held in areas separate from male prisoners.

Insofar as the idea was to confine lawbreakers in silence and solitude, Eastern State worked perfectly. The problem was that the severe confinement also bred loneliness and depression. The facility became known as a breeding ground for mental illness and suicide as much as an opportunity for redemption.

In contrast to the Pennsylvania system, a decade earlier New York State had set in motion a different kind of prison system. The first facility was opened in 1816 in Auburn, and a second in 1826 in Ossining (the prison later called Sing Sing). In the so-called Auburn system, prisoners worked together during the day and ate meals together, though always in strictly enforced silence, and then went to individual cells in the evening. At Auburn, work projects could be much larger than the small trades and crafts performed at Eastern State Penitentiary by individuals in their cells. Workplaces became small factories where prisoners worked together silently in assembly lines to produce goods to fill the orders of organizations beyond the walls. The resulting income to the prison system helped reduce the costs of incarceration. Largely for this reason, other states soon adopted the Auburn system.

As the concept grew of prison as a place not just for punishing but for rehabilitating lawbreakers, it was inevitable that the idea of educating prisoners would take root and develop, as education was viewed as the chief means for accomplishing rehabilitation. The first efforts at prison education were taken late in the eighteenth century with religious ministers teaching prisoners to read. These programs of prison instruction often were called *Sabbath schools.*

The purpose of Sabbath schools was twofold. One objective was to rehabilitate prisoners' character so they would turn away from engaging in criminal activities and become law-abiding citizens once released from incarceration. At the same time, supporters and enactors of prison education often saw their educational mission as providing prisoners the opportunity to achieve religious salvation. It was believed that a condition of achieving either of these goals was to teach prisoners literacy so they could read the Bible, harken to its messages, and transform their spiritual and social lives.

Given the prisoner's dismal living conditions at the time, it is probably safe to say that when the local pastor came for a short while to teach, he was welcome. The pastor provided a Bible—the only reading matter the prisoner was allowed to have in her possession—and typically taught through a grate in a dimly lit cell that the prisoner may or may not have had to share with other prisoners, though in some cases lessons were provided after Sunday services in a prison chapel. The curriculum consisted of learning the English alphabet and grammar, even history and geography, through reading and discussing Bible verses. It is easy to imagine how these sessions may have transpired, with the pastor exhorting prisoners to put aside sinful and unlawful ways, while eagerly teaching them the tools to read the Bible later after the pastor had left. All the while, a guard likely was standing nearby to ensure the proper behavior of the prisoner and safety of the pastor. For the prisoners' part, the fact that someone from the outside world acknowledged that they were alive and deserved human consideration, someone willing to visit them occasionally in the cheerless prison, may have provided powerful motivation to keep their pastoral visitor coming by embracing their lessons through learning how to read.

By the 1820s, education in a few prisons had begun to assume a more secular character, with basic education skills being taught not only in reading, but also writing and mathematics. In 1844, Sing Sing reported teaching not only basic literacy and mathematics skills but also history, geography, astronomy, and physical education. Yet, for the most part, prison education retained a religious nature. At the same time, a number of prison systems had no educational services. According to Gehring, in 1840, the Boston Prison Discipline Society reported that only eleven chaplains in the United States could visit and educate prisoners, and that most of them were in the northeast.

During the 1800s, a notable result of the reform movement occurred when government leaders in New York State legislated that educational programs be mandated in all state prisons. In some other states, too, an increasing number of prisons developed some form of education program for prisoners. At the same time, these programs continued to take on an increasingly secular character. In 1870, the American Prison Association was formed. This organization later became known as the American Correctional Association. In its declaration of principles, it stated its affirmation and support for the value and need of providing education programs in the nation's correctional facilities.

In the early 1900s, with the Industrial Revolution progressing at full strength and speed, the nation's factories evidenced a great need for trained workers. It became obvious to business organizations that one potentially large source of workers was the nation's prisons. They understood that prisoners who developed work skills while incarcerated would be better prepared upon their release to enter a labor force that demanded as many trained workers as possible. That realization helped spur a movement to provide increased vocational education programs in U.S. prisons. This development amounted to a new impetus for increasing prison education—at least vocational education—not stimulated primarily by religious or reform zeal. Rather, the push for increased job skills training for incarcerated individuals amounted to market forces driving the growth of a particular kind of education program within the nation's prisons.[2] Vocational education got a further boost in 1934 with the formation by Congress of Federal Prison Industries to employ prisoners and give them vocational education that could help them secure employment after release.[3]

In the so-called Progressive Era, from around 1900 to 1929, calls for prison reform continued, including more education for prisoners.[4] A significant development for the future of prison education was the formation, in 1930, of the Federal Bureau of Prisons. Austin MacCormick, assistant to the director of the Bureau for Academic and Vocational Training, conducted a nationwide survey to determine the education facilities and practices of correctional institutions. He subsequently formed a standing committee for adult prison education that in time became the Correctional Education Association.[5]

By the 1930s, most U.S. prisons had basic or vocational education programs, but no American correctional institutions had any higher education opportunity for prisoners. Tertiary education did not begin to be offered in any of the nation's prisons until 1965; after that, however, the idea of providing higher education proliferated quickly: by 1982, there were 350 such programs.[6] College programs available included correspondence courses and classes held inside prisons under the auspices of local community colleges and technical schools.

The decades of the 1970s, 1980s, and early 1990s may have marked the height, to date, of the centuries-long push for prison education. The realization that offering a college education to prisoners was an excellent way to prepare them to secure work and enter society on a positive note when they were released had become well accepted. This realization was so strong that the federal government had begun offering Pell Grants and federally guaranteed student loans to eligible prisoners who desired to pursue higher education options while incarcerated but had inadequate funds to pay for tuition.

During that same period, however, development of the tough-on-crime mentality led to a rapid increase in the prison population. This growth in number of people incarcerated, allied with limited money available for U.S. prisons and the rise of a widespread view that prisoners were being provided too many advantages, marked the end of the short-lived era when educational opportunities for prisoners, at least for higher education, were expanded notably. In 1994, Congress passed, and President Clinton signed a law eliminating the issuance to prisoners of Pell Grants and guaranteed student loans.[7] Concurrently, many states prohibited prisoners from taking college correspondence courses.

At present, education in the nation's prisons still is recovering from the significant cutbacks that marked the end of the twentieth century. However, a few points of light have shown through over the past several years. These include the Second Chance Pell Grant program for both state and federal prisoners initiated during the Obama administration. Significant college–prison initiatives have appeared, as has an apparent growing realization among some state and federal leaders of the value of prison education. We will talk much more about some of these developments in later chapters.

CORRECTIONAL EDUCATION TODAY

Today it is well recognized that the educational attainment of those incarcerated in the nation's prisons is considerably below that of the rest of the population. The 2003 National Survey of Adult Literacy comparing the educational achievements and literacy of approximately 1,200 state and federal prisoners to those of 18,000 adult householders found that almost twice as many prisoners (37 percent) had only some high school education or less compared to the nonprisoner adult population (19 percent).[8] It is evident that the prison population, the vast majority of which will be reentering the larger society, needs educational services. It also is widely recognized that offering prison educational programs or even demanding that prisoners participate in education while in prison helps them prepare for their release. Accordingly, most American prisons offer some form of educational programming to incarcerated individuals. Though we have few recent statistics on the number of state prisons offering various forms of prisoner education, the 2005 Census of State and Federal Correctional Facilities noted that 85 percent of all reporting facilities offered one or more formal educational programs to student-prisoners.[9]

Types of Correctional Education

Several forms of prison education are carried on in the nation's prisons. These range from basic education to opportunities for higher education. A brief summary of the main forms of education available in the correctional system follows.

Adult Basic Education (ABE) is one of the main educational programs provided for prisoners in both state and federal prisons. The program is intended for individuals with a reading level below the ninth grade. ABE generally includes instruction in reading, writing, and arithmetic. Instruction in ESL (English as a second language) also is available in some prisons. Soon after admittance to an institution, prisoners are tested to determine their level of reading skill. In some states, partaking in ABE is mandatory for prisoners who test below a given level of reading proficiency. Adult education instruction may be divided into two levels of classes: first through fourth grade, and fifth through eighth grade.

Adult Secondary Education (ASE) is for prisoners who are tested as reading at or above the ninth-grade level. ASE instruction provides high school–level coursework. For the most part, classes focus on preparing the prisoner to take and pass an examination for securing a general educational development (GED) certificate, which is a high school equivalency certificate intended to substitute for a high school diploma.[10] The GED test has four sections—mathematical reasoning, reasoning using language arts, social studies, and science—that include multiple choice questions and require the student to write an essay. The ASE student must complete all four sections successfully to pass the test. Earning the GED certificate not only provides the prisoner with entry to a wider range of employment upon release, but it is also accepted by most U.S. higher education institutions for prisoners who wish to go on to college after release. However, the GED certificate is limited by fewer instructional subjects than the full range of high school courses typically required for a diploma. For this reason, the student may choose to work toward receiving a high school diploma by taking a correspondence course through the mail from one of several organizations offering such instruction. A drawback of working to obtain a high school diploma through correspondence courses while in prison is that the student generally must pay the cost of the course himself. This cost may amount to several thousand dollars. Because many prisoners do not have access to substantial funds, completing a high school diploma through correspondence may be financially out of reach.

Career and Technical Education (CTE). These correctional education programs provide students with targeted skills in a wide variety of professional and technical fields and may offer the prisoner an opportunity to gain certification. Typical fields of training include carpentry, cabinetmaking, drywall, HVAC (heating, ventilating, and air conditioning), administrative services, computer-aided design, masonry, culinary arts, and electronic systems technician. Successfully completing a CTE course generally enables a student-prisoner to qualify for an entry-level job in the selected area of training after release from incarceration and increases the probability of securing living-wage employment.

On-the-Job Training (OJT) through correctional industries programs. When available, these programs connect the correctional system with outside organizations that contract for various kinds of labor or manufactured goods prisoners produce for an attractive cost. Examples of products that prisoners may build and the correctional system may sell are print-shop items such as signs, banners, brochures, and office materials; metal fabrication goods such as metal tables, benches, and signs; office furniture including desks and bookcases; cabinets and countertops; and office panel systems. Manufacture of such items provides the student-prisoner with marketable job skills that can be used to secure employment upon release.

Postsecondary Education (PSE). As explained in the previous section, postsecondary education programs in prisons have diminished compared to what was available a few decades ago. Yet, in some correctional institutions, opportunities still exist for prisoners to enter into a two- or four-year college course that will provide an associate's or bachelor's degree when successfully completed. Individuals may be able to enter such a program in various ways. One is to take a correspondence course from one of a number of educational institutions offering such studies to prisoners. To pay for the courses, the schools themselves or other organizations, such as the Prison Scholar Fund, may offer assistance. The 2012 reinstatement of some Pell Grant eligibility also provides incarcerated students who would otherwise find the cost prohibitive an opportunity to enroll in college coursework.

Some colleges offer innovative programs funded by the state. An example is the partnership between the Ohio Department of Rehabilitation and Correction (ODRC) and Sinclair Community College of Dayton, Ohio, which offers college programs to individuals in ten of Ohio's prisons. Prisoners who apply to enter the Sinclair program are carefully screened by correction officials and, when admitted, attend classes inside their prison. The cost for tuition is $1,950 annually, paid by the state as an investment in preparing offenders to be better able to secure work upon their release and successfully reintegrate into society. Successful reintegration then reduces the probability that released offenders will find their way back to the prison. The Sinclair–ODRC collaboration has had significant success in educating prisoners over its thirty-one years of existence.[11] Several other visionary programs involving other colleges in other states are underway to help prisoners procure a college education. These include innovative prison education programs in California, New York, and elsewhere. We will go into more detail about some exemplary programs in chapter 10.

Digital Education

A widespread educational limitation that impinges on successful societal reentry of incarcerated people, one that is especially important in today's world, is the scarcity of computer and digital education in prison. Having been denied access to the internet, e-mail, and computer networks while serving their time, returning citizens generally have a deficit of computer know-how and little knowledge about online communication and resources. This occurs especially among those who have been incarcerated for several years. Having to wait until release to gain computer skills or learn how to access the wealth of information available on the internet about how to construct résumés and application letters, sit for interviews, and search for and identify employment and educational opportunities is one more roadblock slowing the reentry progress. Computer and digital literacy may have become second nature to most people living outside prison walls, but to gain that status required a learning process that took time. Digital capabilities are advancing constantly, but whereas those outside prison have time to absorb and adjust to changes as they occur, prisoners with no access may be left further and further behind.[12] Returning prisoners who have been incarcerated five, ten, or more years are reentering a technological world where much may seem unfamiliar. The issue of digital illiteracy becomes even more serious given the fact that many jobs expect familiarity with and some degree of proficiency in digital tools.

Safeguarding security is the main reason given for prisoners not being allowed to access the internet or e-mail. The concern is reasonable, but it presupposes that providing prisoners opportunities to gain digital literacy requires full internet and e-mail access. However, the issue need not be an all-or-nothing proposition.[13] Access to digital communications and resources could be limited, via prison intranets, to fully legitimate educational sites that prisoners cannot possibly exploit inappropriately. Prisoners could gain proficiency in programs that might be most useful outside prison walls, such as word processing, image editing, and statistical programs, but do not require online access.

One recent initiative provides prisoners with the opportunity to gain some digital literacy, while at the same time providing educational programming to help them pass the GED or the HiSET exam and even, in some cases, to take college-level courses. Several companies have provided digital tablets for prisoners to access lessons. Prisoners cannot access the internet via the system, but instead are connected to a private, secure network at dedicated facility kiosks where they download educational material and upload prepared lessons. Two such companies are JPay and GTL, both of which were in the prison phone and messaging business and since have added educational programming through tablets. The services also provide entertainment programming such as music and games, as well as messaging capabilities, via the tablets. In promotional material, the companies point out a major benefit: the system keeps prisoners occupied and reduces stress and the potential for violence, which likely adds to overall safety within the institution. However, criticisms of the companies are that though the tablets sometimes are free to prisoners, costs for messaging and entertainment functions are too high for most, who have few financial resources.[14] We are unable to say to what degree the educational services offered counterbalance that concern. Provision of educational programming on the tablets does seem promising, but at this time little research is available on the quality and effectiveness of that programming.

One entrant to the field of prison education via tablets that is smaller than other such companies, but growing, gives some promise of strong focus on providing quality educational services. This is Education Over Obstacles, or EDOVO. Evidence of the company's dedication to providing quality programming is the fact that it has received several grants and start-up investments from organizations interested in social justice innovations.[15] Here too, research is needed to determine the effectiveness of the tablet-based educational services the company provides.

THE FLAWED STATE OF PRISON EDUCATION TODAY

Based on our brief summary of the prevalent forms of education in American prisons, one might conclude that correctional education in the United States is in pretty good shape. After all, prisons provide basic education, secondary education, vocational education, and postsecondary education programs. What more could prisoners want? But our summary does not make clear that correctional institutions differ greatly in which education programs they offer, the quality of the programs, and how many prisoners take advantage of them.

In other words, our summary does not address the messy reality of today's correctional education. That reality includes detrimental factors that place a tremendous drag on efforts to educate prisoners. From our perspective, two main interconnected reasons account for these drawbacks. First is a shortage of knowledge and vision among too many political, correctional, and educational leaders about the enormous value that may accrue to our society of making education a priority in our prisons. That lack of foresight tends to deaden any sense of urgency about the need for prison education. It also results in the second main reason for hindrances to prison education— the perpetual shortage of funds to support correctional education programs, much less expand them.

Before listing some of the detrimental consequences of the lack of vision and funds for prison education, we want to emphasize the dearth of all-inclusive studies that focus on the extent and quality of education available in our nation's more than eighteen hundred prisons. This lack of comprehensive research is understandable, given the complexity of the American corrections establishment. With fifty different state prison systems, each with its own characteristics, along with federal and private prisons, it is difficult to provide definitive measures that might allow us to compare American prison systems across the board in terms of education coverage and quality. It is clear that states differ widely in how important they consider prison education to be, the funding they allocate to it, the programs available to prisoners, and the quality of those programs. It also is evident that numerous correctional systems lag seriously behind in their efforts to educate their prisoners. That said, let us look at some of the main hindrances that beset education in many of the nation's prisons.

One problem is that thousands of would-be students who are eager and ready to enroll in a secondary education program available in their correctional institution, including GED examination preparation, are unable to do so until their name reaches the top of a long waiting list. Although GED prep classes are available to some prisoners in most prisons, in many, class space is limited severely. As a result, people who could be actively preparing for reentry into society by studying, learning, and testing for a GED certificate instead are reduced to marking time until their name pops up on the waiting list. If they are released before that time or before they earn the certificate, then the opportunity to leave prison walls with the GED in hand is lost. Also gone is the increased opportunity to secure a job that would come from having earned the certificate.

Much the same can be said for prisoners who are prepared to advance beyond the secondary level by entering a CTE program. A certificate of completion from such a program could thoroughly lubricate their chances of gainful employment after release. Yet, though they might enter such a program enthusiastically if they could, they are unable to do so, for either of two reasons. First, even if the prison offers a technical/professional program in a field of interest, openings may be limited, so the prisoner is denied entry or must join a waiting list. Another common reason is that CTE programs may be few or simply not offered in the individual's correctional institution. These reasons also often apply to prisoners who want to study in an academic postsecondary field. They may hope to get a head start on entering college after their release or may aspire to attain a two- or four-year degree in their field of interest while incarcerated. In either case, they are unable to do so because their facility offers no postsecondary programs.

Another difficulty that besets many prison education programs is that the quality of instruction and program design suffer from insufficient funding.

Incarcerated students constitute a unique population.[16] They may be taking basic education or high school–level courses, but they are not elementary school or high school students and cannot be treated or taught as such. Understandably, some student-prisoners have issues of trust. They may have cognitive limitations or emotional issues such as dejection and pessimism stemming from their situation. Like any education program, teaching methods and curricula should be designed to fit the students they are aimed at. However, important characteristics of the student-prisoner population may not be taken into account in designing programs. In addition, having dedicated, knowledgeable, and skilled instructors is recognized everywhere as one of the best predictors of student success. However, though prison instructors often do a commendable job, they may lack special training in methods to best teach prisoners.

Yet another problem for prison education is the environment. Prisons tend to be noisy, turbulent places—anything but conducive to studying and learning. Many of America's prisons are aging structures built many decades ago and lack quiet rooms or areas where students can read in peace and focus on their assignments. The only study hall may be the prisoner's cell, surrounded by noise and commotion. Carrying on educational programs in such environments is like trying to teach math or reading on a loud, tumultuous—and sometimes threatening—playground. Yet, the monies may not be available for renovations that a correctional institution may need to create a calm area where student-prisoners can study.

Tackling these problems effectively, of course, will take a greater financial investment in prison education; made wisely, it will pay for itself many times over in reduced recidivism. But to invest wisely, we also require the best thinking of our educators, correctional administrators, business leaders, and politicians. For too long the American prison system has been at the mercy of bankrupt ideas that survive only by turning a blind eye to what is in front of our faces—that providing our prisoners with quality education and training will strengthen their potential for success, will reduce recidivism and its enormous costs, and will make our streets safer. In part II, we will push forward our argument for more and better prison education on the wheels of psychology, sociology, ethics, and financial common sense.

NOTES

1. Information in this section pertaining to the 1700s and 1800s is from several sources, including Thom Gehring, "Characteristics of Correctional Instruction, 1789–1875," *Journal of Correctional Education* 46, no. 2 (June 1995): 52–59; Robert S. Hanser, *Introduction to Corrections* (Thousand Oaks, CA: Sage, 2017); Marilyn D. McShane, *Prisons in America* (New York: LFB Scholarly Publishing, 2008); and Jonathan E. Messemer, "The Historical Practice of Correctional Education in the United States: A Review of the Literature," *International Journal of Humanities and Social Science* 1, no. 17 (2011): 91–100.

2. Messemer, "Historical Practice," 92.

3. Ricky H. Coppedge and Robert Strong, "Vocational Programs in the Federal Bureau of Prisons: Examining the Potential of Agricultural Education Programs for Prisoners," *Journal of Agricultural Education* 54, no. 3 (2013): 116–25, https://www.jae-online.org/attachments/article/1762/2012-0691%20coppedge.pdf.

4. Dominique T. Chlup, "The Pendulum Swings: 65 Years of Corrections Education," *Focus on Basics* 7, no. D (September 2005), http://www.ncsall.net/index.html@id=826.html.

5. Coppedge and Strong, "Vocational Programs," 120.

6. Christopher Zoukis, *College for Convicts: The Case for Higher Education in American Prisons* (Jefferson, NC: McFarland, 2014), 41.

7. Charles B. A. Ubah, "Abolition of Pell Grants for Higher Education of Prisoners," *Journal of Offender Rehabilitation* 39, no. 2 (2004): 73–85, https://doi.org/10.1300/J076v39n02_05.

8. U.S. Department of Education, National Center for Education Statistics, *Literacy Behind Bars: Results from the 2003 National Assessment of Adult Literacy Prison Survey*, by Elizabeth Greenberg, Eric Dunleavy, and Mark Kutner, NCES 2007–473 (Washington, DC, May 2007), table 3.1, http://nces.ed.gov/pubs2007/2007473.pdf.

9. U.S. Department of Justice, Bureau of Justice Statistics, *Census of State and Federal Correctional Facilities, 2005*, by James J. Stephan, Special Report NCJ 222182 (Washington, DC: October 2008), table 6, https://www.bjs.gov/content/pub/pdf/csfcf05.pdf.

10. A few prisons recently have moved from offering GED classes to providing classes to prepare prisoners for a different high school equivalency test called the HiSET (high school equivalency test).

11. Ashley A. Smith, "Momentum for Prison Education," *Inside Higher Ed* (November 6, 2018), accessed April 22, 2020, https://www.insidehighered.com/news/2018/11/06/colleges-push-more-resources-support-prison-education-programs.

12. Eva Marie Toreld, Kristin Opaas Haugli, and Anna Lydia Svalastog, "Maintaining Normality When Serving a Prison Sentence in the Digital Society," *Croatian Medical Journal* 59 (2018): 335–39, https://doi.org/10.3325/cmj.2018.59.335.

13. Toreld, Haugli, and Svalastog, "Maintaining Normality," 337.

14. Victoria Law, "Captive Audience: How Companies Make Millions Charging Prisoners to Send an Email," *Wired*, August 3, 2018, https://www.wired.com/story/jpay-securus-prison-email-charging-millions/.

15. Anne Field, "Edovo, Maker of Tablet-Based Education for Inmates, Aims to Reduce Recidivism and Continues to Grow," *Forbes*, March 12, 2016, https://www.forbes.com/sites/annefield/2016/03/12/edovo-maker-of-tablet-based-education-for-inmates-aims-to-reduce-recidivism-and-continues-to-grow/#3c662f7857b6.

16. Meagan Wilson, Rayane Alamuddin, and Danielle Cooper, *Unbarring Access: A Landscape Review of Postsecondary Education in Prison and Its Pedagogical Supports*, Ithaka S+R Organization research report (May 30, 2019), conclusions, https://doi.org/10.18665/sr.311499.

Part II

Reducing Recidivism

Chapter Six

The Psychological Argument

Intrinsic Motivation, Self-Efficacy, and Post-Release Success

A FUNDAMENTAL QUESTION

One of the most powerful arguments for expanding prisoner education and training focuses on the concept of motivation. The argument is easy to understand, based on scientific evidence, and a veritable slam dunk. It begins with the realization that if we want to reduce recidivism, we need to ask a fundamental question:

> What motivates released prisoners to make choices that will lead to becoming law-abiding citizens who contribute to society?

This question is important because motivation is what moves people to do whatever they do. As we have learned, former prisoners must overcome many challenges to join free society. To successfully meet those challenges, *they must be motivated to do so.* If their motivation to succeed weakens, the chances of being returned to incarceration increase, and the recidivism rate does not go down. Clearly, it is imperative that we learn what we can about the factors that motivate former prisoners to reintegrate into society.

Of course, individual prisoners may be motivated in many specific ways to stay within the law once released. Knowing that family is awaiting his return can steel an incarcerated man's determination to make an honest go of things in the future. A mother's letter reminding a daughter of a dream she had as a teenager can make it evident to her that she must do all she can, once released, to fulfill that dream. Any number of things could motivate a prisoner to decide not to fall back into the cold iron grip of incarceration—a conversation with a fellow prisoner, growing older and thinking about things more clearly, or increasing regret as the months or years go by in prison with no life goals accomplished.

However, we don't need a list of specific factors that may motivate a released prisoner to act within the law. Rather, our job is to comprehend what is most basic about motivation. What elemental factors underlie many, if not all, of the specific motivations prisoners may have to do what they do after their release? We need to understand the fundamentals of motivation.

WHAT MOTIVATES US ALL ALSO MOTIVATES PRISONERS

To understand what motivates returning prisoners to make their choices, we should start by asking what motivates people in general to choose what they choose and do what they do. After all, prisoners are *people*, not a different species. They are individual human beings who have engaged in illegal behavior and been apprehended and sentenced. Some of those criminal behaviors are appalling, others much less so. In any case, though some people might believe that engaging in illegal behavior and being sent to prison amounts to giving up membership in the human community, it does not. So, if we want to understand what fundamental factors influence released prisoners, we need to understand what motivates people in general to make the choices we make.

To better understand motivation, we will outline two powerful theories of motivation set forth by researchers: *the self-determination theory* of psychologists Edward L. Deci and Richard Ryan[1] of the University of Rochester, New York, and the *self-efficacy theory* developed by psychologist Albert Bandura[2] of Stanford University. These two theories of human motivation are not only powerful, but they also share a number of commonalities in their approach to motivation. We want to know first what these models say about what determines human motivation generally, for all of us, and then we want to zero in on what they can tell us about what basic factors affect the motivations of individuals who are or have been incarcerated. As we will see, both theories can tell us a great deal about what to do in our correctional systems to reduce recidivism.

TWO KINDS OF MOTIVATION

We begin with self-determination theory, a well-established framework for understanding human motivation that views motivation as being of two different types: extrinsic and intrinsic. *Extrinsic motivation* means to have an incentive or a reason to perform an action that comes from outside oneself.

We are extrinsically motivated when we engage in an activity for the sake of an external reward or to avoid punishment. On the positive side, we may perform an action to earn an external prize in the form of money, praise, or goodwill. On the negative side, we may be motivated by the desire to avoid a penalty, such as our peers thinking we are strange if we do not act according to their expectations or the probability that we will be fired if we do not do the job we were hired to do. In both cases, our behavior has an external motivator: gaining a reward or avoiding a penalty.

The second kind of motivation is *intrinsic motivation*, an internal incentive or reason to perform an action. Deci and Ryan identify the most basic form of intrinsic motivation as the natural motivation of infants and children to grow and develop psychologically, emotionally, and socially. Development in all of those dimensions begins at birth. Anyone who has witnessed the activities of a newborn over the first few weeks and months has seen the early stages of this development as the child shows initial signs of a natural curiosity about the surrounding world and displays first efforts at attempting to interact with that world. This early motivation to explore and understand the world is innate in all children, deeply embedded in each child's genes. The child is naturally internally inspired to investigate the nearby world while learning how and to what degree she can control the surrounding environment. These efforts to understand and explore the world are done for their own sake, for the personal satisfaction gained from those activities.

Intrinsic motivation continues throughout childhood, especially if nurtured by the child's environment, and in particular by the actions and words of parents and teachers. We can see it operating when children choose to play games and perform tasks simply because they find the activities enjoyable. The young boy who spends hours playing baseball or building model airplanes engages in those endeavors simply for the satisfaction and pleasure he gains. The young girl who likes to play soccer or to practice ballet does so for no other reason than the gratification and delight those activities bring her. Of course, despite all of the intrinsic motivation, extrinsic motivation is certainly not unknown to children. The parent who tells the child that unfinished homework means no video games is using the warning of a potential external loss to motivate the child. The same parent who tells the child that getting a good grade in math will earn a trip to the beach is using an external reward for motivation.

Thankfully, intrinsic motivation continues into adulthood to a considerable degree for most of us, as we typically are motivated internally in many of the choices we make in our lives. We are intrinsically motivated when we decide it is time for a night out on the town or to buy new clothes, or even just to have a cup of coffee or a beer. Those choices come from inside us; they are self-motivated. Many adults are fortunate to work in jobs they are intrinsically motivated to perform. To become a physician, plumber, hairdresser, or IT professional are among many occupations an individual may choose largely because he finds the field attractive and is self-motivated to enter into it. Many other adults, as is common knowledge, find themselves working in occupations they are not intrinsically motivated to choose. They are not particularly attracted to the occupation and not internally motivated to perform the job, but they are in the occupation anyway because they are extrinsically motivated to do the work to gain the external reward of a pay-check.

However, someone in a job only extrinsically moved to perform at first may find that in time he also becomes intrinsically motivated. According to self-determination theory, extrinsic motivations may become internalized and thereby become a second type of intrinsic motivation. To some extent, we may perform the action because we want to earn an external reward or to avoid punishment; at the same time, we also do it because we are internally motivated to perform the action. Many employees can testify to this. Their primary reason for working at a position may be to earn a paycheck—an extrinsic motivation with an external reward. At the same time, they want to do well in their work not just because of the monetary reward but for the sense of self-pride or pleasure they gain. To that extent, the motivation is internal and produces an internal reward. Doing a good job to earn an exter-nal reward may even become integrated into an individual's personal value system so that performing well becomes an important internal goal.

Based on the above distinctions, Deci and Ryan define the overall concept of *self-motivation*,[3] which can be of two types. One type is the natural intrin-sic motivation to perform an action or pursue a goal because doing so brings satisfaction and pleasure. The second type of self-motivation consists of reasons to perform actions and pursue goals that at first may have been only extrinsic but have since become strongly internalized and psychologically incorporated into our value system. We become self-motivated to perform the actions and pursue the goals by their becoming integrated into our self-perception of who we are and our view of what we should do in the world.

WHAT MOTIVATES RELEASED PRISONERS?

Given the distinctions outlined in the previous section, we need to know how they apply to prisoners, especially to prisoners released on parole. What becomes immediately clear when we examine the motivations of released offenders is that many of their motivations are extrinsic—either negative, positive, or both. On the negative side, a main motivator for a parolee to keep an appointment with a supervision officer and adhere to other parole restric-tions is to avoid the penalty of parole revocation, which will lead to being reincarcerated. The parolee also may have positive extrinsic motivations for obeying parole directives, such as eventually obtaining the external reward of completing parole successfully or the more transitory reward of gaining praise from the parole officer.

What is not so clear is to what degree prisoners are self-motivated to negotiate the obstacle course they face upon release. This is essential for us to understand because we have powerful reasons to want released prisoners not to be motivated only by external rewards or penalties; we should also want them to be internally motivated—self-motivated. We should want this because research by Deci, Ryan, and others strongly indicates that self-motivation is positively associated with performance and persistence in undertaking various tasks.[4] These findings are important because former prisoners typically confront formidable challenges following their release. As we have learned, they must find employment despite the fact that their record prohibits them from working for many organizations; locate affordable, decent housing that will accept their presence; follow reporting requirements, restrictions, and regulations while on parole; pay fines and fees associated with their incarceration and release; and fulfill other tasks made difficult because their record follows them wherever they go. To navigate this difficult obstacle course, they will need all the effort, persistence, and resilience they can muster. And those very qualities are heightened if they are self-motivated.

Therefore, it is evident that we should hope former prisoners are not just extrinsically motivated to address the many tasks they must fulfill to merge successfully with society. We should very much want them to be self-motivated, because self-motivation will provide them the best chance for success, the best chance to avoid further criminal involvement, and the best chance not to be back in prison after a year or two. No doubt, the extrinsic motivation to avoid reincarceration typically impacts favorably on many former offenders, fostering post-release success. However, given the arduous demands of parole, it is crucial that released prisoners also be self-motivated. They need to be internally driven to succeed.

If we want released offenders to be self-motivated, then, according to the principles of self-determination theory, we must understand and do our best to address a couple of important issues. The first issue is in regard to the hallmark of incarceration—prisoners' lack of autonomy—because self-motivation is closely connected to autonomy.

SELF-MOTIVATION AND AUTONOMY

To have *autonomy* is to be able to act freely out of one's own self. It is, simply, self-determination. The concept can be understood in terms of being a free agent. According to psychologist Albert Bandura, a fundamental truth about human beings is that we naturally are equipped to be free agents, which means that we have the ability to make decisions about what to do in our lives and then to act on those decisions. Our decisions may regard issues ranging from small to large, anything from whether to have another slice of pizza to marrying our sweetheart. Insofar as we can make such a decision freely, we are self-determined, autonomous agents, masters of our own lives.

The catch is that word "freely." To be an autonomous agent, able to make a choice and act on it, we must be free to do so. Yet, as we all know from experience, we have varying degrees of freedom in our choices in different areas of our lives and at different times, which results in limitations on our ability to act as free agents. We all are limited, even sometimes buffeted, by what happens in our environment as forces and happenings outside our control impinge on our freedom. We are late, so we hurry out in the morning, planning to drive to work; but when we try to start the car, we find we have a dead battery. At that moment we have lost our freedom to drive to our job if we want to get there on time. We still may be free to find another way to work, but the one option we do not have is to drive there ourselves. Our autonomy to choose freely to do so has been taken away by a lifeless battery.

Some people, of course, find themselves in positions where they are more susceptible to the buffeting winds of reality than others, and this clearly is true for prisoners. For the most part, virtually every minute of every day is under the control not of the prisoner, but of prison authorities. The multitude of things outside a prisoner's control include the basics—when and what to eat, where to sleep, whether and when to go outside to get fresh air, and at what points the prisoner's personal living area or physical body is subject to random search. Certainly, prisoners have a small degree of autonomy. Within strict limits, they can make a few decisions and act on them as they carry on their prison lives. For instance, they can choose with which fellow prisoners to attempt to fraternize. They may be able to purchase a few items at the commissary if someone outside sends money to their account. But their autonomy is severely limited, and their freedom to make decisions that might substantially change their situation immediately is totally absent.

It is evident that autonomy—the ability to freely make and act on one's own decisions in some area—goes hand in hand with self-motivation.[5] When people perceive that they have autonomy in some matter, their belief reinforces their self-generated motivation to determine what decisions are best for them in that area. The connection between being an autonomous agent and self-motivation is endorsed by self-determination theory, which identifies the ability to control one's choices and actions—autonomy—as a basic psychological need that is innate and universal among all people.[6]

Research indicates that whether a four-year-old child or a ninety-year-old adult, when the need for autonomy is supported within the surrounding environment, the individual experiences higher perseverance toward behavior change, increased cognitive flexibility, a more positive emotional tone, greater self-esteem and trust, and improved physical and psychological health.[7] In addition, the person's ability to exercise self-motivation in making life choices is strengthened. But when the environment stultifies or fails to support the need for autonomy, self-motivation weakens.

And autonomy, again, is precisely what prisoners do not have. Indeed, that is the essence of their punishment—the ability to govern their own life is taken from them, and taken radically. When prisoners' natural need to self-determine their own lives is frustrated, when they understand that the domain where their choices make any difference has been reduced drastically, their self-motivation, understandably, is weakened. The actions the prisoner undertakes are, for the most part, only extrinsically motivated, while the sphere of self-motivation may become negligible. This is not good if we want our prisoners to succeed in reintegrating into society after their release. We should not expect them to spend time in prison with little self-motivation due to lack of autonomy, feeling like their decisions do not matter, with their self-motivation in hibernation, and then suddenly become fully self-motivated upon release.

The question is, if the essence of punishment by incarceration is for prisoners to lose their autonomy, then how is it possible to simultaneously strengthen their sense of autonomy while they are incarcerated and thereby promote their self-motivation? The answer to that question is manifest. Though in their present circumstances, prisoners have minimal autonomy and can exercise little self-motivation, those circumstances do not imply that they cannot have substantial autonomy—and associated self-motivation—in regard to *their future*.

While still incarcerated, they can work and plan for their release so that when that day comes, they will be ready to attack—with gusto, determination, and a positive outlook—the tough challenges they will face to rejoin society successfully. And an excellent way to promote that autonomy toward the future and inspire prisoners' self-motivation is to give them opportunities to prepare for their release through education. By providing them a chance to exercise autonomy regarding what classes or training to take in preparation for their future, we are at the same time furnishing them occasions for self-motivation—for making choices that will enable them to start working toward post-release life.

Will having educational opportunities engender self-motivation for the future for all prisoners? Of course not. Some, perhaps many, will remain unmoved and may live out their time in prison doing what the authorities tell them to do, barely thinking what they will do once released. These individuals may be the most likely to fail to assimilate into society and be returned to prison not long after they leave. But many others will welcome expanded opportunities for education to prepare themselves for release. They will increase their sense of autonomy and self-motivation, and lessen their chances for returning to prison.

For anyone not yet convinced of the value of expanded education for post-release success, we can take the argument based on self-determination theory another step. According to Deci and Ryan, autonomy is not humans' only basic need, and not the only need closely related to self-motivation. Another fundamental need that all human beings have is for competence.

SELF-MOTIVATION AND COMPETENCE

To have *competence* is to be effective in some area of endeavor. According to self-determination theory, human beings have a fundamental need to feel competent in areas that are important to them.[8] The proof of this is in our everyday lives and all around us: it is obvious that people generally yearn to perceive themselves as competent in various domains, such as in their social life and in their physical abilities. Work is one of the most important areas in which people typically want to feel competent. They crave the knowledge and skills to do the work they perform correctly, if not with excellence, and not just for external reasons such as their employer's expectations. Their desire to feel competent in their work is a basic innate need.

So how does a prisoner's need for competence fare while he is incarcerated? To address that question, we identify three ways an offender may become more competent while in prison. The first we call *environmental competence*, which consists of becoming competent at negotiating the prison environment. Prisoners may be able to increase this competence in a number of ways. For instance, they may learn the meal and shower schedules; how to hold a pillow over their head to block out the clanging, yelling, and screaming when they are trying to sleep; who is in which gang; who to avoid and who to befriend; and how best to protect their belongings from others' opportunistic fingers.

A second kind of competence prisoners may gain while imprisoned is how better to commit crimes and escape detection once they get back into the free world. This is *criminal competence.* Certainly, not all prisoners become more criminally competent in prison, but some do. They talk in low tones with fellow prisoners and discuss the dos and don'ts of some area of criminality, including new techniques and strategies they could employ after release. Relatively naive younger prisoners may learn from older offenders who teach them new ways of criminality. Prisoners may learn tricks of the trade for criminal activity they have never before engaged in. The incarcerated thief may learn some rules for profitably dealing in drugs. The incarcerated drug dealer may learn closely kept secrets of conducting internet scams. Prisoners may get contact information about out-of-prison criminal elements, including crime syndicates, large or small, that may have an eye out for new recruits. Of course, increased criminal competence is not an ability we want prisoners to gain while incarcerated.

The third kind of competence prisoners may be able to gain while incarcerated is *employment competence.* This competence amounts to the ability of prisoners, once released from incarceration, to secure employment in a legitimate job from which they can earn a paycheck. Employment competence is something to be exercised after release. Though some prisoners have jobs in prison, for which they generally get paid extremely little, our focus is not on prisoners' competence for performing prison work but their competence for finding and doing work once released. Gaining employment competence is very important for prisoners because the more they have, the greater their likelihood of gaining post-release employment; and, as we saw in chapter 4, abundant research indicates that former prisoners being employed reduces recidivism.

Research also suggests that the quality of employment former prisoners find after release is another factor associated with reduced recidivism.[9] Higher-quality jobs are more likely to be jobs that pay higher wages A low-wage job, for which so many prisoners must settle, is better than no job at all, but it is not likely to pay a living wage and may not even allow a released prisoner to earn enough money to pay for the most basic necessities along with fees and fines.

A main reason many former prisoners must settle for a minimum-wage job is lack of knowledge and skills to perform work from which they could earn higher pay. In a word, they lack *competence.* The greater released prisoners' employment competence, the greater their likelihood of securing not just any employment, but living-wage employment. It is news to no one that in our society making a living is a basic expectation and necessity for adults. Released prisoners are no exception. Their having employment competence upon return to society is crucial for reducing recidivism because if they cannot secure living-wage employment, the likelihood increases of their committing crimes such as theft or dealing in drugs to gain needed income. The result is a growing probability that the individual will be apprehended and returned to incarceration.

The obvious way to increase prisoners' employment competence is to provide them with academic or technical education to prepare them to find legitimate living-wage employment after release. Although most prisons already offer education and training to some extent, we learned in chapter 5 that it may be restricted to basic and GED education, often limited in their availability and with lengthy waiting lists. We can do much better. Successful prisoner reintegration into society is of such great import that it is vital to raise prisoners' employment competence and prepare them for an increasingly technological and demanding workplace.

Helping prisoners develop employment competence not only has the practical effect of increasing their likelihood of successfully finding post-release employment that pays a living wage. According to self-determination theory, people's inner motivation grows along with their belief in their competence to deal with challenges. When prisoners walk out of the prison walls, we want them to be motivated from the inside to face their new world with the goal of succeeding. If they do not believe they will be able to secure employment—probably their major task after release—their self-motivation to meld successfully with society is likely to take a large hit. That makes two connected reasons we need quality education for prisoners: to provide them with the competence to help them secure a living-wage job after release and to increase their inner motivation to find that job and successfully reintegrate into society.

SELF-MOTIVATION AND SELF-EFFICACY

Training and education programs designed to increase prisoners' employment competence also positively affect their beliefs in what they are capable of achieving—their sense of self-efficacy. This is another concept that can help us understand how education and job training programs increase former prisoners' self-motivation for addressing the challenges they must meet upon release. People's sense of *self-efficacy* consists of their beliefs about their ability to do various things, meet challenges they may confront, and achieve particular goals they set. The concept of self-efficacy is close to the idea of competence.

According to psychologist Albert Bandura, our beliefs about our self-efficacy can either handicap us or help us. In regard to challenges we encounter, if we believe in our ability to deal with them successfully, then we are more likely to be successful. On the other hand, a weak sense of self-efficacy may hinder us as much as limitations in the external environment.

Beliefs in our self-efficacy also profoundly affect our motivations in life. If we want to reach a particular goal and believe we are capable of doing so, we are much more likely to pursue the goal. If we do not believe we are capable of achieving the goal, then, even if we desire to do so, our lack of belief in our ability to reach it puts a pall on even trying. Self-efficacy beliefs affect several key aspects of individuals' motivation and behavior as they make choices and pursue goals. These aspects include the amount of effort the person puts forth and her resilience in sticking to it if she meets difficulties or opposition.[10] It seems likely that a lack of belief in personal self-efficacy may lead a person not to address a challenge at all. A person's sense of self-efficacy may even largely determine what goals she sets. After all, why torture ourselves by even wanting to achieve a particular goal if we believe we can't be successful?

When prisoners are released from incarceration, it is crucial that they have a strong sense of self-efficacy. They will need all of the self-motivation they can muster; and the stronger their sense of self-efficacy, the stronger the inner motivation they can bring to their efforts. The greater their employment competence, the stronger will be not only their belief that they can get a good job, but also their sense that they will be able to perform successfully whatever other tasks they need to complete in adapting to the world outside. Therefore, we come to the same conclusion here as we did in regard to employment competence: the best way to fortify prisoners' sense of self-efficacy is to provide education opportunities to strengthen their employability and their belief in their ability to succeed in free society.

OUR ARGUMENT IN BRIEF

We have been arguing that it is crucial to attend to the psychological factors that determine the choices prisoners make after release. The question that confronts us is this: do released prisoners make choices that promote rejoining society successfully, or do they choose to engage in criminal activity that will likely lead to reincarceration? We claim that a central psychological issue that pertains to all people, including those released from incarceration, is what *motivates* them to make the choices they do. Are they motivated only from the outside, or also from the inside?

We argue that released prisoners face many difficult challenges, and to address those challenges successfully it is not enough to be extrinsically motivated—motivated by such considerations as society's expectations, fear of being reincarcerated, or any other solely extrinsic motivation. Motivation needs to come from inside: they must be self-motivated. But to foster self-motivation in released prisoners, solid psychological grounds indicate that it is crucial to help increase their autonomy, competence, and sense of self-efficacy while they are incarcerated. We have highlighted three fundamental factors that increase prisoners' capacity for self-motivation:

- providing prisoners with a measure of autonomy to make choices in prison geared toward their future helps strengthen their self-motivation;
- providing them with employment competence increases their likelihood of obtaining living-wage employment after release and strengthens their self-motivation to succeed; and
- providing employment competence to prisoners also reinforces their sense of self-efficacy, which, in turn, bolsters their self-motivation.

It is evident that what we can bring to correctional institutions that will strengthen all of these factors is expanded training and education opportunities to help prepare prisoners for post-release life. Training and education promote prisoners' employment competence, sense of self-efficacy, sense of autonomy, and self-motivation. Based on these effects, we can expect providing quality academic and technical education greatly to increase released prisoners' likelihood of reintegrating into society successfully and substantially reduce recidivism.

The alternative is to make no changes. But settling for the status quo is a nonstarter if our goal is to reduce the enormous recidivism rate. If we settle for the present state of affairs, we virtually guarantee that recidivism will stay unacceptably high, demanding billions of dollars annually to house, feed, and guard masses of prisoners who have been returned to incarceration, and imposing tragic personal costs paid by the prisoners, their families, and their communities.

NOTES

1. Edward L. Deci and Richard M. Ryan, "Self-Determination Theory," in *International Encyclopedia of the Social & Behavioral Sciences*, 21, 2nd ed., edited by James D. Wright (Amsterdam: Elsevier, 2015), 486–91.

2. Albert Bandura, "Human Agency in Social Cognitive Theory," *American Psychologist* 44, no. 9 (1989): 1175–84, https://doi.org/10.1037/0003-066X.44.9.1175.

3. Deci and Ryan denote what we are calling "self-motivation" by the term "autonomous motivation."

4. Marylene Gagne and Edward L. Deci, "Self-Determination Theory and Work Motivation," *Journal of Organizational Behavior* 26 (2005): 337.

5. Gagne and Deci, "Self-Determination Theory and Motivation," 333.

6. Deci and Ryan, "Self-Determination Theory."

7. Edward L. Deci and Richard M. Ryan, "The Support of Autonomy and the Control of Behavior," *Journal of Personality and Social Psychology* 53, no. 6 (1987): 1024, https://doi.org/10.1037/0022-3514.53.6.1024.

8. Edward L. Deci and Arlen C. Moller, "The Concept of Competence: A Starting Place for Understanding Intrinsic Motivation and Self-Determined Extrinsic Motivation," in *Handbook of Competence and Motivation*, edited by Andrew J. Elliot and Carol S. Dweck (New York: Guilford Publications, 2005), 579–97.

9. Christopher Uggen, "Ex-Offenders and the Conformist Alternative: A Job Quality Model of Work and Crime," *Social Problems* 46, no. 1 (1999): 127–51, doi: 10.2307/3097165.

10. Bandura, "Human Agency."

Chapter Seven

The Sociological Argument

Strengthening Communities

While incarcerated, every prisoner's "home" is a meager cell and a few common areas shared with many others. But their *real* home is the community out of which they came. That is where their family and friends live, and the location of many places familiar to them—the corner store, the barber one street over from the family home, the basketball court down the block, the schools they attended, the churches, the fast-food outlets. And that is the community to which they likely will return after release.

For most prisoners, their home community is in an urban area that typically is racially segregated, deficient in resources, and with a decaying infrastructure and a high unemployment rate. Such urban neighborhoods, from Seattle to Chicago to New York City, contribute an inordinately high percentage of individuals to the U.S. prison population. Certain neighborhoods may supply ten, twenty, or many times more prisoners than other parts of the same city. Evidence suggests that since the 1980s, during the decades of mass incarceration, the phenomenon of prisoners' homes being concentrated in certain urban communities has become increasingly prevalent.[1] Every year, tens of thousands of individuals are taken from these urban neighborhoods and sent to prison, and every year tens of thousands are released from prison back to the same neighborhoods.

In this chapter, we explain how prisoners' exit from and return to these communities has a powerful bearing on the communities' strength, stability, and fortunes. We also explain how providing incarcerated people with academic and technical education is one of the most effective ways to help these communities benefit—even thrive—from the return of individuals they temporarily had lost to prison. More than that, we argue that delivering good academic and vocational education to prisoners benefits not just communities with a high incarceration rate, but also every community to which former prisoners return.

We begin by emphasizing that the urban communities we're talking about have many good, law-abiding people. Some families there struggle mightily in an environment that perennially is in economic recession, if not depression, to ensure daily food on the table, adequate heat in the winter, and clean clothes for their growing children. Mothers and fathers take their children to church every Sunday and attend parent-teacher conferences to make sure their children receive a proper education. Yet many of these good families are familiar with incarceration, as they lament that a son, daughter, or partner has been sent to prison, do their best to support their incarcerated loved one, and await his or her return.

Of course, others in the community may shed no tears about the loss of the incarcerated individual if he is a local troublemaker. If he was sent away for drug dealing, extortion, armed robbery, or other violent activities, neighbors may breathe more freely after his arrest and conviction. Community members are likely to view their streets as safer and feel more comfortable going out into the neighborhood. By doing so, they increase their opportunities to socialize as they visit with neighbors, shop at local stores, walk to church, and take their children to the park. These activities tend to affirm and strengthen various social networks within the community, add to the residents' sense of neighborhood unity, and promote cooperation among neighbors.[2] It is thus evident that the arrest, conviction, and sentencing to prison of some perpetrators benefits the community by making it a safer, better place to live.

However, many assignments to prison from high-incarceration districts offer little or no sense of increased safety among community residents. Instead of being a major troublemaker, the one sent away more likely was convicted of a nonviolent crime such as drug possession, which many in the community and elsewhere may view as relatively minor. This kind of arrest and conviction has increased greatly during the period of mass incarceration, with many new prisoners being not perpetrators of violence or persistent breakers of the law but rather first-time offenders, often convicted of low-level drug crimes. If that kind of offense was charged against the newly incarcerated one, neighbors may lament, along with the offender's family, what they consider to be a local resident's regrettable transfer from the community to prison—all the more so if they believe that her offense would be better addressed by a sentence that would keep her in the neighborhood, such as being assigned to community service or a drug court.

They may especially deplore the person's exit if it is only the latest of numerous similar removals from the community. And that is likely, because to be a high-incarceration community entails having a high rate of forced social mobility, with a continuous flow of residents being sent to prison and then returning once their term has been served. Indeed, because the possibilities for residents of impoverished urban areas to move voluntarily from a community may be minimal, forced exits from and entrances into the community of people being sent to and leaving prison may be the dominant type of mobility in the area.[3]

Strong evidence shows that a high rate of social mobility within a community tends to lead to adverse outcomes. Based on research in social disorganization theory, Clear and associates argue that within high-incarceration communities, the rate of removal of individuals to prison and their subsequent return is a form of coerced residential mobility that creates disorganization and threatens community stability.[4] One effect of high mobility is that residents tend to live in greater isolation from one another, not knowing, or having only transitory relationships with, their neighbors. This circumstance undermines the community's social integration and cohesion. Also, the greater anonymity that results from a high level of enforced mobility reduces residents' commitment to the neighborhood and their interest in improving the area. Neighbors assist one another less and have decreased possibilities for collective action to deal with neighborhood needs. All of these results impair a community's social stability and the ability of its residents to work together to achieve common aims.[5] Overall, the disorganization and instability that a high rate of incarceration creates weakens the social fabric that ties together the community.

SOCIAL FABRIC

The structure of a community has several aspects. One is its economic structure, including the kinds and numbers of businesses, shops, and commercial services available there, as well as the various ways residents make a living, their income, and the total value of resources they own. Another structural aspect is the community's physical infrastructure, including its buildings, roads, electrical grid, and public transportation options. A third aspect— mainly what concerns us here—is the community's social infrastructure and, in particular, that element of its social infrastructure that arises out of its residents and links the community. We term this element the community's *social fabric.*

We view the social fabric of a community as based on and arising out of the *social networks* of which residents are a part. We are not talking about online, but rather offline social networks—real-world networks that include families but go beyond family ties to comprise any relatively stable, continuing type of relationship that occurs between two or more people in the community. Examples are friendships, groups, clubs, churches, parent-teacher organizations, cooperatives, teams, and other kinds of association. Such networks undergird a community's social fabric by forming bases for communication among residents and tying them together socially in various ways.

A community's social fabric is strengthened by the number and quality of its social networks. These networks give rise to two other important aspects of the community's social fabric. These are its *social norms* and *social capital*, two phenomena whose health is important for the community's strength. These three concepts—social networks, social norms, and social capital—are intimately interrelated. By understanding how they do or do not work together to affect a community's social fabric, we can better understand why the removal to prison of a high proportion of residents can severely damage a community.

Social Networks

People sent to prison out of high-incarceration neighborhoods, especially those convicted of relatively minor offenses, typically have numerous legitimate connections within the community and often contribute to its stability.[6] In the first place, the newly incarcerated person has a family there, parents and perhaps siblings, perhaps a wife or husband and children, and often an extended family including grandparents, uncles, aunts, and in-laws. The newly incarcerated one had relationships with all of those family members, and his enforced exit from the family attenuates those relationships, leaving gaps that may be quite significant, especially with respect to spouses and children. In all probability, the exit to prison does not destroy any of the relationships in the social network that consists of the person's family, but those relationships may be significantly weakened, at least for the duration of incarceration. The family network is likely to be weakened financially, especially if the one incarcerated contributed to the family's finances, as money is needed for prison visits and to support the family member financially while he is incarcerated. If the new prisoner has children, the family network will be weakened by the children lacking the support and guidance no longer available each day from the now-imprisoned parent.

The community member sent to prison has not only a family, but also friends and neighbors, and she likely belonged to various social networks before removal. For instance, she may have been a member of a local church. Churches often are the center of an extensive social network in the community and are socially important because they provide opportunities for residents with different backgrounds, ages, and types of employment to visit with one another, converse, and share ideas. And she may have been active in that church—a member of the choir, a study group, or a neighborhood outreach committee.

A workplace, too, is a social network, with workers and managers joined together not only economically but also in a social system; so, if the new prisoner had a job, he was a member of an employees' network. Local stores are also the locus of social networks, as are recreation centers, schools, libraries, civic organizations, and neighborhood associations, both formal and informal. The individual removed from the community may have been a member of several of those networks, perhaps friendly with the proprietors of an often-frequented corner store, a visitor or volunteer at the local recreation center, or someone who kept in contact with a former teacher or coach who desired a bright future for his former charge. Now, with him in prison, a hole opens in all the social networks of which he was a member.

The existence of those holes brought about by one community member's being sent to prison, when compounded by numerous other gaps in social networks due to the incarceration of other community members, is a serious problem. When many such holes open within a community, when an inordinate number of citizens from a particular neighborhood or area are to be found not in their real home but in a prison cell, and especially when incarcerating those individuals does not lead to any significant increase in public safety, the social fabric that binds the community together is weakened. This weakening then tends to lead to a decrease in safety within the community, as we will learn below.

Social Norms

Arising out of its social networks, a second main element that forms a community's social fabric is its *social norms*—the community's standards for the proper behavior of its members. Community residents have a kind of collective awareness of its social norms, a tacit understanding of the expected appropriate behavior.[7] By helping to guide the community's citizenry, social norms constitute an informal method of social control, which is a major means by which communities promote order and safety among residents. Whereas a low level of incarceration within a community tends to increase public safety, high levels may reduce safety through distorting social norms.[8] By promoting continual community disruption, the removal to prison of a large percentage of residents and their subsequent return hinders the ability of social networks to press for informal social controls. With the most fundamental sources of community control being impaired, community life is undermined.

One result of the weakening of social norms is increased difficulty for community members to reach agreement on shared values and how to address community problems.[9] This is pernicious because a key type of social network gives birth to community actions, such as clearing a corner lot to form a small park, calling on city hall to fix broken streetlights, or forming a group of citizens committed to clearing snow from the walkways of elderly neighbors. By uniting residents to work together to achieve common goals for the community, such networks are especially valuable for strengthening its social fabric. However, the disorganization that high social mobility causes weakens such networks and their ability to motivate members to agree and act on shared social norms.

Another unfortunate result of the attenuation of informal social control is the strengthening of conditions that encourage unlawful activity. Impaired social norms in a neighborhood to which many prisoners return lessens the social penalties for their once again engaging in unlawful activity.[10] When it is not evident to would-be offenders that the other members of the community are firmly against criminality, a hindrance to such activities is absent. For a prisoner returning to these conditions, even if she was incarcerated for a minor drug offense, and especially if her living-wage job prospects are poor, the loosening of community norms against engaging in unlawful behavior may be seen as giving her free rein to step into a criminal endeavor that will provide income. Weak social networks may intensify that temptation, leading returning prisoners to identify less with their community. This exacerbates the problem, because identification with a community encourages residents to embrace social norms opposing unlawful activities.[11] Inversely, lack of identification with the community results in returning prisoners being less likely to accept or adhere to such community norms.

Social norms that favor lawful behavior also suffer when high rates of incarceration generate community members' distrust of the legal system. If many of the arrests and convictions in a neighborhood are considered by residents to be minor crimes that would be better addressed by judgments leaving the offender in the community, sending him to prison may breed lack of confidence in the fairness of the criminal justice system. Distrust leads to reduced respect for law and a weakening of norms that encourage law-abiding behavior; government agencies become viewed as adversaries rather than service providers.[12]

A high level of incarceration in a community means that virtually all of its residents know someone—a parent, relative, neighbor, or friend—who has been sent to prison. Incarceration becomes normalized in such communities. This understanding among residents effectively makes imprisonment into a social institution within the community. Their knowledge that many of the community's residents have been incarcerated—and the possibility that they themselves eventually may be one of those casualties—becomes part of the socialization process for children and youth, affecting development of their norms.[13] Youths who have seen one or more friends or relatives sent to prison, especially if they view the incarceration as somehow unjustified, may decide to ignore community norms against breaking the law. Or, worse, they may embrace a new norm—that becoming an outlaw is the right thing to do.

Social Capital

The impairment of social networks and social norms that occurs in neighborhoods with a high rate of imprisonment also weakens the community's social fabric by severely diminishing the *social capital* available to residents and to the entire neighborhood.[14] Social capital can be viewed at either the individual or the group level.[15] At the individual level, social capital consists of the valuable information, resources, support, and opportunities that accrue to individuals through their membership and activity in social networks. This form of capital grows out of both small and large social associations, including two- and three-person networks up to the entire community, and it is empowered not only by network membership but by mutual trust between and among network members and the norms of reciprocity that they share.[16]

An example of someone benefiting from social capital at the individual level is a job seeker talking with a friend and learning from him that a nearby company is hiring. Another example is a math student at the local community college who is having difficulty with the course and is offered free tutoring by an on-campus organization to which she belongs. Both instances reflect the fact that social capital typically flows out of relationships in social networks and potentially can be of considerable economic or other value.

Social capital can be considered an attribute not only of individuals, but also of groups, a community, or even a society. Generally, the greater the number and variety of social networks in a district or neighborhood and the greater the network membership, the more social capital the area has. As various network members meet, talk, and exchange ideas, the possibilities grow not only for individuals, but also for the network itself gaining advantage from the association. The benefits of social capital may accrue to the entire community when residents form a neighborhood improvement group that focuses on addressing safety, recreational, educational, or other social needs. As we have mentioned, such groups can be especially effective in strengthening the community's social fabric.

Despite its value, however, social capital in high-incarceration neighborhoods tends to be meager due to the attenuation of social networks. Residents often possess minimal amounts of individual social capital, a condition that affects the entire neighborhood. As a result, the information, support, resources, and opportunities that might be provided to community members by their associations with others are diminished or missing. People and families tend to be more socially separated from one another, coping alone with whatever challenges they may face and unable to take advantage of opportunities that might be afforded by their belonging to strong social networks. The group social capital that could be enjoyed as community members come together to address shared problems also likely will be reduced as residents find it more difficult to join forces with others.

For returning prisoners in need of a job, especially those with poor education credentials, reduced social networking and sparse social capital in their home neighborhood is a substantial impediment to finding employment. Whereas neighborhood associations, reintegration organizations, or other social support groups might assist the native son in finding employment by providing information about open positions, introductions, references, or transportation help, a dearth of such networks results in the individual having to go at the typically difficult job-hunting task entirely alone.

RETURNING PRISONERS AND THE SOCIAL FABRIC

No clear remedy appears for the disintegration of social networks, social norms, and social capital that occurs in communities with a high incarceration rate. However, we maintain that at least the beginnings of a remedy can spring from what some may consider an unlikely source. Though the weakening social fabric in such neighborhoods is a serious problem with no easy solutions, one group of potential difference makers could mitigate—even reverse—the social breakdown that high incarceration rates cause. These are the returning prisoners themselves. It is true that they play a large role in bringing about the disorganization and instability that shred the social fabric, but they have the potential, through their attitudes and behaviors, to strengthen that same cloth.

The last statement may raise an eyebrow or two, and we can hear the ensuing question: "Why should we suppose that released prisoners might serve to help mend the social fabric of their community?" After all, these individuals have spent substantial time, often years, in a typically brutal environment. They likely have associated with prisoners who were sentenced for having committed crimes worse than their own. They may have been physically or sexually assaulted while incarcerated. By living in those conditions for a substantial period, with their primary daily associations being other prisoners, they may have mentally and emotionally absorbed less than favorable attitudes toward the criminal justice system and society. Quite possibly, the unforgiving, sometimes violent prison culture has long-term adverse effects on many after their release. In fact, research suggests that the harder the time served, the more detrimental the effects of imprisonment. For instance, a study of more than one thousand individuals released from federal prisons found that the recidivism rate was about double for those who had been transferred from a minimum-security facility to a harsher institution.[17]

As a result of their prison experiences, first-time offenders convicted of a relatively minor crime such as drug possession may return to the community much more callous than when they left. Such a transition may be most dramatic for offenders who were young when sent away, as their ideas, attitudes, and emotional stance toward society may not have been fully formed at the beginning of their incarceration. These young individuals may be more easily affected by the brutal realities of prison and more likely to come back viewing the criminal justice system and society itself through cynical eyes.

Yes, that likely is true of some returning prisoners, but we have no reason to expect that to be true for most individuals. On the contrary, many understandably are long weary of the prison existence and determined never to go back. They return to their neighborhood with a fresh outlook, resolved to make the most of their new freedom. These former prisoners can be a strong resource for their neighborhood. They have the potential to boost the community's social networks by becoming involved in churches, neighborhood associations, and civic organizations. They can become positive role models in the community, demonstrating to children, youth, and others that living an affirmative, law-abiding life is a real, viable, and preferable alternative to becoming involved in activities that eventually may lead to prison. [18]

The former prisoner's position as an authoritative role model may be especially powerful, given that he has been there, done the time, and knows intimately what prison life is like and why it has none of the "romance" that some people, especially some young men, may attribute to it. Going to prison is not cool, not manly, and not noble in any sense: a former prisoner has the authority to say that and be heard by the community. In sum, former prisoners who reenter changed, with the ability to communicate that change, clearly can be a positive community resource when they return home. [19] To the extent that they serve as positive role models and enter into community groups, especially those dedicated to the well-being of the neighborhood, they can help rebuild social networks, strengthen social norms that favor community solidarity and safety, and increase the available social capital.

But former inmates have a problem. No matter how happy they may be to have their freedom again, how resolved they are to lead a lawful and productive life, how eager they are to renew positive old associations and enter into new ones, or how well they are prepared to relay their knowledge of prison life, they first must overcome numerous challenges. If they are sentenced to parole, one major challenge is to adhere to all of its conditions; as we explained in chapter 4, that can demand significant time, money, and effort. Another big challenge for many former prisoners is to reestablish relationships with their family. This may require much effort as these individuals, after a lengthy absence, try to find their way back into their family and redefine themselves as a spouse or parent. Fitting in as a father or mother may be difficult if children have grown into adolescence or adulthood during the former prisoner's incarceration or have been living with foster parents or relatives. Other challenges the released prisoner faces include dealing with the collateral consequences we described in chapter 4, overcoming the stigma associated with incarceration, and, for some, dealing successfully with substance abuse or mental health issues.

Then they have the problem of finding work. This may be, by far, the biggest challenge facing many or most released prisoners returning to their old neighborhood. After being back for a few days, former prisoners are likely to learn that the neighborhood's social fragmentation is no better, and possibly worse, than before. Yet, it is within that broken environment that they must find employment while adhering to all other parole requirements. In trying to locate a job, they may seek out whatever social capital is available—from family, friends, neighbors, or local groups—but find little useful information or tangible help. With a paucity of assistance from others, they may be on their own.

Already hampered by being in a community that may be short on good available jobs, the returning prisoner is held back further by two heavy chains. One is the stigma of having been incarcerated; that simple fact, no matter what the offense, typically is enough to eliminate many job possibilities. A second—and arguably the heaviest—chain may be a deficient education. If, like many others, the former prisoner did not complete a high school education, she is at a disadvantage in finding work. Those who were able to earn a GED or high school diploma while in prison probably are somewhat more likely to land a job paying a minimum wage, but the position may be only part-time and offer no benefits. And it still will be difficult to qualify for full-time employment that pays a living wage.

The inability to find a decent-paying job puts a tremendous burden on the backs of former prisoners and, often, their families. With lodging, food, and other necessities to pay for, along with possible restitution and supervision fees, they have only two legitimate options if they cannot find a job: either rely on their family or go off the grid and become homeless. Either horn of this dilemma adds additional stresses to the community's social fabric. In the first case, intimate partners, who typically are female and already are financially disadvantaged, must now support a returned prisoner, leaving fewer resources for themselves or the rest of the family. The partner may have to take a second or third job, leaving little time to raise any children or to associate with others in the community. If there are children, a chronically out-of-work father at home will constitute a poor role model for them to follow as they mature, likely reducing their chances to succeed in the community.

On the other horn of the dilemma, homelessness is a further breach of the community's social fabric and obliterates a returning prisoner's chance to become a positive resource for the community. And, of course, either outcome contributes to the likelihood that a returning prisoner who is unable to secure a living-wage job eventually will engage in criminal activities to bring in money. If so, a return to incarceration may be only a matter of time.

It is abundantly clear that whatever good intentions they may have, former prisoners who cannot obtain secure employment after they return to their former neighborhood are unlikely to be a significant positive community resource. Though they may rise to other challenges, including adhering to parole restrictions, reconnecting with family members, and convincing other community members that they have changed, finding employment is far from being a given. That inability to get a job is disastrous for returned prisoners, their family, and their community. Conversely, it is abundantly clear that if former prisoners can secure a good job upon their return to their neighborhood, that is the principal step in melding with the community and becoming a positive force to strengthen its social fabric. Getting a job—a decent job— is key.

EDUCATION AND HUMAN CAPITAL

A system that removes numerous people from a community, imprisons them for a time, then reinserts them into the same community need not and should not close its eyes to the ways those actions create social disorder in the community, imperil its social fabric, and reduce community safety. The system should seek ways to alleviate the destructive effects of these actions and help communities withstand the effects of mass incarceration. We believe that one of the very best ways to do that is to empower former prisoners who return to these communities to conquer their greatest challenge—to get a living-wage job—and thereby enable them to become a positive force in their community. And the obvious way to do that is through providing quality vocational and academic education to prepare them for getting that job.

By educating prisoners, we increase their personal human capital and the human capital available to their communities for growth. Human capital consists of the "knowledge, skills, competencies, and attributes that allow people to contribute to their personal and social well-being, as well as that of their countries."[20] Increasing the human capital of a returning prisoner correlates positively with the probability of obtaining a better job, greater community social involvement, and economic growth in the community, all valuable outcomes we should want for the health of our communities. Education is that key to human capital.[21]

Textbox 7.1: Hon. Terry Barnard, chairman, Georgia State Board of Pardons and Paroles

The Georgia State Board of Pardons and Paroles recognizes that the basis for successful reentry is derived from an offender's preparation during the incarceration period. Stable employment is a cornerstone of success for offenders being released back into society. Research shows that for every day an offender is employed, the percentage drops regarding that offender's likelihood of committing a new crime. Inmates who participate in educational upgrades such as obtaining a GED, achieving a high school diploma, or receiving certification in one of the several job skills programs offered by the Georgia Department of Corrections reflect positively on the goal of reducing prison recidivism.

But education is precisely where the great majority of prisoners are deficient. Once they leave prison, that deficiency, unless it has been addressed by academic and/or technical education while they were incarcerated, virtually dooms them, for a lifetime, to the lowest rungs of the economic ladder. Their fate begins immediately after they come home. Those who return to high-incarceration communities typically find it a practically insurmountable challenge to secure living-wage employment. Their potential to help strengthen their community's social fabric quickly becomes minuscule. Instead, their return puts further strain on a fabric already in tatters. Worse, their inability to locate decent work due to deficient knowledge and skills sets them up for a greater likelihood of returning to prison. If that occurs, they will, in time, again return to their community after a period of incarceration—possibly to repeat the pattern again. It is all very reminiscent of the tale of Sisyphus, except the protagonist is not a character in a Greek myth, but a human being sentenced, by lack of education, to repeat a dreary fate over and over. One difference, however, is that not only is the prisoner condemned to the terrible pattern, but so is his community.

The way out of this dreary narrative is education. Prisoners obviously are a captive audience, so time and opportunity are there to provide them quality education. And money to finance that education can be there, too, once we realize that the public financial cost of providing good education to prisoners is substantially less than that of recidivism. All that is left is the will to invest that financial capital in human capital. High-incarceration communities may prove to be one of the greatest beneficiaries of that will to invest, as former prisoners return to the community with much more human capital than when they left, a greater likelihood of finding a good job, and a higher potential for becoming a positive resource that weaves some steel thread into the community's social fabric.

But what about former prisoners who do not return to one of the high-incarceration neighborhoods? What if the prisoner comes home to a small town in Georgia or a small city in Idaho or Wisconsin? We believe that the force of the argument for education remains strong for all home communities. Released prisoners with deficient education who return to virtually any community in the United States will have a hard time finding a good job. And not finding such employment will make it much more difficult for them to blend with the community and contribute to its social fabric. It also will substantially increase the likelihood of again becoming involved in criminal activity and reincarceration. Conversely, those prisoners who return to any community with greater human capital than when they left, due to having benefited from prison education, are much more able to find good jobs, become active members of positive social networks, strengthen beneficial community norms by acting as positive role models for youth and others, and add to the community's social capital. In sum, they are much more likely to become the productive, law-abiding, involved citizens who are a boon to any community.

NOTES

1. Jeremy Travis, Bruce Western, and F. Stevens Redburn, eds., *The Growth of Incarceration in the United States: Exploring Causes and Consequences* (Washington, DC: National Academies Press, 2014), 283–88, https://johnjay.jjay.cuny.edu/nrc/NAS_report_on_incarceration.pdf.

2. Dorothy E. Roberts, "The Social and Moral Cost of Mass Incarceration in African American Communities," faculty scholarship paper 583 (Philadelphia: University of Pennsylvania Law School, 2004), https://scholarship.law.upenn.edu/cgi/viewcontent.cgi?article=1582&context=faculty_scholarship, 1286.

3. Todd R. Clear et al., "Coercive Mobility and Crime: A Preliminary Examination of Concentrated Incarceration and Social Disorganization," *Justice Quarterly* 20, no. 1 (2003): 37, https://doi.org/10.1080/07418820300095451.

4. Clear et al., "Coercive Mobility," 37.

5. Clear et al., "Coercive Mobility," 36.

6. Roberts, "Social and Moral Cost," 1283.

7. Adrienne Chung and Rajiv N. Rimal, "Social Norms: A Review," *Review of Communication Research* 4 (2016): 1–29, https://doi.org/10.12840/issn.2255-4165.2016.04.01.008.

8. Roberts, "Social and Moral Cost," 1285.

9. Roberts, "Social and Moral Cost," 1286–87.

10. Jeffrey D. Morenoff and David J. Harding, "Incarceration, Prisoner Reentry, and Communities," *Annual Review of Sociology* 40 (2014): 419, https://doi.org/10.1146/annurev-soc-071811-145511.

11. S. Alexander Haslam, Stephen D. Reicher, and Michael J. Platow, *The New Psychology of Leadership: Identity, Influence and Power* (New York: Psychology Press, 2013), 69.

12. Roberts, "Social and Moral Cost," 1287.

13. Roberts, "Social and Moral Cost," 1288–89.

14. Todd R. Clear, *Imprisoning Communities: How Mass Incarceration Makes Disadvantaged Neighborhoods Worse* (New York: Oxford University Press, 2007), 90.

15. Michael Tzanakis, "Social Capital in Bourdieu's, Coleman's and Putnam's theory: Empirical Evidence and Emergent Measurement Issues," *Education* 23, no. 2 (2013): 2, http://www.educatejournal.org/index.php/educate/issue/view/42.

16. Douglas D. Perkins, Joseph Hughey, and Paul W. Speer, "Community Psychology Perspectives on Social Capital Theory and Community Development Practice," *Journal of the Community Development Society* 33, no. 1 (2002): 33, https://doi.org/10.1080/15575330209490141.

17. M. Keith Chen and Jesse M. Shapiro, "Does Prison Harden Inmates? A Discontinuity-based Approach," discussion paper no. 1450 (New Haven, CT: Cowles Foundation for Research in Economics, Yale University, January 2004), http://cowles.yale.edu/sites/default/files/files/pub/d14/d1450.pdf.

18. Dina R. Rose and Todd R. Clear, "Incarceration, Reentry and Social Capital: Social Networks in the Balance," in *Prisoners Once Removed: The Impact of Incarceration and Reentry on Children, Families, and Communities*, edited by Jeremy Travis and Michelle Waul (Washington, DC: Urban Institute Press, 2003), 331.

19. Rose and Clear, "Incarceration," 331.

20. Brian Keeley, *Human Capital: How What You Know Shapes Your Life* (Paris, France: Organization for Economic Cooperation and Development, 2007), 3, https://www.oecd.org/insights/humancapitalhowwhatyouknowshapesyourlife.htm.

21. Keeley, *Human Capital*, 3.

Chapter Eight

The Ethical Argument

Many Good Consequences

In the previous two chapters, we presented powerful psychological and sociological reasons for delivering more and better academic and technical education to our incarcerated population. Those chapters set the stage for a third type of reason—perhaps the most powerful of all—for prison education. In this chapter, we explain and defend a multifaceted argument, from an ethical and moral perspective, for prison education. The argument's conclusion is that providing quality education to men and women while they are incarcerated is morally right and a duty of society.

First, however, with an eye to a few objections our argument may prompt, we need to write about the most common justifications for incarceration that are put forward, some of which may be cited as bases for *not* improving prison education. Our purpose in doing that is to make clear that those rationales are not without major problems. They typically leave unaddressed important issues about the value of incarceration and how we should deal with our incarcerated population. So, we begin the chapter with an overview of the main justifications given for incarcerating individuals who break the law.

FOUR RATIONALES SUPPORTING INCARCERATION

The four main rationales for incarcerating people who commit felonies are incapacitation, deterrence, retribution, and rehabilitation. Let's have a closer look at each of them.

Incapacitation

Of the rationales put forward for incarcerating people, incapacitation may be the most straightforward; that is, by placing convicted lawbreakers behind prison walls (or in a jail cell), society makes it impossible for them to commit any further crimes outside their confinement. Though they still may be able to engage in criminal activity inside prison—such as theft, larceny, assault, dealing in drugs, or murder—the larger society outside need not fear law-breaking from those who are behind prison walls. Plainly, those who make this claim are correct. Incapacitating lawbreakers by locking them up prevents them from committing new crimes in communities outside as long as they stay locked up.

But what about after they are released?

Incapacitation works only for as long as the prisoner is incarcerated. Though serial killers, violent rapists, and other confirmed bad guys may be sentenced to a lifetime of incarceration, the great majority of prisoners are far from being such hard-core criminals. And surely, we do not want to throw everyone convicted of committing a crime—including burglary, drug possession, forgery, and many more nonviolent felonies—into prison for life. Sooner or later, the great majority of prisoners will be released into free society, where they will no longer be incapacitated. What happens then? In addressing that issue, a key question to ask is: does having been imprisoned for a period make it less likely for an offender to break laws later, after release? One answer to that question often is given by a second main argument for incarceration: future deterrence.

Deterrence

This rationale comes in two forms. First is the claim that imprisonment deters convicted lawbreakers from committing additional crimes not only while they are incarcerated, but also after their release. Supporters of the deterrence rationale hold that punishing those convicted of violating a law through incarceration will "teach them a lesson." Prisoners will learn firsthand what happens when they commit a crime. As a result, they will decide not to violate any laws after release in order to avoid being sent again to prison. One problem with this rationale is obvious: the three-year recidivism rate for those who have spent time in prison is close to 50 percent. So, almost half of released prisoners are undeterred from committing future crimes by having been previously incarcerated, which strongly suggests that though the future deterrence rationale may apply to some prisoners, it certainly does not apply to all.

Worse, evidence is that rather than being a deterrent, imprisonment actually is a criminogenic factor. That is, incarceration may make the chances of future offending more likely. Evidence for this conclusion comes from a meta-analysis of eighty-five studies.[1] Those studies compared the results of sentencing lawbreakers to custodial sanctions, such as incarceration, with sentencing them to noncustodial sanctions such as fines, community service, or electronic monitoring. Among those who were sentenced to custody, the recidivism rate was 14 percent higher than those given noncustodial sentences. The researcher concluded that incarcerating individuals may worsen the problem that it is supposed to help solve by making future criminal activity more, not less, likely.

Those who view the prison experience as being criminogenic, and therefore a poor deterrent, cite several main considerations.[2] One is the prevalence within prisons of a subculture that opposes authority and into which prisoners are socialized. Becoming a member of that subculture may help entering prisoners adjust to the severely restrictive realities of prison, including the radical reduction in autonomy. Within the subculture, prisoners are able to associate with others who support norms and values that differ greatly from those in the larger society, including individuals who endorse various types of criminal activity and criminality as a way of life. Due to these associations, prisons can become learning centers for criminality, especially for young prisoners who are first-time offenders. What may strengthen the prison subculture is that entering prisoners import into the prison environment attitudes and beliefs that they learned, affirmed, and perhaps lived by on the street. This may include bringing in gang membership and a high regard for appearing tough to others. Antisocial attitudes and beliefs may be transmitted from prisoner to prisoner through their interactions. Prison thereby constitutes a social learning environment that may reinforce an orientation toward future criminality.

A second mechanism by which incarceration may be criminogenic is the labeling effect. Labeling incarcerated individuals as *criminals* and *felons* amounts to publicly disparaging and stigmatizing them, which may lead those who are so labeled to see themselves in the same ways.[3] This self-labeling mechanism can be strengthened by prolonged association with others labeled as criminals and felons. A prison sentence provides a substantial period of time in which the self-attributions can be reinforced and accepted by those who are labeled, making it more likely that those conceptions will govern their conduct once they are released. These self-images then may become self-fulfilling prophecies, encouraging released prisoners to perform actions consistent with the images. In this way, incarceration may empower what it intends to suppress—crime.

After release, the mechanism may be further reinforced as the social stigma of having been a former prisoner continues, resulting in job discrimination and difficulties in restoring bonds to conventional social and political institutions. The likelihood of a return to criminality is further strengthened if criminal associations are readily available in the neighborhoods to which prisoners are released, which they often are.

A third explanation for findings that imprisonment has a criminogenic effect focuses on the loss or attenuation of informal social bonds, including family bonds, that prisoners typically experience.[4] Outside prison, such bonds have a positive effect by helping to prevent potential offenders from thinking they are free to perform criminal acts. This positive function is weakened if the bonds are loosened, which they generally are when the prisoner becomes incarcerated. Limited visiting hours, the distance of the prison from home, and meager financial resources all can severely reduce contact with family members and others in the outside world with whom a prisoner has social connections. The natural crime-preventing effect of social bonds with individuals outside thus is diminished or even lost, leaving prisoners in an environment in which criminality is held to be a value by new associates whose attitudes and beliefs the prisoners may incorporate.

Again, this results in incarceration itself making future crime more likely for many prisoners. The evidence that incarceration does little to prevent future crime and may actually be criminogenic strongly suggests that being sent to prison is an inappropriate way to deal with the bulk of the prison population who will be released into society at some point. What is needed in addition to incarceration is targeted prison programs for which good evidence shows a deterrent effect. More on this later.

A second form of the deterrence rationale for incarceration is the claim that imprisoning a lawbreaker is an object lesson for other individuals who might be tempted to break the law. Knowing that sentenced offenders get sent to prison for a period supposedly will make potential offenders "think twice" about violating the law. In regard to this rationale, it is fair to ask the following two questions. To what extent are potential lawbreakers deterred from future crime by observing that apprehended and sentenced offenders are sent to prison? And to what extent will that observation convince them to plan their criminal activity carefully so that they will not be apprehended?

The argument that people will refrain from committing crimes for fear of being incarcerated certainly is correct to an extent. However, that extent may be small or even absent for many at the time they decide to break a law. The claim for deterrence is based on a presumption that people are logical reasoners who will consider carefully the pros and cons of performing a crime. Supposedly, as a result of their reasoning, they will decide that the advantage they would gain by committing the proposed criminal act is not worth the disadvantage of spending a year or more in prison. But this supposition frequently is mistaken: potential offenders often do not reason in that way when they are considering breaking a law. Though they likely are rational, the reasoning process they go through may not concern the price they would pay were they caught, but rather the likelihood of their being caught and having to pay that price.

This way of thinking about whether to perform a crime is present in the *fraud triangle* model that sets forth conditions for committing a financial fraud such as embezzlement.[5] The fraud triangle model holds that a person who commits a financial crime reasons that (1) he has a need to commit the crime (such as a need for money) and (2) an opportunity to commit the crime. If the person can (3) rationalize committing the crime, then he likely will commit it. The second part of the triangle—opportunity—includes the person's reasoning of the probability that he will or will not be caught. Research supports the conclusion that the more powerful considerations that influence whether individuals commit a crime are those that involve how likely they are to be caught, not the possibility of being incarcerated if they are caught.[6]

Further, any reasoning process that the potential criminal employs often is diminished by being under the influence of alcohol or drugs. And many crimes, especially those of a violent nature, are committed while in the passion of anger, where reasoning may play little part. Given these considerations, it is naive to suppose that the possibility of being sent to prison is the main consideration in the mind of many potential lawbreakers. For them, that consideration does little to deter them from criminal activity if they believe they can escape detection or are in the grip of anger, alcohol, or drugs.

Retributive Justice

This justification for incarceration is about restoring a kind of balance that is held to be lost when people break laws. Because a crime brings harm to the victim(s) and breaks the legal rules of society, it is viewed by the retributionist as causing an imbalance in the scales of justice. To redress the grievance and restore balance, the perpetrator of the crime must be made to experience some form of punishment. Being incarcerated for a period, of course, is one very common form of punishment. By a prisoner losing a great deal of her freedom of movement for that period, the balance that was lost due to committing a criminal act is held to be restored.

To an extent, we agree with that argument. We, too, affirm that society has a right—and perhaps an obligation—to require a perpetrator to pay a price for committing a crime, and in many cases the price may rightly be incarceration for a period in which the offender gives up freedom. However, a problem with the rationale is that punishment by incarceration in our society consists of much more than a loss of freedom. Offenders typically are imprisoned in austere and overcrowded environments where they are subject to humiliation and intimidation by corrections officers and others, and where victimization through extortion and physical and sexual violence are common. A retributionist may claim that these other adverse aspects of incarceration can be regarded as further parts of the punishment that lawbreakers should undergo. However, this claim seldom is backed by any train of reasoning; instead, it seems to arise from a perception of prisoners as being unfit to be treated humanely. One argument brought forward by retributionists is that by being so thoroughly dreadful, incarceration deters prisoners from committing future crimes. But as noted above, evidence is that imprisonment is criminogenic, and making conditions of imprisonment harsher only adds to its criminogenic effect. Multiple studies have found that the harsher the environments in which prisoners are incarcerated, the greater the chances of recidivism.[7] Thus, the attempt to justify harsh prison conditions by their alleged deterrent effect is an argument not based in reality.

If retributionists continue to declare that awful prison conditions are justified simply because lawbreakers deserve to live in those conditions, their rationale goes directly against one principle of retributive justice—the principle of proportionality. This principle holds that retribution should be proportional to the crime. An individual sentenced to incarceration for shoplifting should not be punished to the same degree as someone convicted of violent rape. Though a degree of proportionality probably means the shoplifter being given a shorter sentence than the rapist, the conditions in which the two individuals are incarcerated may be the same or similar, so the type of punishment is not proportional. Here, too, the retributionist's supposed justification for forcing prisoners to live in inhumane condition turns out to be poor.

Our conclusion is that we have no rational grounds for holding that the principle of retribution justifies forcing prisoners to be warehoused for long periods in ugly, overcrowded, demeaning environments where they may undergo terrible experiences. Rather, the claim seems simply based on an emotional reaction characterized by malice toward lawbreakers.

Rehabilitation

This is a justification for incarceration only in the sense that incarcerating offenders creates an opportunity to provide interventions to make it less likely that they will commit crimes after release. Rehabilitation, therefore, can be viewed as having an objective of deterrence. Supporters of rehabilitation believe that the best way to gain that objective is to provide prisoners with tools and motivations that promote their reintegration into law-abiding society. Advocates of rehabilitation also often are inspired by other considerations, such as assisting the offender to achieve personal recovery, redemption, or emancipation. Rehabilitation champions generally believe in the worth of prisoners as part of the brotherhood of humans and support providing interventions that can improve their lives after release.

Academic and technical education, of course, constitutes two rehabilitative tools proven to positively affect prisoners' lives following their release, strengthening them and providing resilience as they negotiate the mine field that awaits them. Other interventions also have a positive effect on prisoners, as measured by reduced recidivism, including substance abuse programs, cognitive-behavioral programs to rewire the brain and thinking of prisoners, and ongoing post-release support.[8]

Due to limited funds and the belief that higher risk individuals will profit most from an intervention, the risks-needs-responsivity (RNR) model often is used to decide which prisoners will be provided these programs.[9] Using the RNR model, interventions may be deemed not needed, or not needed as much for prisoners judged to be at low risk of reincarceration. However, for those at low risk, a danger of not being able to enter a rehabilitation program is that incarceration may prove to be criminogenic and turn them from low to high risk.

The findings of a 2016 study support the effectiveness of evidence-based prison interventions, including postsecondary programs.[10] Researchers followed more than fifty-five thousand prisoners who were released from Minnesota prisons from 2003 to 2011 to compare recidivism rates of those who simply were warehoused with no rehabilitation programs to those who participated in one or more such programs. Warehoused prisoners numbered 17,804 (30.7 percent) of the total. Researchers found that having entered one rehabilitation program reduced the odds of recidivating by 12 percent, while entering two programs reduced the odds by 26 percent. This and much additional research shows abundant evidence of the effectiveness of a number of programs for rehabilitating prisoners.

Of course, implementation of rehabilitation programs requires a monetary investment, which may be put forward as a reason for not expanding academic and technical education opportunities. But this is a shortsighted complaint. The amount of money saved in annual incarceration costs is far greater than the financial investment required to implement most such interventions. Education programs are, of course, evidence-based interventions we are emphasizing in these pages. In the next chapter, which presents the financial argument for prison education in some detail, we will see that these programs more than pay for themselves by reducing the rate of recidivism and thereby the more than thirty-thousand-dollar average annual cost of maintaining one person in prison.

THE FOUR JUSTIFICATIONS CONSIDERED TOGETHER

Our overview indicates that of the four primary justifications given for incarceration, only two rest on reasonable grounds. One is incapacitation, for it is true that while imprisoned, an offender cannot commit further crimes outside prison. But this fact begs the question of what occurs when the individual is released into free society. The answer to this question may cite the second justification, which is deterrence. However, the deterrence argument is weak when applied to those already incarcerated. Evidence strongly suggests that instead of deterring released prisoners from new criminal activity, incarceration is criminogenic and makes new lawbreaking more likely. As for the possibility of being incarcerated deterring others from committing crimes, what determines whether potential offenders commit a crime has more to do with estimating the chances of being apprehended than any fear of being incarcerated; and in many cases, it results more from being under the influence of alcohol or drugs, passion, or rage than any reasoning process.

As for retribution as a justification for incarceration, we agree with this rationale to a point. However, those who emphasize the principle of retribution often leave important issues unaddressed, including inhumane punishment and proportionality. When the retribution argument shows itself as being an attempt to legitimize a desire for revenge, we step away. At that point, the rationale often has more to do with an unthinking emotional reaction to lawbreakers than it does with plausible supporting reasons.

The rationale for incarceration most clearly warranted is that spending time in prison provides an opportunity to rehabilitate the offender. Here, we have a justification that makes practical sense. Based on abundant research showing that applying evidence-based rehabilitative interventions reduces the chances of a recurrence of lawbreaking, it is clear that rehabilitation is a strong justification, not so much for incarceration itself, but for effectively using incarceration time to reduce future criminality and recidivism. One such evidence-based intervention is to provide prisoners with more quality education programs. In the rest of this chapter we argue that rehabilitation through education not only makes practical sense, it is the right thing to do.

THE MORALITY OF EXPANDING PRISON EDUCATION

Several ethical arguments can be marshaled in favor of the rightness of providing prisoners academic and technical education opportunities. These include reasons based on concepts such as fairness, human rights, and God's command. We choose to focus on a *consequentialist* argument—that educating prisoners is morally right because its consequences are good and, in fact, far better than not doing so. One reason for our focus on consequences is that throughout this book, we have been laying the foundation for that argument. A second reason is that by using a consequentialist lens, we also are able to identify other main arguments for the rightness of educating prisoners.

The good consequences of expanding prison education are manifold. They comprise positive results for prisoners, their families, their communities, and American society.

We start with the prisoners themselves. Yes, they broke laws, and society insists that they pay a price for their actions. The radical loss of freedom they experience by being incarcerated is one main part of that price. However, as we have touched on several times, they pay other huge prices. Foremost, in their incarceration, they are forced to live alone in austere and brutal conditions. Separated from their family and sources of social support, and relegated to an intimidating, dangerous environment, they lose virtually all autonomy. They are told what to do, as well as when and how to do it. They are under close surveillance constantly. They regularly may be subjected to demeaning demands such as body cavity searches. The worst aspect of imprisonment for many may be having little to occupy their minds and relieve the day-after-day tedium. Living for an extended period in such an environment is worse than stressful. Humiliating, mind-numbing punishment that stretches on for months or years is psychologically damaging and may lead to depression or other mental health problems and exacerbate antisocial tendencies.

Textbox 8.1: A prisoner

Worlds apart. You have to understand that prison is different than the free world. In the free world to be kindhearted, empathetic, and forgiving are qualities to be admired, because in the free world you are surrounded by decent people with only a few trying to take advantage of you. In prison these same traits are weaknesses, because you are surrounded by people trying to take advantage of you.

The nature of institutionalization in today's prisons has numerous pernicious psychological consequences. First, imprisonment fosters extreme dependence on the institution, its rules, and its employees, which can cause self-initiative to atrophy. Many prisoners capitulate psychologically to this dependence, to the point where it begins to seem natural for the institution to make all of their choices. This submission to authority in virtually all aspects of their life can weaken some prisoners' self-initiative to the point that they become virtually incapable of planning and exercising self-originated behavior. Total institutional control, allied with constant surveillance that can result in immediate punishment for violating any of the many limits set for prisoners, can result in a prisoner's internal controls withering or, for young prisoners, not developing.[11] This weakening of self-initiative is in direct opposition to the need for prisoners to develop self-motivation to increase the likelihood of successfully maneuvering through the many obstacles they will encounter after their release, as we argued in chapter 6.

Prisoners often develop a kind of constant hypervigilance that fosters distrust and suspicion of others.[12] Hypervigilance becomes a habit for many in a perilous environment where others always are nearby, ready to exploit any perceived weakness or carelessness. They feel they constantly must be alert, watchful for signs that they are in personal danger. Their hypervigilance naturally results in distrust of and distancing oneself from others. They learn to mask their emotions to protect themselves from being perceived as weak. They may work to create an image of themselves as a potential threat and project a tough veneer that keeps all others at a distance. For protection, often prisoners consider it necessary to restrain their emotional reactions to what they experience, carefully tempering emotional responses to others. They may begin to feel that an emotional investment in any relationship is risky. Continuous donning of an emotion-concealing mask in prison eventually may result in persistent emotional vapidity in their demeanor with others, leading to almost total social withdrawal and isolation. To help ensure their safety, some attempt to become practically invisible to others, engage in only required social interaction, and withdraw into themselves. This occurs most often in prisoners serving longer rather than shorter terms. The emotional countenance of some of these individuals is similar to someone who is clinically depressed.

For some prisoners, the psychological harm that incarceration fosters exhibits in post-traumatic stress reactions.[13] The incarceration experience is so psychologically hurtful that it rises to the level of trauma resulting in post-traumatic stress symptoms once they are released. This may occur more often among prisoners who suffered childhood trauma, which has been found to correlate with later offending and incarceration.[14] Prisons, with their harsh, unfeeling, and demanding environments, may retrigger these childhood traumas.

Is any of this what we want? It is one thing to deprive offenders of their freedom for a time for having committed an unlawful act—a sentence that may be just. It is something else to force them to serve that time in bleak and pitiless conditions that induce or even compel psychological and spiritual decline.

At this point in our argument we will leave, for a moment, our consequentialist focus to insist on another kind of ethical rationale for prisoner education. Call it the argument for human decency, which claims that the kind of punishment awaiting our prisoners violates the sanctity of human life and is, in a word, inhumane. Some would say it amounts to treating incarcerated people as if they were a lower species. Some would point out that all major religions condemn such punishment. The argument from human decency's conclusion is simply that it is morally right to educate prisoners in need because they are fellow human beings—and doing so helps provide a partial respite from the otherwise stark and remorseless prison conditions they must face.

Attending classes provides prisoners a small degree of autonomy as they choose to gain knowledge and skills that they will sorely need once released. It provides short-term goals to engage them in the otherwise bland, monotonous conditions of prison life. In doing so, it is a partial antidote to the psychological deterioration that often results from long periods in prison. In brief, providing prisoners with academic and technical education opportunities humanizes them. This is a major positive way education benefits prisoners, as we have repeatedly emphasized, by providing them with new knowledge and skills, an increased chance to obtain living-wage employment after release, and a reduced likelihood of reverting to criminal activity to support themselves or their families.

An additional positive consequence for prisoners is that education increases their motivation and will to overcome obstacles they will encounter after release as they attempt to reintegrate successfully with society. At the same time, education helps build their sense of personal responsibility, also crucial to successful reintegration. Those sentenced at an early age may enter prison confused about who they are and who they can be, with a minimal sense of personal responsibility for their actions and little concern for how those actions may affect others. Many still are at a very impressionable age and easily may fall prey to the ideas and attitudes of prison acquaintances who endorse criminality.

Education is a counteracting force. It can help socialize young prisoners into a different kind of culture and open their minds to realize that there is a walkable pathway besides criminality. Focusing on and learning subjects, completing assignments, taking tests, or perfecting new skills can be transforming for prisoners as they realize they are capable of learning new things. This realization can help overcome their tendencies to label themselves negatively and instead instill personal pride in their accomplishments. The idea that they were responsible for learning a subject or developing a skill likely will promote growth in their sense of personal responsibility for all of their actions.

Prison education may provide especially large benefits to prisoners who are economically and socially deprived, two factors that research indicates are criminogenic.[15] Providing education to those prisoners goes a considerable way toward redressing early disadvantages and conditions that increase the likelihood of committing a crime. We don't claim that background, lack of education, or personal circumstances excuse a perpetrator or erase society's right to penalize him for breaking the law; we embrace the concept of personal responsibility and the right of society to sanction lawbreakers.

However, a great deal of research certifies the existence of environmental and social factors that result in an individual being more likely to commit unlawful acts.[16] These include the neighborhood and home environment in which the individual grew up, quality of local schools, degree of education, peer pressure, the presence of neighborhood gangs, and employment prospects in the area. A fundamental presupposition of such research is that effectively dealing with crime is not simply a matter of assigning personal responsibility; it is also a matter of learning how external factors influence the thoughts, attitudes, and decisions of individuals and determine to what degree they assume personal responsibility for their actions. Young people often have not had the time, influences, or opportunities to help them mature into responsible members of society, especially young adults who grew up in a socially and economically deprived environment. Personal responsibility does not magically appear in a person at age eighteen, twenty, or even fifty; it must be nurtured. If personal responsibility is important, then so are the factors that help build it or impede its development. Whether or not a student is from a deprived area, prison education helps build a more knowledgeable, skillful, and mature person who is better equipped to accept personal responsibility for future actions.

All of the beneficial consequences of education for prisoners that we have identified—alleviating stark prison conditions and creating a more human experience, increasing motivation for success, providing new knowledge and skills that increase the chances of post-release employment, and fostering a sense of personal responsibility—are highly desirable outcomes in themselves. They are of great value to prisoners because they increase the likelihood of success after release. Our claim is that these beneficial consequences for prisoners constitute a strong moral reason to provide them with the opportunity to receive effective academic and technical education while incarcerated.

Prison education also benefits families by increasing the likelihood of a successful and permanent post-release reunion. These families have been without the prisoner for months or years, dealing with life's vicissitudes by themselves. They, too, have had to endure the incarceration period; many pay a large financial and emotional price. Prisoners' spouses, children, siblings, and parents all hope that the period of imprisonment will be the last that their loved one—and they—will have to bear. The release of former prisoners promises a potential new avenue for improving their families' financial health if they can land a job. The likelihood that they can secure employment and stay crime free increases substantially if they have greater motivation and opportunity for success gained from education while incarcerated.

The main beneficiaries of returned prisoners' success may be the children they can again parent. As we learned in chapter 3, children of an imprisoned parent pay a large price in emotional and cognitive growth. Parents who return from prison with new knowledge, skills, motivation, and self-understanding more likely will be positive influences in their growing children's lives as they negotiate the challenges they often face. Clearly, greater probability of successful family reunification that results from prisoner education is a second strong moral reason for providing those opportunities.

A third beneficiary of prisoner education is the community that returning citizens reenter. We learned about these benefits in chapter 7, which presented the sociological argument for academic and technical education for prisoners. The conclusion of that argument was simply this: released prisoners who are educated are much more likely to become assets to their communities rather than liabilities. This is important for all communities to which former prisoners return, though it is most obvious for those that suffer from substantial economic and social deprivation. It is those communities to which a majority of released prisoners return, and it is those that urgently need released prisoners to be positive additions. They certainly do not need individuals who will find themselves in the revolving door that takes them back to prison. The increased likelihood of released prisoners successfully reentering and strengthening their community is thus a third beneficial consequence of quality prison education.

A fourth positive consequence of educating our prisoners is that doing so benefits American society. In reducing the chance of recidivism, providing prisoner education is good not only for prisoners and their families and communities, but also for society as a whole by strengthening the nation's social and economic fabric. Every individual who commits an unlawful act and is sentenced to prison constitutes a weak thread in that fabric. With almost 1.5 million individuals in our prisons, the fabric is weak in many places; but every former prisoner who successfully rejoins society strengthens that portion of the fabric for which she is responsible. As a society, we need to reinforce our weak threads to make them stronger. Effective prison education strengthens the nation's social and economic fabric by producing good consequences.

Former prisoners have a greater likelihood of finding decent jobs that can help them resettle into society socially and economically. Families of former prisoners are strengthened by the greater probability that the prisoner is coming home to stay. Communities gain stronger social cohesion and increased social capital resulting from former prisoners who successfully reenter the community and help stabilize and build it. These are results that we all should desire.

Prison education is not the complete solution to the serious problems of bleak, overcrowded prisons and recidivism, but it is a major part of the solution. By educating our prisoners, we help empower them to become more than they were when they committed a crime and were incarcerated. It is a sign of a principled and wise society if it recognizes that imprisoning a citizen for breaking the law without providing resources for rehabilitation is not only immoral, but also pointless. Providing prisoners with opportunities to receive effective academic and technical education is, without doubt, morally and ethically right. By giving prisoners a better chance to succeed, we strengthen not only them but also our entire society.

NOTES

1. Cheryl Lero Jonson, "The Impact of Imprisonment on Reoffending" (PhD diss., University of Cincinnati, 2010).

2. Daniel S. Nagin, Francis T. Cullen, and Cheryl L. Jonson, "Imprisonment and Reoffending," *Crime and Justice* 38, no. 1 (2009): 115–200, https://doi.org/10.1086/599202.

3. Nagin, Cullen, and Jonson, "Imprisonment and Reoffending," 126–27.

4. Nagin, Cullen, and Jonson, "Imprisonment and Reoffending," 127.

5. Donald R. Cressey, *Other People's Money: A Study in the Social Psychology of Embezzlement* (Glencoe, IL: Free Press, 1953).

6. Jeremy Travis, Bruce Western, and F. Stevens Redburn, eds., *The Growth of Incarceration in the United States: Exploring Causes and Consequences* (Washington, DC: National Academies Press, 2014), 4, https://johnjay.jjay.cuny.edu/nrc/NAS_report_on_incarceration.pdf.

7. Lawrence L. Bench and Terry D. Allen, "Investigating the Stigma of Prison Classification: An Experimental Design," *Prison Journal* 83, no. 4 (2003): 367–82, https://doi.org/10.1177/0032885503260143; M. Keith Chen and Jesse M. Shapiro, "Do Harsher Prison Conditions Reduce Recidivism? A Discontinuity-Based Approach," *American Law and Economic Review* 9, no. 1 (Spring 2007): 1–29, https://doi.org/10.1093/aler/ahm006; Gerald G. Gaes and Scott D. Camp, "Unintended Consequences: Experimental Evidence for the Criminogenic Effect of Prison Security Level Placement on Post-Release Recidivism," *Journal of Experimental Criminology* 5, no. 2 (2009): 139–62, https://doi.org/10.1007/s11292-009-9070-z.

8. U.S. Department of Justice, Archives, *Prison Reform: Reducing Recidivism by Strengthening the Federal Bureau of Prisons*, last modified March 6, 2017, https://www.justice.gov/archives/prison-reform.

9. James Bonta and D. A. Andrews, *Risk-Need-Responsivity Model for Offender Assessment and Rehabilitation 2007–06*, report for Public Safety Canada (Ottawa, 2007), http://www.courtinnovation.org/sites/default/files/documents/RNRModelForOffenderAssessmentAndRehabilitation.pdf.

10. Grant Duwe and Valerie Clark, "The Rehabilitative Ideal Versus the Criminogenic Reality: The Consequences of Warehousing Prisoners," *Corrections* 2, no. 1 (2017): 41–69, https://doi.org/10.1080/23774657.2016.1240596.

11. Craig Haney, "The Psychological Impact of Incarceration: Implications for Post-Prison Adjustment," paper prepared for the From Prison to Home Conference, January 30–31, 2002, Bethesda, MD, 81, http://webarchive.urban.org/UploadedPDF/410624_PyschologicalImpact.pdf.

12. Haney, "Psychological Impact," 81–82.

13. Haney, "Psychological Impact," 83–84.

14. Nancy Wolff and Jing Shi, "Childhood and Adult Trauma Experiences of Incarcerated Persons and Their Relationship to Adult Behavioral Health Problems and Treatment," *International Journal of Environmental Research and Public Health* 9, no. 5 (May 2012): 1909, https://doi.org/10.3390/ijerph9051908.

15. Corina Graif, Andrew S. Gladfelter, and Stephen A. Matthews, "Urban Poverty and Neighborhood Effects on Crime: Incorporating Spatial and Network Perspectives," *Sociology Compass* 8, no. 9 (2014): 1140, https://doi.org/10.1111/soc4.12199.

16. Graif, Gladfelter, and Matthews. "Urban Poverty," 1140–41.

Chapter Nine

The Financial Argument

The ROI of Prison Education

INTRODUCTION

In the preceding three chapters, we have argued vigorously for the value of providing expanded education to prisoners. We have provided multiple reasons based on an understanding of human psychology and motivation as they apply to the situations of prisoners and their release. We have offered reasons founded on the evidence that educated prisoners are more likely to secure decent jobs after their release, stay crime free, and become positive influences in their communities. These favorable outcomes contrast with what often happens to prisoners released without adequate education who are more likely to become a continuing burden to their community, lower its safety, and add to its disintegration. And chances increase that in a year or so they will return to prison, the next stop in a vicious repeating cycle.

We also have provided a many-sided ethical argument that entreats society and its members to have compassion for fellow human beings who have fallen on hard times. Yes, it may be true that for the most part they got themselves there, "making their own bed to lie in." But perhaps it is time we drop that tired old mantra and set aside the guilt trips so easily laid on this population. They do no good for anyone. Perhaps it is time we ask ourselves as a society who we are if we do not offer prisoners a strong helping hand. Of course, we cannot *force* those who are incarcerated to become law-abiding citizens after release, but we can help them by providing educational opportunities to enable them to meld fruitfully with their communities. And we can provide that help while being certain of its logic, knowing that the evidence clearly shows that educating prisoners is proven to prepare them for a successful return to society.

In this chapter, we provide one of the strongest reasons for educating our prisoners. Our conclusion is simply this:

The more we expand prisoners' educational opportunities,
the more money we will save.

On the way to that conclusion, we will set before you an array of solid evidence showing that what we spend to educate prisoners is far less than the financial penalty if we don't. First, we will examine several important meta-analyses that have been conducted over the past twenty years about the relationship of prison education to recidivism.

THE VIRTUE OF META-ANALYSES

A meta-analysis, as you may well know, focuses on the results of other studies about some matter. A meta-analysis about the relation of prison education to recidivism examines prior studies that have investigated whether there is a connection between these two variables. Many such studies have been undertaken over the past four decades, and one big reason for that is clear: money spent on housing prisoners has grown enormously over those years, taking a huge bite of state budgets and burdening the federal budget. Clearly, state and federal government officials have a keen interest in policies they could enact to reduce prison populations and the huge amount of money spent on them.

All along, providing prisoners with education programs to reduce recidivism has seemed a possibly effective strategy. As a result, many studies have been conducted to determine the effects of prison education on the recidivism rates of prisoners.

However, one problem is that those studies have shown mixed results. One might show that providing academic education to prisoners is associated with a significant reduction in their three-year recidivism rate after release, compared to the three-year recidivism rate of a control group of prisoners who were not given that treatment. Another study that uses different samples of prisoners might find no significant difference in recidivism between the treatment and control groups. When results of the studies about the effects of prison education programs differ, confusion ensues about the value of education for reducing recidivism.

Adding to the confusion, the quality of the methodology is different in different studies. A portion have been true experimental studies using randomized control groups and sophisticated analytic methods to control for variables that might affect the results, such as age and length of sentence. Others are less rigorous in their methodology; they do not use randomized control groups or take care to ensure that the treatment and control groups are well matched in characteristics that might bias the findings. As a result, how much trust should be placed in the outcomes of the more rigorous studies compared to those with looser research designs is uncertain.

Existence of these sorts of concerns about the results of studies investigating prison education in relation to recidivism leads to indecision among state and federal policymakers about prison education programs. If researchers' findings don't agree, if we can't agree which studies are the ones whose results we should most trust, then it is difficult for those with decision-making powers about prison education programs to reach consensus about whether to put more funds into those programs.

The virtue of a well-done meta-analysis of studies about the relation of prison education to recidivism clears away a lot of this confusion. A meta-analysis is a big job. It examines numerous studies conducted about how the variables of interest are related. After identifying a number of eligible studies for the meta-analysis, the authors begin to investigate by looking carefully at the research designs of each study. They apply sophisticated tools to determine the quality of the research designs, eliminate studies whose designs they consider poor, then consider the findings of each remaining study.

It doesn't matter whether a particular study's results showed a positive, negative, or no relationship between the variables. The results of all of the studies that pass the quality test are taken into account. Finally, after thoroughly scrutinizing each study and putting their findings together, the meta-researchers come to a conclusion about what the studies show about the relationship between prison education programs and recidivism.

But how do we know that the meta-analysis was not biased? How do we know the authors did not consciously or unconsciously desire a certain conclusion and make judgment calls in their analyses of some studies that gave more weight to the conclusion they favored? Because the completed meta-analysis is then published in scientific journals and other publicly accessible vehicles. Not just the final results are published, though. The names and details of the studies examined are also presented, along with the methods the authors used in analyzing those studies. All of the major details of the meta-analysis, how it proceeded, what judgments were made and why, are there for the authors' peers and other interested persons to review. And you can bet that if any peers find a problem with the meta-analysis, if they decide that it is biased in some way, they will let the world know by writing a paper that criticizes whatever aspect of the meta-analysis they take issue with. Writing such a paper is one way that people rise in the academic world. And it is one way that science progresses: scientists in a particular field of study check on each other and keep one another honest.

So, to repeat, our first step toward our conclusion in this chapter is to look closely at the major meta-analyses conducted since 2000 that have examined studies to learn the relationship between prison education programs and recidivism. The overwhelming conclusion of each study we review is that prison education programs significantly reduce recidivism. But the real evidence is in the details, so we hope you will read through our brief accounts of each study to see how strong the evidence is and to learn just how great a reduction in recidivism we can expect from expanding prison education programs.

Our second goal is to explain how much the reduction in recidivism that comes about through prison education programs means in terms of money saved from reincarceration. What cost reduction can be expected from providing quality prison education programs to, say, one hundred thousand prisoners? What reduction in taxes paid could we enjoy each year as a result of providing expanded educational opportunities to prisoners? We will set before you well-developed figures that show the expected average costs of educating incarcerated individuals. Then we will compare the two figures: the costs of educating prisoners versus the savings realized from reducing recidivism. That comparison will support our conclusion that the bang for the buck we get for providing education programs to prisoners is phenomenal.

THREE META-ANALYSES OF PRISON EDUCATION AND RECIDIVISM

Our first meta-analysis was published in 2000 by David Wilson, Catherine Gallagher, and Doris MacKenzie at the University of Maryland.[1] These scientists examined thirty-three studies published since 1975 that dealt with the relation of prison education programs to recidivism. Most of the studies examined had experimental or quasi-experimental designs; a treatment group of prisoners who participated in an education program was compared to a control group of prisoners who did not.

Several important features marked that analysis. First, researchers considered not just whether a study showed some association (positive or negative) between a prison education program and recidivism; they also took into account the size of that association. Another feature was that the quality of each study they reviewed was considered using the Maryland Scientific Methods Scale (SMS), which the team helped to develop. It rates the quality of a study's methodology on a scale of one to five, with higher numbers indicating higher quality. The research team reviewed only those studies with at least a score of two. They also took into account the methodology of each of the remaining thirty-three studies in determining to what degree study results might be attributed not to a difference between treatment and control groups but to a feature of the study's design.

Their conclusion was that the preponderance of evidence from the studies showed that on average, those who were provided an academic prison program were about 11 percentage points less likely to recidivate than those who were not. Academic programs considered included Adult Basic Education, GED education, and postsecondary programs.

A second meta-analysis of studies about the relation of prison education to recidivism was published in 2006 by Doris MacKenzie, a coresearcher in the 2000 meta-analysis.[2] This new analysis dealt only with studies published since 1980 and included several that had been published since the 2000 review. It also included only studies that scored at least three on the Maryland SMS scale, thereby eliminating some studies that had reached only level two in the previous meta-analysis. The results of this 2006 meta-analytic review agreed with those of the 2000 study in respect to the association of prison academic education with a reduced likelihood of recidivism, but found the association to be greater. MacKenzie found that taking part in a prison academic education program predicted a 16 percent lower probability of released prisoners recidivating than not. She also was able to determine an association of vocational education and recidivism, concluding that prisoners who participated in a vocational education program while incarcerated were 24 percent less likely to recidivate than those who did not.

Also in 2006, a meta-analytic review of studies about various initiatives for reducing criminal activity among adults and juveniles was published by a scientific team working out of the Washington State Institute for Public Policy.[3] This review included 571 studies reaching as far back as 1970 and published before 2005 that had a quality score of three or above on the five-point Maryland SMS scale. The team reviewed studies about the relation to recidivism of a variety of prison interventions such as cognitive-behavioral therapy, drug courts, and drug treatment. They included an analysis of studies on the relation of prison education programs to recidivism. Seventeen studies about prison general education and four studies about prison vocational education were included in this meta-analytic review.

The findings of the Washington State team agreed with those of the other 2006 meta-analysis, though the researchers' estimates of the association of prison education with reduced recidivism were less. The Washington State team concluded that both academic and vocational education in prison were associated with reduced recidivism, estimating that prisoners who participated in a general education program were 7 percent less likely to recidivate compared to nonparticipants, while taking part in a vocational education program predicted a 9 percent reduction in recidivism. In a second study, the team also projected how many dollars would be saved based on the predicted recidivism reduction and the dollars per prisoner required for education or training.[4] Their aim was to estimate the financial benefit gained from each type of education. We will return to these estimates later when we move to the next step in our argument.

THE RAND STUDY

A fourth meta-analysis was conducted by researchers at the RAND Corporation and published in 2013.[5] This undertaking is considered by many to be the current gold standard for meta-analyses of research comparing prison education programs with recidivism. For that reason, we want to take a little more space to examine the study's results.

The RAND study was sponsored by the Bureau of Justice Assistance, indicating that the Department of Justice had faith that the RAND Corporation would conduct a first-rate meta-analysis. Given the history and credentials of the corporation, the department had every reason for that belief. RAND is a nonpolitical nonprofit research organization devoted to research and analysis that can help inform the decision-making process for policy makers and others. RAND has offices in the United States, Europe, and Australia. Most of its funds come from U.S. government branches, including the U.S. Departments of Defense, Homeland Security, Health and Human Services, the Army, and the Air Force.[6]

The RAND review covered fifty studies conducted between 1980 and 2011 that examined recidivism or other outcomes of prison education programs. Only studies scoring two or above on the Maryland SMS scale and meeting RAND eligibility standards regarding research design, type of intervention, and measured outcomes were reviewed. Several studies included more than one comparison of prison education to recidivism, so seventy-one effect sizes were found in the accepted studies. Like the Washington State team, the RAND authors used their findings to provide a further analysis comparing the cost of educating a prisoner with projected savings from reduced recidivism.

As in the meta-analyses reported earlier, the RAND review showed a relationship between participation in several types of prison education program and reduced recidivism. Taking into account the results of all fifty studies, no matter what the rigor of their study design, the RAND team found that for prisoners participating in prison education programs, the odds of recidivating were 36 percent less than the odds of recidivating for prisoners who did not participate in prison education.

To address any suggestion that this result may have been due to the presence of lower-quality studies that were biased toward showing a positive effect of prison education programs, the RAND team then reanalyzed the studies including only those that reached a level of four or five on the SMS scale. This group included seven studies. Two were experiments that used randomized controls, and five were quasi-experiments in which the treatment and control groups were matched on key variables. The authors found that when only the studies with high-quality experimental designs were included in their analysis, prisoners who take part in education programs are 43 percent less likely to recidivate than prisoners who do not.

Using these results and the estimate of national three-year recidivism rate of 43.3 percent provided by the Pew Charitable Trust,[7] the RAND scientific reviewers found that participation in prison education programs predicts a three-year recidivism rate reduction of 12.9 percent.[8] That is, given one hundred thousand released prisoners who otherwise would return to prison after three years, we can expect that if they had taken part in an educational program while incarcerated, almost thirteen thousand would not be reincarcerated during that period. It is important to emphasize that neither the RAND nor the other meta-analyses guarantee that a prisoner who participates in an education program while in prison will not return to prison. But they do give excellent evidence for a significant reduction in the *likelihood* that a participating prisoner will recidivate. When applied to a large segment of the 1.5 million people incarcerated in U.S. prisons, that leads to a very substantial reduction in recidivism.

The RAND scientists also provided reincarceration probabilities for four types of prison education program that were the focus of various studies: vocational education, adult basic education, high school or GED education, and postsecondary education. Because some reviewed studies dealt with education programs that spanned more than one category, the RAND team noted that the categories in their breakdown should not be considered pure examples of each type. Given that proviso, they estimated that the odds of recidivating were 36 percent lower for those who took part in vocational education compared to those who did not, 33 percent lower for adult basic education, 30 percent lower for high school or GED education, and 51 percent lower for postsecondary education.[9]

Notably, the RAND team also considered the reviewed studies from the perspective of the type of instruction in an educational program. Among the programs, the ones with the lowest odds ratios—and thereby the greatest reduced likelihood of participants recidivating—were programs that connected prisoners with the world outside prison walls, such as programs with classes taught by an external teacher within the prison.

An update and extension of the 2013 RAND meta-analysis was published in 2018, its authors including three who had performed the original analysis and one new member of the team.[10] Reviewing studies conducted from 1980 to 2017 and only studies that earned at least a level two on the Maryland SMS, the researchers added seven studies to the update, including several done since the original RAND report in 2013. This made fifty-seven studies with eighty-one effects in the review.

The results of the updated meta-analysis were similar to those of the original. Considering the results of all fifty-seven studies, the new RAND team found those who take part in prison education have 32 percent less chance of recidivating than those who do not. Restricting the analysis to only those studies considered to have the most rigorous experimental designs, the team found a 28 percent lower rate of recidivating for prisoners participating in education programs. By type of education program, the updated RAND meta-analysis showed lower odds of recidivism of 32, 31, 25, and 48 percent, respectively, for vocational, adult basic, high school or GED, and postsecondary prison education. [11]

SAVING MONEY BY EDUCATING PRISONERS

Based on the results of the five meta-analyses we have summarized, evidence is very good that as a society we would be wise economically to invest substantially more money in educating our prisoners. How much? A couple of the meta-analysis teams have done the calculations for us based on the results of their review. The Washington State team estimated the cost of providing vocational education in 2006 dollars as $1,182 per participant and the value gained by reducing recidivism by 9 percent as $14,920—a net estimated long-term gain of $13,738 per prisoner educated. Similarly, the Washington State team found that a 7 percent reduction in recidivism based on academic education resulted in a net gain of $10,669 after accounting for the estimated $962 cost per participant. [12]

The scientific team that performed the 2013 RAND meta-analysis also calculated the financial gains that could be realized from providing education programs for prisoners. First, based on two respected studies on the costs of prison education, researchers gave a lower cost estimate of $1,400 and a higher estimate of $1,744 for educating a prisoner. Second, based on two other respected studies, they provided both a lower and higher estimate of the cost of one prisoner being reincarcerated for 2.4 years, the average length of incarceration based on Department of Justice statistics. [13] The lower estimate was $67,975; the higher, $75,086.

Finally, based on their finding of a 12.9 percent recidivism reduction, they calculated the difference in recidivism costs between one hundred released prisoners who participated in prison education and one hundred who were released but did not participate, using both sets of estimates. Based on the most conservative figures—the lower reincarceration cost estimate and the higher education cost estimate—the difference in reincarceration cost between the two sets of one hundred prisoners was $870,000, but the cost of educating one hundred prisoners was $174,000.[14] The net gain was $696,000. In other words, using the most conservative estimates, investing $174,000 in educating one hundred prisoners would provide a return on investment (ROI) of 400 percent.

And, of course, by reducing recidivism by almost 13 percent among a group of one hundred prisoners through engaging them in education, we do more than save ourselves the financial cost of reincarcerating about thirteen released individuals. Because they have been provided education or training while incarcerated, those individuals can be expected to find jobs and start paying taxes. Even if the average tax each one pays is only, say, $2,000 per year, that amounts to about $26,000 annually for all of them together. Over ten years, that totals to $260,000 and brings our long-term ROI up to about 550 percent. And as they go about their law-abiding business, purchasing housing, food and drink, utilities, entertainment, and much more, they lubricate the economy, paying money to landlords, grocers, and other retailers that will add to the payees' bottom line and the taxes they pay. These returning citizens also can be expected to stay crime free, which reduces money needed to fight crime, another savings.

Due to the many variables involved, we cannot estimate the total financial value of increased economic participation by almost 13 percent of released prisoners who will not return to incarceration due to participation in a prison education program. Nor can we estimate the financial value of reduced need for money to fight and prosecute crime for this 13 percent. But these amounts likely are substantial. What we can know is that the money saved on reincarceration is much more than the cost of providing that education and training.

Our very best argument here may be to repeat the well-evidenced figures as starkly as we can.

So, what happens if we expand our group of released educated prisoners from the one hundred that the RAND team used for comparison to a much larger number, say one hundred thousand? Immediately, we can see that the 12.9 percent three-year reduction in recidivism due to participation in education amounts to an estimated 12,900 released prisoners not reincarcerated. As a conservative estimate, this would save $870 million from reincarceration expenses, not to mention the other considerable financial benefits. And the cost to provide the education would be one-fifth of that, resulting in a net savings of almost $700 million. Our society could put that money to good use—reduce our taxes, or build roads, highways, bridges, and other good works that benefit all of our lives.

The financial argument for providing more and better education and training to our prisoners is very strong. First, the scientific evidence for prison education and training reducing recidivism is indisputable. Second, the cost of educating and training our prisoners to bring about reduced recidivism is far less than the savings to be gained by that reduction. So why don't we make that investment? Is it a lack of understanding?

If so, we are doing our best to remedy that in this chapter by emphasizing the large financial benefit federal and state governments and the people of this country would gain by investing in prison education. And here is the best part. Not only will we save a lot of money in the long run while boosting the economy by providing prisoners with effective education and training. We also will provide strong tools that returning prisoners can use to reintegrate successfully into the world outside prison, while at the same time strengthening their families, their communities, and our society.

NOTES

1. David B. Wilson, Catherine A. Gallagher, and Doris L. MacKenzie, "Meta-Analysis of Corrections-Based Education, Vocation, and Work Programs for Adult Offenders," *Journal of Research in Crime and Delinquency* 37, no. 4 (November 2000), https://doi.org/10.1177/0022427800037004001.

2. Doris MacKenzie, *What Works in Corrections: Reducing the Criminal Activities of Offenders and Delinquents* (New York: Cambridge University Press, 2006).

3. Steve Aos, Marna Miller, and Elizabeth Drake, *Evidence-Based Adult Corrections Programs: What Works and What Does Not*, document no. 06-01-1201 (Olympia: Washington State Institute for Public Policy, January 2006), http://www.wsipp.wa.gov/ReportFile/924.

4. Steve Aos, Marna Miller, and Elizabeth Drake, *Evidence-Based Public Policy Options to Reduce Future Prison Construction, Criminal Justice Costs, and Crime Rates*, document 06-10-1201 (Olympia: Washington State Institute for Public Policy, October 2006), https://www.wsipp.wa.gov/ReportFile/952/Wsipp_Evidence-Based-Public-Policy-Options-to-Reduce-Future-Prison-Construction-Criminal-Justice-Costs-and-Crime-Rates_Full-Report.pdf.

5. Lois M. Davis et al., *Evaluating the Effectiveness of Correctional Education: A Meta-Analysis of Programs That Provide Education to Incarcerated Adults* (Santa Monica, CA: Rand Corporation, 2013), https://www.rand.org/pubs/research_reports/RR266.html.

6. RAND Corporation, *How We're Funded*, accessed May 19, 2020, https://www.rand.org/about/clients_grantors.html.

7. Pew Center on the States, *State of Recidivism: The Revolving Door of America's Prisons* (Washington, DC: Pew Charitable Trusts, April 2011), https://www.pewtrusts.org/en/research-and-analysis/reports/0001/01/01/state-of-recidivism.

8. Davis et al., *Evaluating the Effectiveness*, 22.

9. Davis et al., *Evaluating the Effectiveness*, table 3.3.

10. Robert Bozick et al., "Does Providing Inmates with Education Improve Postrelease Outcomes? A Meta-Analysis of Correctional Education Programs in the United States," *Journal of Experimental Criminology* 14 (2018): 389–428, https://doi.org/10.1007/s11292-018-9334-6.

11. Bozick et al., "Providing Inmates with Education," table 3.

12. Aos, Miller, and Drake, "Evidence-Based Public Policy Options," exhibit 4.

13. U.S. Department of Justice, Bureau of Justice Statistics, *Sourcebook of Criminal Justice Statistics 2002*, by Kathleen Maguire, Ann L. Pastore, and Johnna Christian (Washington, DC, 2004), https://www.hsdl.org/?abstract&did=711164.

14. Davis et al., *Evaluating the Effectiveness*, 37–38.

Chapter Ten

Today's Trailblazers in Prison Education

We have been contending that American society can no longer socially, morally, or economically afford the tough-on-crime mentality that has bloated our prisons. We need better thinking, focused on evidence-based approaches to help our returning citizens integrate with and become productive members of society. A key element of this new approach is to provide vastly expanded quality prison education.

Over the past two decades, we have seen auspicious signs that these necessary changes in mentality have begun and are generating promising new programs in prison education. These developments include various forward-thinking initiatives in some U.S. correctional institutions that point the way to what is possible for all. They include new prison technical preparation programs that prepare student-prisoners in growth industries that pay a living wage, college–prison joint ventures, new methods of providing prison education, and government initiatives. Together, these efforts make clear that numerous officials, educators, and organizations have recognized the need for increasing the availability and quality of prisoner education. What's more, not satisfied with recognizing the problem, some have applied their best thinking and significant resources to this vital issue and have developed effective programs to tackle it. In this chapter, we identify and describe some of these notable initiatives.

COLLEGE–PRISON PARTNERSHIPS

Several exciting prison education initiatives focus on providing college-level courses to incarcerated students. Such efforts are especially needed in our prisons after the extreme reduction in postsecondary prisoner education that occurred in 1994 with the passage of the Violent Crime Control and Law Enforcement Act. This law, another product of the tough-on-crime mentality, made it illegal for any prisoner to receive a federal Pell Grant to finance higher education while imprisoned. The Pell Grant had allowed prisoners with few financial resources to pay for and work on correspondence courses offered by various colleges, preparing themselves for eventual release. But after 1994, with Pell Grant assistance gone, those same prisoners had no way to pay for tuition, instruction, and materials. Following enactment of the law, what had been several hundred prisons with a higher education program quickly dwindled to barely a handful.

But it is hard to keep a good idea down forever, evidenced by the fact that the federal government has recently reintroduced the Pell Grant in the experimental Second Chance Pell (we will have more on this later in the chapter). And even before the Second Chance Pell, the idea of postsecondary education for prisoners had remained very much alive. Following 1994, some prisons were able to circumvent the legislative myopia by developing postsecondary programs. What has made possible a number of these programs is a prison's partnering with an accredited college or university. The deal often includes expert instructors ready to share their knowledge. In other cases, it includes a digital learning system that allows student-prisoners to access online coursework and resources over a private network.

The Prison University Project

One correctional institution that has formed an effective partnership with a college is San Quentin State Prison, a four-thousand-strong, male-only medium-security institution less than twenty miles north of San Francisco. San Quentin has a storied history and a reputation of being one of America's most brutal and violent prisons. Yet today, it is among the vanguard of efforts to bring quality higher education to prisoners.

The prelude to this initiative began quietly in 1996 when San Quentin began offering two postsecondary education classes to carefully screened prisoners. Within a few years, this modest beginning became the Prison University Project, funded entirely by private donations from foundations, organizations, and individuals. The project began by partnering with Patten University, a private, accredited, for-profit institution in Oakland, California. It now offers an array of college-level classes, as well as the opportunity to earn a two-year associate of arts degree. Instructors in the program include numerous volunteers from universities and colleges in the San Francisco Bay area. Students pay no fee, and supplies are provided by the project, including books that publishers donate.[1]

Classes are held on the prison grounds rather than through correspondence courses. In that way, San Quentin learners get closer to having a full academic higher education experience. According to the Prison University Project website, an average of three hundred incarcerated students enroll in the program each semester, representing more than 7 percent of the prison population. To enter the program, all that is required academically is that the student-prisoner have a high school degree or GED certificate. Most students admitted to the program first must take college preparatory classes in writing and math and show satisfactory progress before being allowed to take courses that earn college credit.

The project's website also indicates that students in the program are provided the first two years of a true liberal arts education, as well as academic preparation for further study in math and science. Twenty courses for college credit are taught per semester, mostly in the afternoons and evenings. On most evenings, study halls are offered where students can do homework and consult with tutors and volunteer teachers. Besides math and science classes, the Prison University Project offers coursework in the humanities and social sciences. Most of the courses are transferable to four-year colleges and universities. To earn the associate degree, students must satisfactorily complete five courses in English, four courses in the social sciences, five courses in the humanities, two science courses, at least one with a laboratory, and intermediate algebra.

The Prison University Project's association with Patten University ended recently. As a result, the project was required to seek accreditation from another source. As of May 2020, the project has been accepted as a candidate for accreditation by the Accrediting Commission for Community and Junior Colleges. Currently it is transitioning to become an independent educational institution named Mount Tamalpais College. [2]

The Bard Prison Initiative

Even more impressive than the San Quentin Prison University Project is the Bard Prison Initiative (BPI), another groundbreaking college–prison partnership. The program began offering its first classes, for sixteen prisoners, in 2001. Since then, BPI has grown to provide college-level courses to more than three hundred male and female prisoners in New York state prisons. [3] The academic home of BPI is Bard College, a private liberal arts college in Annandale-on-Hudson, New York, founded in 1861 as St. Stephens College. However, the academic home for student-prisoners enrolled in the program is the institution where they are incarcerated and attend classes. At this writing, that academic home is one of six different prisons in the state, all seventy miles or less from Bard College. Participants come from five male-only medium- and maximum-security prisons (Coxsackie, Eastern, Fishkill, Green

Haven, and Woodbourne correctional facilities) and the all-female medium-security Taconic Correctional Facility in Bedford Hills.[4]

Students incur no costs for taking the courses or for books and materials. Almost all of the monies for the program are provided by grants and private donations. The college education offered through the initiative is designed to be as rigorous and comprehensive as that provided to main-campus students. Bard professors who teach the courses speak highly about teaching in the BPI program, noting that students enrolled are remarkably engaged and diligent in their classes and coursework. This high regard is evidenced by the waiting list of professors who want to teach in the program.[5]

The Bard program curriculum is impressive. According to the BPI Comprehensive academic engagement Web page, the program is wide ranging, with courses divided into four major areas: science, mathematics, and computing; languages, literature, and the humanities; social studies; and the arts. It strongly emphasizes effective written communication and critical thinking and analysis skills; students are required to take at least six writing courses. A brief sample of the courses offered testifies to the curriculum's level of sophistication: dynamical systems (math); biology of infectious disease (science); Python programming (computer science); contemporary political philosophy (social studies); beginning, intermediate, and advanced Chinese (languages); Homer's *Iliad* and *Odyssey* (literature); and histories of architecture and design (the arts).

Students who are accepted into the two-year program can earn the associate of arts degree awarded by Bard College. If they then are accepted to continue their studies in the program, they may pursue a bachelor's degree in their chosen field, also granted by Bard. As they progress toward the bachelor's degree, they narrow their area of interest to a specific approved topic. In their final year, they must complete a senior thesis, just as all Bard College students at the main campus traditionally have been required to do.

The Bard Prison Initiative also provides students the opportunity to focus on several curricular specializations that help them prepare for a career. These include a seven-course Public Health specialization, which prepares students for careers in the healthcare, public health, and community health areas. An Urban Farming and Sustainability program prepares students for careers in farming and in the areas of regional food systems, sustainability, and food justice. Along with academic coursework, the program includes gardening experience at organic gardens maintained at two of the BPI prisons. Students can prepare for jobs in computer science or for computer-focused jobs in other fields by specializing in a concentrated computer science curriculum. Finally, BPI students can prepare for post-release work in teaching for the New York City TASC high school equivalency examinations.

Although the Bard program is committed to offering a college education on its prison campuses equal in quality to that supplied by Bard College on its traditional campus, BPI obviously cannot provide the range of extracurricular activities available at the home college. Yet the program does offer a few art and cultural extracurricular activities in BPI prisons. These include an annual performance in one of the prisons by the Bard Conservatory Orchestra and appearances by the Bill T. Jones/Arnie Zane Dance Company, open to the general prison population. BPI students also have a debate team at Eastern New York Correctional Facility. The quality of the team is reflected in the fact that it has won debates against prestigious teams, including one from Harvard University.[6]

Further noteworthy about the Bard Prison Initiative is its reentry assistance offered to student-prisoners after their release from incarceration. This help begins with providing the reentering student participant in BPI with a detailed reentry handbook full of practical information and how-tos on tasks to be undertaken in the early days of release, such as reporting to a parole officer, obtaining a cell phone, and creating a résumé. Also, the program's director of reentry spends time with each returning student in one-on-one consultation, focusing on how the individual can best take advantage of the education received while incarcerated.

These options may include completing undergraduate education if the individual was released before completing the BPI program. Many students return to New York City and enroll in the City University of New York system, where they can complete their baccalaureate degree. For those who completed the bachelor of arts degree while in prison, reentry counseling may aid them in deciding whether to enroll in a graduate school and, if so, where. Former BPI students have entered graduate schools including Columbia University, New York University, and Cornell University. Others obtain employment in private companies or other organizations.[7]

Significantly, the recidivism rate for graduates of the Bard Prison Initiative is less than 3 percent. This is outstanding, especially when compared to the three-year national recidivism rate of close to 50 percent. The founder and current executive director of BPI, Max Kenner, downplays this very encouraging statistic, indicating that participating in the BPI program doesn't simply move participants away from illegal behavior but, more importantly, it changes their lives in profound ways.[8]

We agree that the program clearly changes the lives of many participants in positive ways—a deeply heartening result. But we also believe that the outcome of radically reduced recidivism among program graduates should be brought to the front and emphasized because it is important to marshal as many good arguments as possible to rally society to champion the need for more and better education for incarcerated citizens. That the quality postsecondary education the BPI program provides greatly reduces recidivism—and its many costs to society—is one of the most compelling practical arguments to win over those who remain unconvinced by ethical, psychological, and sociological considerations. It is powerful because it is geared toward tax-payers' legitimate concern for their pocketbooks. This argument can be stated simply and cogently:

- Abundant evidence indicates that improved prison education would re-duce recidivism, lowering the prison population and thereby saving mil-lions, even billions, of tax dollars.
- The cost of education leading to those savings is far less than the savings themselves, resulting in a net decrease in tax dollars spent on incarcera-tion.
- Those saved tax dollars can be used for important societal needs such as improved infrastructure.
- Consequently, improving prison education is a patently good idea for anyone who wants tax dollars spent wisely.

The Consortium for the Liberal Arts in Prison

The Bard Prison Initiative has been so successful that its principles and methods, under BPI's guidance, have spread to other colleges and univer-sities. This expansion follows from the establishment, in 2009, of the Consortium for the Liberal Arts in Prison. Through the consortium, BPI partners with other institutions of higher education to create college pro-grams in prisons in their own localities. To date, BPI has helped more than a dozen colleges and universities establish such programs.[9]

The Bard Initiative National Projects website explains that the consortium adheres to the foundational principle that the postsecondary education of student-prisoners must put academics first, expecting education excellence in the prison location equal to the traditional college classroom. To that end, consortium members are expected to develop college-level prison programs that have identical demands and quality as the same courses taught on the member's main campus. Members partner with correctional systems to present courses within prisons that are taught by fully qualified instructors, including home institution professors and graduate students, while adhering to specific tenets and aspirations. These include:

- Do not just bring college courses into the prison environment; help stu-dent-prisoners feel part of the main campus by incorporating them into its intellectual, creative, and political life.
- Focus on providing a liberal arts curriculum, education, and degrees.

- Strive to make the full-time academic engagement of student-prisoners the main aspect of their incarceration at every moment while they are enrolled in the postsecondary program.
- Make academic requirements, expectations, and evaluations of student-prisoners identical to those for students on the institution's main campus, and do not alter any part of the curriculum based on unverified ideas about the abilities, aspirations, or possibilities of the participants. [10]

At this writing, thirteen higher education institutions have joined the consortium, ranging geographically from the University of Vermont to the Freedom Education Project of the University of Puget Sound, Washington, for incarcerated women. Descriptions of these initiatives are available on BPI's National Projects website. To provide a flavor of what is being done, we briefly highlight a consortium partnership that started in 2012, when BPI began a collaboration with Notre Dame University, Holy Cross College at Notre Dame, and the Indiana Department of Corrections. This initiative resulted in establishing the Moreau College Initiative at Westville Correctional Facility, a multi-security prison for adult males in Westville, Indiana. More than fifty students are enrolled full-time at Westville, with a curriculum that includes courses in literature, science, mathematics, theology, business, and political science. Classes are held within the prison, with most faculty coming from Notre Dame. Commencement ceremonies are held at the Westville Correctional Facility campus for students who have graduated from the associate of arts or the bachelor of arts degree programs.

Ashland University

A college–prison partnership substantially different from BPI and the Prison University Project involves Ashland University, a private institution associated with the Church of the Brethren located in Ashland, Ohio. The Ashland correctional education program, which began in 1964, claims to be the oldest continuous postsecondary prison education program in the United States. [11] The program began at the Ohio State Reformatory in Mansfield, fifteen miles from the school, and subsequently also was offered at nearby Grafton Correctional Institution and the Richland Correctional Institution. [12] At that time, the program was partly funded by Pell Grants awarded to student-prisoners. When the Pell Grant was made unavailable by the 1994 law, Ashland University continued to maintain the program, aided by state funding. At that time, courses for which students could earn a certificate of accomplishment were offered in person at prison locations.

When the Second Chance Pell Grant program was authorized to begin in 2016, the Ashland correctional education program was able to expand in Ohio. It is now offered to male and female adult prisoners in institutions in the Ohio Department of Rehabilitation and Correction and to juvenile offenders assigned to the Ohio Department of Youth Services. By incorporating digital distance learning into its educational methodology, Ashland was able to extend its reach into out-of-state locations. According to the Ashland University Correctional Education Web page, the program is now also offered in prisons in ten states and the District of Columbia and has more than three thousand students.

What has enabled the Ashland program to expand so widely is a learning system that students can access on an electronic tablet provided by the company JPay, which we briefly mentioned in chapter 5, in association with Ashland and participating prisons. Through the tablets, students can access lessons, course material, and tests, as well as submit their completed assignments to and communicate with Ashland instructors. These connections to the learning system are not via the internet, which prison regulations generally will not allow prisoners to access, but by students connecting their tablets to JPay's private learning network.[13] Because the Ashland program offers primarily online education, it does not provide the student-instructor face-to-face interchange that the Prison University Project and the Bard Prison Initiative offer and thus may not provide the same level of instructional quality. As we noted in chapter 5, questions have arisen about the company providing the services. Before beginning to offer educational services, JPay already was providing prisoners with e-mail capabilities, music, and video through its tablets. Critics have claimed that the JPay services are priced exorbitantly and take advantage of what is, literally, a captive audience.[14] Yet, the program reaches widely and provides postsecondary educational opportunity to many prisoners who otherwise would not have it.

Other College–Prison Partnerships

Several other noteworthy postsecondary prison education programs currently are operating, three within New York State. They are the Prison-to-College Pipeline (P2CP), the Cornell Prison Education Program (CPEP), and Hudson Link.

The P2CP program was established by the Institute for Justice and Opportunity (formerly the Prisoner Reentry Institute) of John Jay College of Criminal Justice, in New York City. The program brings City University of New York (CUNY) instructors some eighty miles to Otisville Correctional Institute, a men's medium-security prison in Mount Hope, New York, to teach accredited college-level courses. P2CP also provides a developmental education program to improve students' reading and writing skills. The program helps released students transition into further education, advising them on their opportunities and helping them with needed paperwork for entering college in the community. Transition is aided by the fact that incarcerated students who pass their courses in the P2CP program are guaranteed acceptance into a CUNY campus upon their release. [15]

The John Jay P2CP program Web page reports that the program includes a *Learning Exchange* element. Once each month, students from John Jay's Manhattan campus take part in classes held at the Otisville institution. The program gives student-prisoners experience in a setting similar to that of a traditional college, while allowing visiting students direct contact with prisoners and aspects of prison life.

The P2CP program's Learning Exchange is an instance of the Inside-Out Prison Exchange movement. The movement began at Philadelphia's Temple University in 1997, with a class taught in the Philadelphia prison system that included incarcerated students and traditional students from Temple University. The program was expanded to Graterford prison in 2000; then other colleges and universities, both public and private, in collaboration with nearby prison systems, began to join the movement. [16] Today, the Inside-Out Center at Temple University has become the hub of an international movement. The center encourages colleges to establish semester-long courses in which incarcerated students sit beside students from home institutions, and it provides training in establishing such programs. Today, the Inside-Out movement has grown to involve more than 140 private and public colleges and universities in thirty-six U.S. states and includes institutions in Canada, the United Kingdom, Australia, Denmark, Mexico, and the Netherlands. [17]

Cornell University in Ithaca, New York, an Ivy League institution, conducts the Cornell Prison Education Program (CPEP), which educates postsecondary students in two upstate New York men's prisons. In 1999, the university began to offer credit-bearing college-level classes to student prisoners at Auburn Correctional Facility, a maximum-security prison thirty-five miles north of Ithaca, charging no tuition or fees. Course offerings increased gradually, and in 2010, the CPEP program was established. Supported by grants from the Sunshine Lady Foundation and other donors, as well as the university, the program began to offer twelve credit-bearing courses per semester, while expanding to nearby medium-security Cayuga Correctional Facility. A liberal arts curriculum is taught in the prisons by volunteer Cornell faculty members and graduate students. Participants can earn an associate degree awarded by Cayuga Community College. [18] CPEP also provides the opportunity for staff from seven New York prisons to earn college credits from Cornell. [19]

A third force in New York State prison postsecondary efforts is Hudson Link for Higher Education. Begun in 1998, the nonprofit Hudson Link organization now works with a number of colleges and universities to provide postsecondary and college preparatory courses at five New York state prisons. The organization also helps prisoners who were unable to complete their studies while incarcerated transition to colleges and universities to continue their education after release. Over its lifetime, seven hundred college degrees have been awarded to prisoners through the Hudson Link program. Notably, the recidivism rate of Hudson Link graduates is 2 percent, compared to 43 percent for all former New York state prisoners. [20]

Among other noteworthy prison education projects is the Philemon Fellowship, founded in 2015 to provide free postsecondary education to prisoners in Georgia correctional institutions. The Fellowship's name refers to the New Testament book of Philemon, a letter written by the disciple Paul to his wealthy associate Philemon, asking him to accept back and forgive the runaway slave Onesimus, who had wronged Philemon. The Fellowship grew out of the efforts of Dr. Roger Byrd, coauthor of this book, in coordination with Baptist Brewton-Parker College in Mt. Vernon, Georgia, where he is an associate professor, and other professors and local pastors who volunteer to teach college-level classes in nearby prison facilities.

The program, though only a few years old, has had good success, with the Philemon Fellowship currently operating in two Georgia prisons, offering free postsecondary in-prison education classes to approximately fifty incarcerated students. The organization's Facebook page makes clear that the Fellowship also works to educate the community on reentry issues that returning prisoners encounter "so that once an offender's debt is paid, he—like Paul desired for Onesimus—can be received back into society as a more productive and responsible citizen, rather than as a slave to past transgressions." [21]

What College–Prison Partnerships Provide Student-Prisoners

The college-in-prison programs we have described are some of the most heartening developments in prisoner education. The benefits of postsecondary education—especially programs in which instructors come face-to-face with prisoners—are many. One of the most obvious is that completing college-level courses—possibly even an associate of arts or baccalaureate degree—helps students prepare for their release into the larger world outside. Once out of prison, they can use what they have learned in their search for employment and possibly for continued higher education. The college preparatory courses alone, required of many participants before they can enroll in credit-bearing courses in a program such as San Quentin's Prison University Project, can further their skills in reading, writing, and math. These are all necessary competencies in an increasingly technological workplace and ones that make returning citizens more employable.

Another benefit of these programs is that student-prisoners must learn and practice the discipline of study, perhaps for the first time in their lives. To succeed in the courses requires not only brain work, but also time management, perseverance, flexibility, and resilience, especially in the crowded, noisy, restrictive prison environment with its daily distractions and disturbances. Just having the discipline to complete college-level courses while incarcerated may be enough to impress a potential employer with a former prisoner's diligence and tenacity, tipping the scales in the applicant's favor.

What also is obvious is that these programs provide participants with meaning, purpose, and goals within an otherwise bleak environment where the only previous aim may have been to wait, wait, wait until their sentence ends. But the opportunity to take college-level courses brings many new objectives: books to read, papers to write, tests to prepare for. It is easy to imagine a student coming out of a class with a mind full of what must be done before the next meeting, planning where and when to study, or trying to determine a topic for an upcoming paper. If the student is having difficulty grasping something in the book or lecture, perhaps he will devise questions to ask whoever presides at an evening study hall or at the next class meeting. Although the student is in the same old environment, surrounded by impenetrable walls, that world will likely seem less harsh because something new has replaced the ever-present commotion, noise, and austerity in his mind.

Not least of the benefits for prisoners enrolled in these programs is something that should never be forgotten about education: it is transforming. People have a natural tendency to refer all that they learn in school and in life to themselves. It is the same with participants in college-in-prison programs. Coursework they take is not simply a bag of information dumped into their brains. Courses deliver new concepts, ideas, and ways of thinking that they try on for size to determine whether and how it fits them and their life.

Education provides student-prisoner insights into who they have been, are now, and can be in the future. Education makes people who they are and who they will be, as does its lack. People's presence in prison is a function of how they thought about themselves, other people, and the world before they committed whatever crime landed them in prison. The college-level courses they take in prison introduce them to new ways of understanding that likely will impact their view of themselves in relation to the world. Even the fact that they are enrolled in such courses is very likely to affect their self-concept positively.

Speaking of student-prisoners' self-concept, recall what we learned in chapter 6 about the importance of a prisoner's sense of self-efficacy and competence as a catalyst for securing work and integrating into society after release. Success in a prison postsecondary program brings with it a heightened sense of self-efficacy and increased competency. These empower the individual's self-generated motivation to succeed when returning to and merging with society. Simply by being part of such a program, prisoners arguably already are taking steps to connect to the world outside as they are doing what millions of people on the outside do—taking real college courses in an unusual, yet a true academic setting.

Other significant advantages follow from postsecondary education programs in prison. They aid prison staff in controlling the incarcerated population. Guards need to worry less about what prisoners may be "up to" when they are in class, studying for their next one, or busy writing a paper. It is the kind of control prison staff should crave: the self-control of prisoners engaged in legitimate projects that are important to them. Students spending their time learning what is being taught in a college-level course that they choose to take means they are not out on the floor learning from someone else how to be better at a criminal pursuit. That is, prisoners making the most of their opportunity to learn math, writing, science, and history have much less time available to learn what we do not want them to learn. Engaged student-prisoners are unlikely even to want to learn to be better criminals.

As for the instructors, they find incarcerated students to be some of their very best. Student-prisoners may have environmental challenges that traditional college students do not, but they do not have the campus life distractions that may interfere with traditional students' studies. They probably have as much or more time to put into studies, while their motivation to learn and succeed in their courses is apt to be high. This all makes for energized and serious students, the very thing that college instructors desire and appreciate. No wonder the Bard program has a waiting list for instructors and many volunteers are ready to teach in prison.

College-in-prison programs that have an inside-out element also provide important rewards for traditional college students who take courses sitting beside incarcerated classmates. Traditional students learn about prison and prisoners firsthand, a superior and potentially eye-opening opportunity. That inside-out courses provide substantial benefits to traditional students is evidenced by the movement's spread to thirty-six states and six more countries over the past two decades.

One of the greatest rewards of college-in-prison programs is the humanizing of prisoners. To treat prisoners as more than numbers, more than just "lawbreakers and bad guys," is to think and feel beyond simplistic categories. It is to recognize and respect them as valuable human beings, worthy of being provided with decent tools to increase their chance of success upon release. This humanizing effect may be as important to the goal of reintegration as the college courses themselves. Students enrolled in college-in-prison programs learn that active, influential people and organizations in our society reject the idea that they are pariahs. Rather, these individuals and organizations see them as fellow citizens in need of education while incarcerated, and they are willing to put their resources, time, and efforts into substantively supporting those ideals. That fact itself, when student-prisoners recognize it, is likely to promote their desire to fully integrate into a society that includes those concerned about and willing to work for their future success.

Finally, consider again the very substantial reward that college-in-prison programs provide of reduced recidivism. The programs furnish student-prisoners with essential resources they will need when they reenter society. This package of resources includes new knowledge, skills, and understandings of themselves in relation to others and society, increased self-efficacy, empowered motivation to succeed, and justified hope. Gaining these resources will give them a much better chance to find suitable employment and reintegrate successfully into society. The result will be substantially decreased rates of recidivism, which will greatly benefit the released citizens themselves, as well as their families and communities, and will significantly reduce prison populations and the enormous amounts spent on incarceration.

GOVERNMENT INITIATIVES

Several encouraging government initiatives, both federal and state, in the realm of prison education have occurred recently. To the degree that our government officials represent the will—or at least the sentiments—of our nation toward its incarcerated citizens, these initiatives suggest that the tough-on-crime mentality is giving way to a better understanding of the penalties mass incarceration places on our society.

Federal Actions

That the federal government is gradually abandoning the tough-on-crime approach and developing a new, more realistic attitude toward the need for prison reform is evidenced by several recent developments. For example, passage of the First Step Act in 2018 applies to prisoners in the federal correctional system. While the law does not focus primarily on the need for prison education, it does address several other issues of importance to federal prisoners. These include sections on sentencing reform, including reductions in mandatory minimum sentences for some drug offenders, greater flexibility for judges in sentencing, and making the Fair Sentencing Act of 2010 retroactively apply to prisoners previously sentenced to especially lengthy terms for possession of crack cocaine. Among other provisions, the law gives some nonviolent prisoners the opportunity to earn good-time credits for participating in evidence-based recidivism-reducing programs, including job training.[22]

The most notable recent federal government initiative recognizing the need for more and better prison educational opportunities has been reintroduction of Pell Grant eligibility for up to twelve thousand prisoners in the federal and state systems. The pilot program, proposed by the Obama administration, is the Second Chance Pell. Beginning in 2016, the program has allowed as many as sixty-seven colleges and universities nationwide to provide Pell Grants to prisoners who typically are incarcerated in nearby correctional facilities. The Pell, a need-based educational grant amounting to more than $6,000 per academic year, goes directly to the educational institution to pay for the student's tuition, fees, books, and other educational expenses. For the most part, classes are taught face to face inside prison walls, but some institutions offer online classes. Prisoners most likely to receive the award are those who are expected to be released within five years.[23]

At this writing, the Second Chance Pell program has been in operation for more than two years, with sixty-three colleges and universities currently providing the award. In the program's first two years, the Pell was granted to around eighty-eight hundred incarcerated students; however, a full-scale evaluation of the Pell's success is yet to come.[24] Nevertheless, the program recently was extended by the Trump administration to the 2019–2020 academic year. The present secretary of education, Betsy DeVos, has called for an increase in the number of colleges and universities authorized to award the Second Chance Pell and has publicly announced her view that Congress should permanently reinstate the availability of the Pell Grant for prisoners.[25]

On April 9, 2019, The Restoring Education and Learning (REAL) Act to permanently reinstate federal Pell Grant availability for prisoners was introduced in the U.S. House of Representatives and referred to the House Committee on Education and Labor. The REAL Act has yet to be voted on in the House; however, the fact that the bill has both Democratic and Republican cosponsors indicates a degree of bipartisan support for the prospect of permanently restoring the Pell Grant program for incarcerated individuals who aspire to postsecondary education.[26] Continued support of the Second Chance Pell pilot program by the next administration would be a further positive impetus for passage of the REAL Act.

State Initiatives

The massive increase in state prison populations over the past several decades has led to necessary increases in state budget monies devoted to correctional systems. From the 1979–1980 fiscal year to 2012–2013, expenditures on state and local corrections increased 324 percent from $17 billion to $71 billion annually, straining many state budgets.[27] In various states, budget crunches have led to policies focused on restructuring sentencing guidelines and other legislative and administrative changes aimed at reducing prison populations. In Texas, for instance, the Council of State Governments helped the state develop policies since 2007 that resulted in new drug courts, reduced the incarceration of nonviolent offenders, increased substance abuse treatment in prison, and offered new vocational and academic education options. These actions reduced prison population growth by thirty thousand individuals and resulted in closure of eight prisons.[28] Other states that have significantly reduced their prison populations over the past decade through various actions, including altering sentencing and release policies, include California, Connecticut, Michigan, Mississippi, New Jersey, New York, Rhode Island, and South Carolina.[29]

In an increasing number of states, officials have become convinced that education is a key to reducing recidivism, resulting in new efforts to provide increased educational opportunities for prisoners. These include not only new postsecondary initiatives, but also—very important—improved career and technical education programs, often called vocational or occupational programs. Of course, CTE under any name has long been a mainstay of prison education programs, as many prisoners are not academically inclined and prefer to be trained in an occupation or career that will provide them an advantage immediately in searching for employment after release. In the past, such programs sometimes have been questioned as to whether they have much real-world applicability.[30] Over the past several decades, however, realization has been increasing about the importance of ensuring that CTE programs impart to student-prisoners skills that are needed in the job market as they prepare for specific types of employment, especially jobs that pay a living wage. Career and technical education programs that prepare prisoners to become electricians, plumbers, carpenters, HVAC professionals, or computer support specialists potentially are very beneficial as these occupations are expected to grow faster than average through 2028.[31]

An illustration of a forward-looking vocational program is provided by Colorado, which backs an innovative prison education program, the Fresh Start Initiative, that teaches entrepreneurship. The state has invested several million dollars in the program; the Pikes Peak Small Business Development Center provides classes to prisoners to teach them how to start and run their own business after they are released. One idea motivating the program, according to a Fresh Start instructor, is that even if a released prisoner does not start a business, she will be better prepared to locate a supervisory position by being able to read financial statements and understand and deal with business concepts such as cash flow.[32]

Georgia is another state taking steps toward improving prison education. Under Governor Nathan Deal, Georgia increased spending for correctional education by $12 million, including money to expand a charter school program enabling prisoners to receive not just a GED but an official high school diploma while incarcerated.[33] Georgia also has increased its vocational training programs, partnering with local technical colleges to offer courses in diesel mechanics, commercial driving, and more than twenty other CTE programs.[34] In addition, the state's correctional system works with the Georgia State University Prison Education Project to bring college-preparatory and college-level classes to several prisons and a transitional center.[35]

A third state clearly making efforts to increase prisoner education is Tennessee. In 2019, Governor Bill Lee announced that in association with the Tennessee Higher Education Commission, $10.5 million would be invested over three years to provide increased technical and career credentials to prisoners in areas such as computer information technology and building construction.[36] The Tennessee Department of Corrections also is working with the nonprofit organization Tennessee Higher Education Initiative to provide in-prison postsecondary education classes leading to an associate degree in business administration, psychology, or political science through Nashville Community College. All credits and degrees prisoners earn are valid at any Tennessee Board of Regents college or university.[37]

Partnering with one or more higher-ed institutions to present academic or vocational classes is the main way that not only Georgia and Tennessee, but also many other states, are improving prisoner education. California is an outstanding example of a state that has made significant strides. It offers a number of CTE programs in its prisons, including computer coding, electrical construction, electronics and network cabling, HVAC, plumbing, and fifteen more career tracks. According to California's Division of Rehabilitative Programs, all CTE programs "provide industry-recognized certification and an employment pathway to a livable wage. . . . Many programs include green employment skills relevant to solar, geothermal and smart energy management practices."[38]

The California Department of Corrections and Rehabilitation also began collaborating with the state higher education system in 2014 to expand postsecondary education programs in the state's prisons. As of early 2020, the number of prisons offering instructor-taught college-level classes in California prisons had gone from one (the Prison University Project at San Quentin) to thirty-four of the state's thirty-five prisons.[39] State prisons at every security level are included, with almost forty-five hundred prisoners enrolled in the classes in 2017. The educational backbone of the programs is a number of the state's 114 community colleges. These institutions offer prisoners classes that can lead to an associate degree, accepted by all of the state's higher education institutions. Many community colleges have begun on-campus support groups and associations for former prisoners, helping them adjust to their new educational context. In the California state university system, Project Rebound, a program to assist former prisoners in adjusting to college life, has expanded to nine campuses.[40]

New York is another state that is a model for how higher education can be integrated substantially into a state correctional system. College-level programs operate in twenty-seven New York Department of Corrections prisons. They largely are partnerships between the corrections department and a number of New York colleges and universities, both public and private. Other than the higher education institutions operating in the state's prisons described earlier in this chapter, involved colleges and universities include Columbia University, the State University of New York (SUNY), and New York University, for a total of more than thirty colleges and universities.[41] Face-to-face programs held inside prison walls are funded by private donations and the Second Chance Pell program. In addition, the state has awarded $7.3 million over five years for prison educational programming and reentry services to fund twenty-five hundred student-prisoners in seventeen New York facilities for college education and job training.[42]

Despite promising initiatives taken to improve prison education, opportunities remain far too limited for both academic and technical education in numerous prisons. Though many states have added CTE courses that appear to be well-matched to job and career opportunities outside prison, the courses are offered in too few facilities and are limited in size, making them practically unavailable to many prisoners. Those eager to enroll in a vocational course of study often are on long waiting lists that place course entry effectively out of reach. Availability of nearby colleges to partner with a facility to present a technical education course is an important factor that limits courses offered. In Illinois, for instance, a number of community colleges are in and around the Chicago area, while the southern part of the state has fewer, limiting the availability of technical course offerings in prisons located there. Of course, lack of funds is a major limitation on whether and what vocational courses a facility can offer. The same can be said of prison academic education. The postsecondary initiatives we have identified in this chapter are encouraging, but a great deal of work remains to be done. As of May 2020, the National Directory of Higher Education in Prison Web page of the Prison Studies Project reports that twenty-one states have no higher education program in any of their prisons.

Overall, evidence is that an array of points of light brighten the landscape of prisoner education. At the same time, positive change remains slow and uneven.

Despite some progress on the vocational and academic fronts over the past few decades, limitations on both types of opportunity in our prisons is troubling considering the increasing data-driven consensus that prisoner education is a strong promoter of post-release success, an inhibitor of recidivism, and therefore a major money saver for state governments. The limitations also provide some evidence that the tough-on-crime mentality still pulls at budget strings in many statehouses.

NOTES

1. "Academics," Mount Tamalpais College, accessed September 29, 2020, https://www.mttamcollege.org/academics/admissions/.

2. "Accreditation," Mount Tamalpais College, accessed September 29, 2020, https://www.mttamcollege.org/about/accreditation/. In September, 2020, the Prison University Project officially changed its name to Mount Tamalpais College.

3. Bard Prison Initiative, *Who We Are*, accessed May 30, 2020, https://bpi.bard.edu/who-we-are/.

4. Bard Prison Initiative, *The College: Comprehensive Academic Engagement*, accessed May 30, 2020, https://bpi.bard.edu/the-work/the-college/.

5. Steve Giegerich, "Exercise in Student Activism Opens Doors to Academic Achievement," *Focus*, Fall 2016, https://focus.luminafoundation.org/exercise-in-student-activism-opens-doors-to-academic-achievement/.

6. Leslie Brody, "Three Prison Inmates Beat Harvard in a Debate. Here's What Happened Next," *Wall Street Journal*, October 19, 2019, https://www.wsj.com/articles/three-prison-in-mates-beat-harvard-in-a-debate-heres-what-happened-next-11571490001.

7. Steve Giegerich, "Unlocking Lives: Postsecondary Programs Go Behind Prison Walls to Forge New Futures," *Focus*, Fall 2016, 22, https://focus.luminafoundation.org/wp-content/up-loads/2016/04/Focus-Fall-2016-web.pdf.

8. Giegerich, "Unlocking Lives," 23.

9. Bard Prison Initiative, *National Projects: Creating Educational Opportunities in Prison Nationwide*, accessed May 30, 2020, https://bpi.bard.edu/our-work/national-projects/.

10. Bard Prison Initiative, *National Projects*, Principles.

11. "Correctional Education," Ashland University, accessed May 19, 2020, https://www.ashland.edu/coas/programs/correctional-education.

12. Dylan Sams, "AU Extends Prison Education Programs to 3 states, D.C.," *Times-Gazette*, February 23, 2018, https://www.times-gazette.com/special/20180228/au-extends-prison-educa-tion-programs-to-3-states-dc.

13. Meagan Wilson, Rayane Alamuddin, and Danielle Cooper, *Unbarring Access: A Land-scape Review of Postsecondary Education in Prison and Its Pedagogical Supports*, Ithaka S+R Organization research report, May 30, 2019, Technological Interventions, https://doi.org/10.18665/sr.311499.

14. See, e.g., Mack Finkel and Wanda Bertram, "More States Are Signing Harmful 'Free Prison Tablet' Contracts," Prison Policy Initiative Briefing, last modified December 23, 2019, https://www.prisonpolicy.org/blog/2019/03/07/free-tablets/.

15. "Prison-to-College Pipeline," Institute for Justice and Opportunity at John Jay College, accessed May 20, 2020, https://justiceandopportunity.org/educational-pathways/prison-to-col-lege-pipeline/.

16. "History," Inside-Out Prison Exchange Program, accessed May 20, 2020, https://www.insideoutcenter.org/history-inside-out.html.

17. "Higher Education Partners," Inside-Out Prison Exchange Program, accessed May 20, 2020, https://www.insideoutcenter.org/higher-education-partners.html.

18. "About Us," Cornell Prison Education Program, accessed May 20, 2020, https://cpep.cornell.edu/about-us/our-history/.

19. David Skorton and Glenn Altschuler, "College Behind Bars: How Educating Prisoners Pays Off," *Forbes*, March 25, 2013, https://www.forbes.com/sites/collegeprose/2013/03/25/college-behind-bars-how-educating-prisoners-pays-off/#4359e3727077.

20. "Fact Sheet," Hudson Link, accessed May 20, 2020, http://www.hudsonlink.org/what-we-do/fact-sheet/.

21. The Philemon Fellowship on its Facebook page, accessed May 31, 2020, https://www.facebook.com/PhilFellowship/.

22. Congressional Research Service, *The First Step Act of 2018: An Overview*, March 4, 2019, 5, https://fas.org/sgp/crs/misc/R45558.pdf.

23. Ellen Wexler, "Prisoners to Get 'Second Chance Pell,'" *Inside Higher Ed*, June 24, 2016, https://www.insidehighered.com/news/2016/06/24/us-expands-pell-grant-program-12000-prison.

24. Andrew Kreighbaum, "Education Department Urged to Evaluate Second-Chance Pell," *Inside Higher Ed*, April 5, 2019, https://www.insidehighered.com/quicktakes/2019/04/05/edu-cation-department-urged-evaluate-second-chance-pell.

25. Andrew Kreighbaum, "Taking Stock of Pell Grants Behind Bars," *Inside Higher Ed*, July 16, 2019, https://www.insidehighered.com/news/2019/07/16/full-repeal-pell-ban-prisons-top-mind-annual-convening-second-chance-pilot.

26. Michael T. Nietzel, "Congress Should Pass the REAL Act and Make Prisoners Eligible for Pell Grants Again," *Forbes*, April 15, 2019, https://www.forbes.com/sites/michaeltnietzel/2019/04/15/congress-should-pass-the-real-act-and-make-prisoners-eligible-for-pell-grants-again/#55be52212f0c.

27. U.S. Department of Education, Policy and Program Studies Service, *State and Local Expenditures on Corrections and Education*, July 2016, https://www2.ed.gov/rschstat/eval/other/expenditures-corrections-education/brief.pdf.

28. Hannah Wiley, "Trump Administration Looks to Texas as It Pushes a Criminal Justice Reform Bill," *Texas Tribune*, December 3, 2018, https://www.texastribune.org/2018/12/03/first-step-act-prison-reform-texas-criminal-justice/.

29. Dennis Schrantz, Stephen DeBor, and Marc Mauer, *Decarceration Strategies: How 5 States Achieved Substantial Prison Population Reductions* (Washington, DC: Sentencing Project, September 5, 2018), Executive Summary, https://www.sentencingproject.org/publications/decarceration-strategies-5-states-achieved-substantial-prison-population-reductions/.

30. See, for example, Robert Martinson, "What Works—Questions and Answers about Prison Reform," *Public Interest* 35 (Spring 1974): 28, https://www.nationalaffairs.com/public_interest/detail/what-works-questions-and-answers-about-prison-reform.

31. U.S. Bureau of Labor Statistics, *Occupational Outlook Handbook*, last modified April 10, 2020, https://www.bls.gov/ooh/.

32. Bryan Grossman, "Innovative Prison Programs Help Inmates Prep for Successful Careers," *Colorado Springs Independent*, June 12, 2019, https://m.csindy.com//colorado-springs/innovative-prison-programs-help-inmates-prep-for-successful-careers/Content?oid=19794049.

33. Greg Blustein, "Education at Heart of Georgia's Next Wave of Change in Criminal Justice," *Atlanta Journal-Constitution*, April 19, 2015, https://www.ajc.com/news/state--regional-govt--politics/education-heart-georgia-next-wave-change-criminal-justice/0sEjraPmg357K1YqntiyFI/.

34. "Career, Technical, and Higher Education," Georgia Department of Corrections, accessed May 20, 2020, http://www.gdc.ga.gov/Divisions/InmateServices/Vocational.

35. Georgia State University Prison Education Project, *Bringing Higher Education into Prisons*, accessed May 20, 2020, https://perimeter.gsu.edu/gsupep/.

36. "Gov. Bill Lee Announces Strategies to Improve Criminal Justice System," Tennessee Office of the Governor, February 28, 2019, https://www.tn.gov/governor/news/2019/2/28/gov--bill-lee-announces-strategies-to-improve-criminal-justice-system.html.

37. "Turney Center Industrial Complex," Tennessee Higher Education Initiative, accessed May 20, 2020, thei.org/tcix.

38. "Career Technical Education," California Division of Rehabilitative Programs, accessed May 23, 2020, https://www.cdcr.ca.gov/rehabilitation/cte/.

39. "Post-Secondary Education," California Division of Rehabilitative Programs, accessed May 20, 2020, https://www.cdcr.ca.gov/rehabilitation/pse/.

40. Debbie Mukamal and Rebecca Silbert, *Don't Stop Now*, Corrections to College California, March 2018, 5–7, https://correctionstocollegeca.org/assets/general/dont-stop-now-report.pdf.

41. Trevor Craft et al., *A Second Chance: College-in-Prison Programs in New York State* (Albany, NY: Rockefeller Institute of Government, June 4, 2019), 7, https://rockinst.org/wp-content/uploads/2019/06/5-30-19_CLPS-Report-College-in-Prison.pdf.

42. "College-in-Prison Reentry Programs," Criminal Justice Investment Initiative, August 7, 2017, http://cjii.org/college-prison-reentry-programs/.

Chapter Eleven

Work to Be Done

You may already have been a supporter, even a champion of the cause for more and better education in our nation's prisons. If not, we hope that we have convinced you with our multifaceted argument from the standpoints of psychology, sociology, ethical concerns, and financial practicality of the wisdom and just plain common sense of providing more and better educational opportunities to the people who comprise our enormous prison population. Perhaps at least we have given you powerful considerations in favor of prison education that you feel are worth pondering. But it is one thing to provide arguments for a position and quite another to deal with implementation.

So, it is fair to ask, what practical steps need to be taken to make improved prison education a reality? In this final chapter of the book, we address that question.

RESEARCH

One essential task to be done is research. Lots of it. Though we have cited a good number of studies in making our argument, a great deal of additional research needs to be conducted to understand how best to make substantial improvements in academic and technical education programs for prisoners. The research needs are many. For instance, it is important to understand how to select those individuals who will be most responsive to different types of programs, such as academic versus technical education. Key factors no doubt include a prisoner's interests, aptitudes, and enthusiasm for a course of study. But at this point, we know too little about what the factors are or how to measure them.

Research also is essential on the effectiveness of different educational methodologies in the prison environment. Investigations should compare the relative effectiveness of face-to-face teaching to the modified online learning recently implemented in a number of prisons. We should not assume that because online learning may be less expensive, possibly easier to implement, and, as a result, might be made available to more prisoners, therefore it is better. We need to think about what "better" or "more effective" means in the context of educating people who are incarcerated.

Our standpoint should be clear by now: we have argued for the importance of preparing student-prisoners to increase their likelihood of securing living-wage employment after release. Though this is not the only criterion, we believe that it is the main one by which to measure the effectiveness of prison education. The adjective "living-wage" here is crucial. We should not be satisfied to prepare prisoners for jobs after release; we should demand that, insofar as possible, these be good jobs that pay a wage or a salary that makes their post-release lives financially sustainable, a job in which they can see a future. Preparing prisoners for such employment is how prison education can have the most powerful influence on individuals' lives outside prison and the strongest effect of reducing recidivism.

In regard to academic education, several organizations have taken leadership roles in identifying factors that should be taken into account to assure quality in prison postsecondary education. One leader, the nonprofit Lumina Foundation, emphasizes the importance of assuring that postsecondary prison education programs do not just amount to offering prisoners a few classes for "enrichment." Rather, higher education programs should provide a clear pathway for the student to earn a high-quality credential at the conclusion of the program, one that carries with it substantial employment opportunities.[1] The Lumina Foundation recently provided financial support to two other leaders in prison postsecondary education—the Prison University Project, which we wrote about in chapter 10, and the Alliance for Higher Education in Prison—for preparing a report, *Equity and Excellence*, on quality standards that should define prison postsecondary education. The report identifies seven areas, such as program design, curriculum, and pedagogy, and lists quality components applicable to each area. These quality components are intended to support the objectives of achieving equity, excellence, and access in postsecondary prison education.[2]

The attention postsecondary prison education has received recently from the Lumina Foundation and others likely has been motivated partly by the lack of clarity attending issues such as what should be the objectives and design of such education. Career and technical education programs in prisons may not suffer from as many questions because the objectives of particular programs and what counts as program quality generally are more clear-cut.

However, much research also is needed for CTE programs. The post-release outcome of different programs is one obvious area for investigation.

We have many questions. What factors and criteria determine the CTE programs offered within a prison system? How much do the ease of presenting the course or the fact that the prison has long had such a course play in its presence? Which programs are best suited for students to obtain employment after release? To what degree does the applicability of the course to real-world job needs determine whether to provide it? The only way to answer such questions is through well-designed research. Even just in the area of prison CTE education, unanswered questions are sufficient to power dozens of potentially valuable research projects whose findings could help inform the decisions of authorities who decide which prison education programs to implement.

LEGISLATION

Too often, correctional system heads must make decisions about prison education with little assistance from government leaders. Without buy-ins from governors and legislatures on the value of prison education, thin budgets often leave little room for educational programs that would make a positive difference not only to prisoners but also to a state's bottom line. To expand and improve prison education programs will require increases in prisons' budgets. This can be a hard sell. Legislators and governors answer to constituents, and constituents often believe that prison is for punishment, not education. Governor Andrew Cuomo proposed spending state money on providing postsecondary education in ten New York state prisons in 2014, arguing that the programs would more than pay for themselves, but he soon was forced politically to abandon the idea, at least temporarily. Fortunately, five years later, Cuomo was able again to announce an initiative for prison education by using funds generated by criminal asset proceeds largely from settlements from banks.[3]

Cuomo's prior attempt to finance prison postsecondary education illustrates the difficulties that government leaders often face when presenting initiatives that may be spun by those who are opposed as a proposal that favors offenders at the expense of citizens. Political expediency won the 2014 battle, as it surely does in many other statehouses. However, Cuomo's continuing push for prison education and the inventive way by which he skirted some opposing arguments illustrates how government leaders who understand the value of prison education programs can take an effective stand to support them.

Other recent examples of state political leaders recognizing and acting on proposals favoring prison education include California's legislature passing law SB 1391, which allowed the state's community colleges to offer in-person classes in prisons. A key aspect of the 2014 bill was the provision that colleges could be fully reimbursed by the state for the prison classes the same as if they had been offered to students on the main campus. This feature made offering classes in prisons a financially sound proposition for colleges.[4] As a result, as we reported in chapter 10, a number of California community colleges now offer classes in thirty-four state prisons. Another law, SB 622, passed by the Virginia legislature and signed by the governor in April 2020, specifies that the director of the Department of Corrections may allow prisoners who are deemed trustworthy temporary release from confinement to work for pay or for educational purposes, with the proviso that they travel directly to the workplace or educational institution and remain there during the allotted time.[5] Passage of these measures demonstrates that state leaders can—and sometimes do—recognize the value of providing incarcerated people with educational opportunities and act on that recognition.

What may have made the 2014 California law, Virginia's 2020 law, and Cuomo's 2019 proposal more amenable to constituents was society's gradual move away from the tough-on-crime mentality to a less judgmental view of prisoners. It is also possible that more people are aware today of the basic costs versus benefits reasoning we have been emphasizing. It is clear that though positive change often may come from both the bottom and the top, those at the bottom of the system, in this case the prisoners, have very little power to enact change. It must come from the top, which is why we need many more leaders to recognize the myriad reasons to support more and better prison education and commit themselves to achieve that objective. All of the arguments in this book can provide tools leaders may use to support such commitments. Perhaps the most politically useful argument, based on cost considerations, is return on investment. Strongly pressing that argument forward may defuse a considerable amount of opposition by demonstrating that those who oppose prison education might be characterized as misguided spendthrifts who would waste the people's tax dollars.

EDUCATIONAL OUTREACH

It probably goes without saying that it is important to disseminate information about the value of prison education to as many people as possible. We began this book with the observation that it is easy for people to disregard our prisons and their inhabitants. Correctional institutions often are built in low-populated areas, walled off, and off limits to most people outside. As a result, those inside are easy to disregard. The stigma that accompanies law-breaking and imprisonment prevents many people from making much, if any, effort to think about those imprisoned. But the prisoners are there, hundreds of thousands of them.

The more we can do to remind people outside about the many incarcerated individuals who live out each day in terrible conditions, perhaps especially of a psychological nature, the more our prisoners may gain some consideration. The more who become aware of the difficulties that former prisoners experience after their release, and especially how the obstacles they face create serious reintegration problems that promote recidivism, the more compassion our prisoners may receive. And the more who become aware of how prison academic and technical education can help to humanize incarceration, prepare prisoners for living-wage jobs after their release, power reintegration, and reduce recidivism, the more those insights are likely to power positive advances in prison education.

Education, evidently, is the key not only in prison, for prisoners; it is also the key outside of prison, for the rest of us. Educating the public about the many benefits of providing good academic and technical education opportunities to incarcerated men and women may be the most basic way to make substantially expanded and improved prison education a reality. How best to provide that those outside prison is a tremendous challenge.

One of the main impediments to educating the public may be the tough-on-crime mentality, which still is widespread. Simplistic characterizations of prisoners as dreadful, undeserving people is another encumbrance; it closes minds to rational arguments and creates a lack of empathy. It may be too much to think we can break through such prejudices with books, articles, videos, classes, or information conveyed by some other medium. But providing such materials at least may *weaken* biases and simplistic ideas. Accordingly, we hope that our readers who accept the reasons we have presented for prison education will spread those ideas to others in whatever way they can.

PRISON EDUCATION IS ONLY PART OF THE SOLUTION

In this book we have mentioned initiatives other than education that have had some success in reducing the prison population and in combating recidivism over the past two decades. These include changes in sentencing policies, the provision of drug courts, and evidence-based programs other than education to help rehabilitate prisoners. In regard to rehabilitation programs, one Washington State study we described in chapter 9 found that several noneducation programs reduced recidivism, including drug treatment and cognitive-behavioral therapy in the community or in prison and treatment-oriented intensive supervision programs. All of these were estimated to more than pay for themselves due to the money saved from reduced recidivism.[6]

We have not spoken more about such developments for the simple reason that our purpose has been to focus on the topic of academic and technical prison education and do our best to provide strong arguments to support it. However, we know that education is only one type of program needed in our correctional system. We also heartily applaud changes in sentencing laws and the increase in judges' ability to use discretion in sentencing, as we believe these are moves toward fairer sentencing.

In closing, we wish to emphasize that we consider expansion of prison education to be only one facet of the larger goal of reforming our justice system. The overall goal should be to make the system *more* just while making our prisons more humane and focused on providing evidence-based rehabilitation methods. Providing much-expanded educational opportunities to our incarcerated population is one method that should be in the forefront.

NOTES

1. Haley Glover, *Equity and Excellence—Quality Matters in Prison Higher Education* (Indianapolis: Lumina Foundation, June 4, 2019), https://www.luminafoundation.org/news-and-views/equity-and-excellence-quality-matters-in-prison-higher-education/.

2. Tanya Erzen, Mary R. Gould, and Jody Lewen, *Equity and Excellence in Practice: A Guide for Higher Education in Prison* (San Quentin, CA: Prison University Project; and Denver, CO: Alliance for Higher Education in Prison, November, 2019), Executive Summary, https://assets.website-files.com/5e3dd3cf0b4b54470c8b1be1/5e3dd3cf0b4b5492e78b1d24_Equity%2BExcellence-English-web.pdf.

3. Ethan Geringer-Sameth, "With Push from Cuomo and Funding from Vance, New York College-in-Prisons Program Is Flourishing," *Gotham Gazette*, December 3, 2019, https://www.gothamgazette.com/state/8959-5-years-after-abandoned-cuomo-plan-college-in-prisons-program-is-flourishing-behind-bars-vance.

4. Debbie Mukamal, Rebecca Silbert, and Rebecca M. Taylor, *Degrees of Freedom: Expanding College Opportunities for Currently and Formerly Incarcerated Californians* (Berkeley, CA: Opportunity Institute Renewing Communities Initiative, February 2015), 11, https://www.law.berkeley.edu/files/DegreesofFreedom2015_FullReport.pdf.

5. LIS Virginia Law, Bill Text: VA SB622, 2020 Regular Session, Chaptered, sec. 53.1-60, https://legiscan.com/VA/text/SB622/2020.

6. Steve Aos, Marna Miller, and Elizabeth Drake, *Evidence-Based Public Policy Options to Reduce Future Prison Construction, Criminal Justice Costs, and Crime Rates*, document no. 06-10-1201 (Olympia: Washington State Institute for Public Policy, October 2006), https://www.wsipp.wa.gov/ReportFile/952/Wsipp_Evidence-Based-Public-Policy-Options-to-Reduce-Future-Prison-Construction-Criminal-Justice-Costs-and-Crime-Rates_Full-Report.pdf.

Bibliography

American Bar Association, Criminal Justice Division. *Collateral Consequences of Criminal Convictions Judicial Bench Book*, NCJRS no. 251583. Chicago: American Bar Association, March 2018. https://www.ncjrs.gov/pdffiles1/nij/grants/251583.pdf.

American Civil Liberties Union. *91 Percent of Americans Support Criminal Justice Reform, ACLU Polling Finds.* November 16, 2017. https://www.aclu.org/news/91-percent-americans-support-criminal-justice-reform-aclu-polling-finds.

———. *Smart Justice Campaign Polling on Americans' Attitudes on Criminal Justice.* Accessed May 23, 2020. https://www.aclu.org/report/smart-justice-campaign-polling-americans-attitudes-criminal-justice.

Aos, Steve, Marna Miller, and Elizabeth Drake. *Evidence-Based Adult Corrections Programs: What Works and What Does Not.* Document no. 06-01-1201. Olympia: Washington State Institute for Public Policy, January 2006. http://www.wsipp.wa.gov/ReportFile/924.

———. *Evidence-Based Public Policy Options to Reduce Future Prison Construction, Criminal Justice Costs, and Crime Rates.* Document no. 06-10-1201. Olympia: Washington State Institute for Public Policy, October 2006. https://www.wsipp.wa.gov/ReportFile/952/Wsipp_Evidence-Based-Public-Policy-Options-to-Reduce-Future-Prison-Construction-Criminal-Justice-Costs-and-Crime-Rates_Full-Report.pdf.

Bandura, Albert. "Human Agency in Social Cognitive Theory." *American Psychologist* 44, no. 9 (1989): 1175–84. https://doi.org/10.1037/0003-066X.44.9.1175.

Bannon, Alicia, Mitali Nagrecha, and Rebekah Diller. *Criminal Justice Debt: A Barrier to Reentry.* New York: Brennan Center for Justice at New York University School of Law, 2010.https://www.criminallegalnews.org/media/publications/brennan_center_for_justice_re entry_report_2010.pdf.

Bard Prison Initiative. *The College: Comprehensive Academic Engagement.* Accessed May 30, 2020. https://bpi.bard.edu/the-work/the-college/.

———. *National Projects: Creating Educational Opportunities in Prison Nationwide.* Accessed May 30, 2020. https://bpi.bard.edu/our-work/national-projects/.

———. *Who We Are.* Accessed May 30, 2020. https://bpi.bard.edu/who-we-are/.

Beckett, Katherine, and Alexes Harris. "On Cash and Conviction: Monetary Sanctions as Misguided Policy." *Criminology and Public Policy* 10, no. 3 (2011): 509–38. https://doi.org/10.1111/j.1745-9133.2011.00726.x.

Bench, Lawrence L., and Terry D. Allen. "Investigating the Stigma of Prison Classification: An Experimental Design." *Prison Journal* 83, no. 4 (2003): 367–82. https://doi.org/10.1177/0032885503260143.

Berg, Mark T., and Beth M. Huebner. "Reentry and the Ties that Bind: An Examination of Social Ties, Employment, and Recidivism." *Justice Quarterly* 28, no. 1 (2011): 382–410. https://doi.org/10.1080/07418825.2010.498383.

Blumstein, Alfred, and Kiminori Nakamura. *Potential of Redemption in Criminal Background Checks*. Final Report to the U.S. Department of Justice, Report no. 232358, September 2010. https://www.ncjrs.gov/pdffiles1/nij/grants/232358.pdf.

Blustein, Greg. "Education at Heart of Georgia's Next Wave of Change in Criminal Justice." *Atlanta Journal-Constitution*, April 19, 2015. https://www.ajc.com/news/state--regional-govt--politics/education-heart-georgia-next-wave-change-criminal-justice/0sEjraPmg357K1YqntiyFl/.

Bonta, James, and D. A. Andrews. *Risk-Need-Responsivity Model for Offender Assessment and Rehabilitation 2007–06*. Report for Public Safety Canada. Ottawa, 2007. http://www.courtinnovation.org/sites/default/files/documents/RNRModelForOffenderAssessmentAndRehabilitation.pdf.

Bowlby, John. *Attachment and Loss*, vol. 1. New York: Basic Books, 1998.

———. *A Secure Base*. New York: Basic Books, 1988.

Bozick, Robert, Jennifer Steele, Lois Davis, and Susan Turner. "Does Providing Inmates with Education Improve Postrelease Outcomes? A Meta-Analysis of Correctional Education Programs in the United States." *Journal of Experimental Criminology* 14 (2018): 389–428. https://doi.org/10.1007/s11292-018-9334-6.

Brody, Leslie. "Three Prison Inmates Beat Harvard in a Debate. Here's What Happened Next." *Wall Street Journal*, October 19, 2019. https://www.wsj.com/articles/three-prison-inmates-beat-harvard-in-a-debate-heres-what-happened-next-11571490001.

Brooks, Lisa E., Amy L. Solomon, Rhiana Kohl, Jenny Osborne, Jay Reid, Susan M. McDonald, and Hollie Matthews Hoover. *Reincarcerated: The Experiences of Men Returning to Massachusetts Prisons*. Washington, DC: Urban Institute, 2008. https://www.prisonlegalnews.org/media/publications/uijpc_report_reincarcerated_men_returning_to_ma_prisons_apr_2008.pdf.

Brown, Russell R., III. *Expungement and Collateral Sanctions*. Cleveland, OH: National Center for State Courts, 2006. https://ncsc.contentdm.oclc.org/digital/collection/criminal/id/75/.

Bucklen, Kristofer B., and Gary Zajac. "Success and Failure Deprivation and Thinking Errors as Determinants of Parole but Some of Them Don't Come Back (to Prison!)." *Prison Journal* 89 (2009): 239–64. https://doi.org/10.1177%2F0032885509339504.

Bush, George W. State of the Union Address, January 20, 2004. *Washington Post*. Accessed May 25, 2020. https://www.washingtonpost.com/wp-srv/politics/transcripts/bushtext_012004.html.

Byrd, Roger C. "Secondary Education and Offender Recidivism in Middle Georgia: An Analysis of Perspectives of Community Supervision Officers." PhD diss., Valdosta State University, 2018.

California Division of Rehabilitative Programs. "Career Technical Education." Accessed May 23, 2020. https://www.cdcr.ca.gov/rehabilitation/cte/.

———. "Post-Secondary Education." Accessed May 20, 2020. https://www.cdcr.ca.gov/rehabilitation/pse/.

Campaign for Youth Justice. *Jailing Juveniles: The Dangers of Incarcerating Youth in Adult Jails in America* (November 2007). http://www.campaignforyouthjustice.org/Downloads/NationalReportsArticles/CFYJ-Jailing_Juveniles_Report_2007-11-15.pdf.

CASA (The National Center on Addiction and Substance Abuse at Columbia University). *Behind Bars II: Substance Abuse and America's Prison Population*. New York: The National Center on Addiction and Substance Abuse at Columbia University, 2010. https://files.eric.ed.gov/fulltext/ED509000.pdf.

Chen, M. Keith, and Jesse M. Shapiro. "Does Prison Harden Inmates? A Discontinuity-Based Approach." *American Law and Economic Review* 9, no. 1 (Spring 2007): 1–29. https://doi.org/10.1093/aler/ahm006.

———. "Do Harsher Prison Conditions Reduce Recidivism? A Discontinuity-Based Approach." *American Law and Economic Review* 9, no. 1 (2007): 1–29. https://doi.org/10.1093/aler/ahm006.

Chin, Gabriel J. "Collateral Consequences of Criminal Conviction." *Criminology, Criminal Justice, Law & Society* 18, no. 3 (2017): 1–17.

Chlup, Dominique T. "The Pendulum Swings: 65 Years of Corrections Education." *Focus on Basics* 7, no. D (September 2005, updated July 27, 2007). http://www.ncsall.net/index.html@id=826.html.

Chung, Adrienne, and Rajiv N. Rimal. "Social Norms: A Review." *Review of Communication Research*, 4 (2016): 1–29. https://doi.org/10.12840/issn.2255-4165.2016.04.01.008.

Clear, Todd R. *Imprisoning Communities: How Mass Incarceration Makes Disadvantaged Neighborhoods Worse.* New York: Oxford University Press, 2007.

Clear, Todd R., Dina R. Rose, Elin Waring, and Kristen Scull. "Coercive Mobility and Crime: A Preliminary Examination of Concentrated Incarceration and Social Disorganization." *Justice Quarterly* 20, no. 1 (2003): 33–64. https://doi.org/10.1080/07418820300095451.

Collins, Brett. "Projections of Federal Tax Return Filings: Calendar Years 2011–2018." *Statistics of Income Bulletin* 3, no. 3 (Winter 2012): 181–90. https://www.irs.gov/pub/irs-soi/12winbul.pdf.

Committee on Health Care of Underserved Women, American College of Obstetricians and Gynecologists. *Reproductive Health Care for Incarcerated Women and Adolescent Females.* Committee Opinion no. 535, 2012, reaffirmed 2019. https://www.acog.org/clinical/clinical-guidance/committee-opinion/articles/2012/08/reproductive-health-care-for-incarcerated-women-and-adolescent-females.

Congressional Research Service. *The First Step Act of 2018: An Overview.* March 4, 2019. https://fas.org/sgp/crs/misc/R45558.pdf.

Coppedge, Ricky H., and Robert Strong. "Vocational Programs in the Federal Bureau of Prisons: Examining the Potential of Agricultural Education Programs for Prisoners." *Journal of Agricultural Education* 54, no. 3 (2013): 116–25. https://www.jae-online.org/attachments/article/1762/2012-0691%20coppedge.pdf.

Couloute, Lucius. *Nowhere to Go: Homelessness among Formerly Incarcerated People.* Northampton, MA: Prison Policy Initiative, August 2018. https://www.prisonpolicy.org/reports/housing.html.

Craft, Trevor, Nicholas Gonzalez, Kevin Kellehe, MIKI Rose, and Ofu Takor. *A Second Chance: College-in-Prison Programs in New York State.* Albany, NY: Rockefeller Institute of Government, June 4, 2019. https://rockinst.org/wp-content/uploads/2019/06/5-30-19_CLPS-Report-College-in-Prison.pdf.

Cressey, Donald R. *Other People's Money: A Study in the Social Psychology of Embezzlement.* Glencoe, IL: Free Press, 1953.

Criminal Justice Investment Initiative. "College-in-Prison Reentry Programs." August 7, 2017. http://cjii.org/college-prison-reentry-programs/.

Criminal Justice Policy Program. *Confronting Criminal Justice Debt: A Guide for Policy Reform.* Cambridge, MA: Harvard Law School, 2016.

Davis, Lois M., Robert Bozick, Jennifer L. Steele, Jessica Saunders, and Jeremy N. V. Miles. *Evaluating the Effectiveness of Correctional Education: A Meta-Analysis of Programs That Provide Education to Incarcerated Adults.* Santa Monica, CA: RAND Corporation, 2013. https://www.rand.org/pubs/research_reports/RR266.html.

Deci, Edward L., and Arlen C. Moller. "The Concept of Competence: A Starting Place for Understanding Intrinsic Motivation and Self-Determined Extrinsic Motivation." In *Handbook of Competence and Motivation*, edited by Andrew J. Elliot and Carol S. Dweck, 579–97. New York: Guilford, 2005.

Deci, Edward L., and Richard M. Ryan. "Self-Determination Theory." In *International Encyclopedia of the Social & Behavioral Sciences*, vol. 21, 2nd ed., edited by James D. Wright, 486–91. Amsterdam: Elsevier, 2015.

———. "The Support of Autonomy and the Control of Behavior." *Journal of Personality and Social Psychology* 53, no. 6 (1987): 1024–37. https://doi.org/10.1037/0022-3514.53.6.1024.

Durnescu, Ioan. "Pains of Probation: Effective Practice and Human Rights." *International Journal of Offender Therapy and Comparative Criminology* 55, no. 4 (2011): 530–45. https://doi.org/10.1177/0306624X10369489.

Duwe, Grant, and Valerie Clark. "The Rehabilitative Ideal Versus the Criminogenic Reality: The Consequences of Warehousing Prisoners." *Corrections* 2, no. 1 (2017): 41–69. https://doi.org/10.1080/23774657.2016.1240596.

Erzen, Tanya, Mary R. Gould, and Jody Lewen. *Equity and Excellence in Practice: A Guide for Higher Education in Prison.* San Quentin, CA: Prison University Project; and Denver, CO: Alliance for Higher Education in Prison, November 2019. https://assets.website-files.com/5e3dd3cf0b4b54470c8b1be1/5e3dd3cf0b4b5492e78b1d24_Equity%2BExcellence-English-web.pdf.

Ewert, Stephanie, and Tara Wildhagen. "Educational Characteristics of Prisoners: Data from the ACS." Working paper no. SEHSD-WP2011-08 (Washington, DC: U.S. Census Bureau, April 2011). https://www.census.gov/library/working-papers/2011/demo/SEHSD-WP2011-08.html.

Federal Bureau of Investigation Uniform Crime Reporting Program. *2016 Crime in the United States*, table 1. Accessed January 28, 2020. https://ucr.fbi.gov/crime-in-the-u.s/2016/crime-in-the-u.s.-2016/topic-pages/tables/table-1.

———. UCR Tool, years 1997–2014. Accessed January 27, 2020. https://www.ucrdatatool.gov/.

Federal Bureau of Prisons. *BOP Implementing Modified Operations.* Accessed May 28, 2020. https://www.bop.gov/coronavirus/covid19_status.jsp.

———. Notice. "Annual Determination of Average Cost of Incarceration." *Federal Register* 83, no. 83 (April 30, 2018). https://www.govinfo.gov/content/pkg/FR-2018-04-30/pdf/2018-09062.pdf.

———. *Population Statistics.* Accessed May 7, 2020. https://www.bop.gov/about/statistics/population_statistics.jsp.

———. "Sleep Soundly. We'll Be up All Night." Accessed February 21, 2020. https://www.bop.gov/about/facilities/federal_prisons.jsp.

Fedock, Gina. "Number of Women in Jails and Prisons Soars." *University of Chicago School of Social Service Administration Magazine* 25, no. 1 (Spring 2018). https://www.ssa.uchicago.edu/ssa_magazine/number-women-jails-and-prisons-soars.

Field, Anne. "Edovo, Maker of Tablet-Based Education for Inmates, Aims to Reduce Recidivism and Continues to Grow." *Forbes*, March 12, 2016. https://www.forbes.com/sites/annefield/2016/03/12/edovo-maker-of-tablet-based-education-for-inmates-aims-to-reduce-recidivism-and-continues-to-grow/#3c662f7857b6.

Finkel, Mack, and Wanda Bertram. *More States Are Signing Harmful "Free Prison Tablet" Contracts.* Northampton, MA: Prison Policy Initiative, last modified December 23, 2019. https://www.prisonpolicy.org/blog/2019/03/07/free-tablets/.

Gaes, Gerald G., and Scott D. Camp. "Unintended Consequences: Experimental Evidence for the Criminogenic Effect of Prison Security Level Placement on Post-Release Recidivism." *Journal of Experimental Criminology* 5, no. 2 (2009): 139–62. https://doi.org/10.1007/s11292-009-9070-z.

Gagne, Marylene, and Edward L. Deci. "Self-Determination Theory and Work Motivation." *Journal of Organizational Behavior* 26 (2005): 331–62.

Gehring, Thom. "Characteristics of Correctional Instruction, 1789–1875." *Journal of Correctional Education* 46, no. 2 (1995): 52–59. https://www.jstor.org/stable/23292023?seq=1.

Gelb, Adam, Karla Dhungana, Benjamin Adams, Ellen McCann, and Kathryn Zafft. *Max Out: The Rise in Prison Inmates Released without Supervision.* Philadelphia: Pew Charitable Trusts, 2014. https://www.pewtrusts.org/-/media/assets/2014/06/04/maxout_report.pdf.

Georgia State University Prison Education Project. *Bringing Higher Education into Prisons.* Accessed May 20, 2020. https://perimeter.gsu.edu/gsupep/.

Geringer-Sameth, Ethan. "With Push from Cuomo and Funding from Vance, New York College-in-Prisons Program Is Flourishing." *Gotham Gazette*, December 3, 2019. https://www.gothamgazette.com/state/8959-5-years-after-abandoned-cuomo-plan-college-in-prisons-program-is-flourishing-behind-bars-vance.

Giegerich, Steve. "Exercise in Student Activism Opens Doors to Academic Achievement." *Focus*, Fall 2016. https://focus.luminafoundation.org/exercise-in-student-activism-opens-doors-to-academic-achievement/.

————. "Unlocking Lives: Postsecondary Programs Go behind Prison Walls to Forge New Futures." *Focus*, Fall 2016. https://focus.luminafoundation.org/wp-content/uploads/2016/04/Focus-Fall-2016-web.pdf.

Glover, Haley. *Equity and Excellence—Quality Matters in Prison Higher Education.* Indianapolis: Lumina Foundation, June 4, 2019. https://www.luminafoundation.org/news-and-views/equity-and-excellence-quality-matters-in-prison-higher-education/.

Graif, Corina, Andrew S. Gladfelter, and Stephen A. Matthews. "Urban Poverty and Neighborhood Effects on Crime: Incorporating Spatial and Network Perspectives." *Sociology Compass* 8, no. 9 (2014): 1140–55. https://doi.org/10.1111/soc4.12199.

Gramlich, John. "The Gap between the Number of Blacks and Whites in Prison Is Shrinking." *Fact Tank*. Philadelphia: Pew Research Center, April 30, 2019. https://www.pewresearch.org/fact-tank/2018/01/12/shrinking-gap-between-number-of-blacks-and-whites-in-prison/.

Grossman, Bryan. "Innovative Prison Programs Help Inmates Prep for Successful Careers." *Colorado Springs Independent*, June 12, 2019. https://www.csindy.com/coloradosprings/innovative-prison-programs-help-inmates-prep-for-successful-careers/Content?oid=1979404 9.

Hager, Eli. *At Least 61,000 Nationwide Are in Prison for Minor Parole Violations.* New York: Marshal Project, April 23, 2017. https://www.themarshallproject.org/2017/04/23/at-least-61-000-nationwide-are-in-prison-for-minor-parole-violations.

Haney, Craig. "The Psychological Impact of Incarceration: Implications for Post-Prison Adjustment." Paper presented at the From Prison to Home Conference, Bethesda, Maryland, January 30–31, 2002. http://webarchive.urban.org/UploadedPDF/410624_PyschologicalImpact.pdf.

Hanser, Robert S. *Introduction to Corrections*. Thousand Oaks, CA: Sage, 2017.

Haslam, S. Alexander, Stephen D. Reicher, and Michael J. Platow. *The New Psychology of Leadership: Identity, Influence and Power*. New York: Psychology Press, 2013.

Henrichson, Christian, and Ruth Delaney. *The Price of Prisons: What Incarceration Costs Taxpayers*. New York: Vera Institute of Justice, 2012. https://www.vera.org/publications/price-of-prisons-what-incarceration-costs-taxpayers.

Horowitz, Jake, Connie Utada, and Monica Fuhrmann. *Probation and Parole Systems Marked by High Stakes, Missed Opportunities*. Philadelphia: Pew Charitable Trusts, 2018. https://www.pewtrusts.org/research-and-analysis/issue-briefs/2018/09/probation-and-parole-systems-marked-by-high-stakes-missed-opportunities.

Inside-Out Prison Exchange Program. *Higher Education Partners*. Accessed May 20, 2020. https://www.insideoutcenter.org/higher-education-partners.html.

————. *History*. Accessed May 20, 2020. https://www.insideoutcenter.org/history-inside-out.html.

Institute for Justice and Opportunity at John Jay College. "Prison-to-College Pipeline." Accessed May 20, 2020. https://justiceandopportunity.org/educational-pathways/prison-to-college-pipeline/.

Jackson, Angie, and Kristi Tanner. "Infection Rate at Michigan Prison Exceeds New York, Chicago Jail Hot Spots." *Detroit Free Press*, updated April 16, 2020. https://www.freep.com/story/news/local/michigan/2020/04/16/infection-rate-michigan-prison-exceeds-new-york-chicago-jail-hotspots/2987935001/.

John, Arit. "A Timeline of the Rise and Fall of 'Tough on Crime' Drug Sentencing." *The Atlantic*, April 22, 2014. https://www.theatlantic.com/politics/archive/2014/04/a-timeline-of-the-rise-and-fall-of-tough-on-crime-drug-sentencing/360983/.

Johnson, Rucker C. "Ever-Increasing Levels of Parental Incarceration and the Consequences for Children." In *Do Prisons Make Us Safer? The Benefits and Costs of the Prison Boom*, edited by Steven Raphael and Michael A. Stoll, 177–206. New York: Russell Sage Foundation, 2009.

Jonson, Cheryl Lero. "The Impact of Imprisonment on Reoffending." PhD diss., University of Cincinnati, 2010.

Kang-Brown, Jacob, Eital Schattner-Elmaleh, and Oliver Hines. *People in Prison in 2018*. New York: Vera Institute of Justice, April 2019. https://www.vera.org/downloads/publications/people-in-prison-in-2018-updated.pdf.

Bibliography

Keeley, Brian. *Human Capital: How What You Know Shapes Your Life.* Paris, France: Organization for Economic Cooperation and Development, 2007. https://www.oecd.org/insights/humancapitalhowwhatyouknowshapesyourlife.htm.

Kennedy, Anthony M. "Speech Delivered by Justice Anthony M. Kennedy at the American Bar Association Annual Meeting, August 9, 2003." *Federal Sentencing Reporter* 16, no. 2 (December 2003): 126–28. https://doi.org/10.1525/fsr.2003.16.2.126.

Kessler, Robert C., Wai Tat Chiu, Olga Demler, and Ellen E. Walters. "Prevalence, Severity, and Comorbidity of Twelve-Month DSM-IV Disorders in the National Comorbidity Survey Replication (NCS-R)." *Archives of General Psychiatry* 62, no. 6 (2005): 617–27. https://doi.org/10.1001/archpsyc.62.6.617.

Kreighbaum, Andrew. "Education Department Urged to Evaluate Second-Chance Pell." *Inside Higher Ed*, April 5, 2019. https://www.insidehighered.com/quicktakes/2019/04/05/education-department-urged-evaluate-second-chance-pell.

———. "Taking Stock of Pell Grants behind Bars." *Inside Higher Ed*, July 16, 2019. https://www.insidehighered.com/news/2019/07/16/full-repeal-pell-ban-prisons-top-mind-annual-convening-second-chance-pilot.

Lahey, Jessica. "The Steep Costs of Keeping Juveniles in Adult Prisons." *The Atlantic*, January 8, 2016. https://www.theatlantic.com/education/archive/2016/01/the-cost-of-keeping-juveniles-in-adult-prisons/423201/.

Latessa, Edward J., and Christopher Lowenkamp. "What Works in Reducing Recidivism?" *University of St. Thomas Law Journal* 3, no. 3 (2006): 521–35.

Latessa, Edward J., Paula Smith, John T. Whitehead, Kimberly D. Dodson, and Bradley D. Edwards. *Prisons, Probation and Parole in America: How Punishment Changes Behavior.* Routledge Free Book, 2016. https://www.crcpress.com/rsc/downloads/Prisons,_Probation_and_Parole_in_America.pdf.

Law, Victoria. "Captive Audience: How Companies Make Millions Charging Prisoners to Send an Email." *Wired*, August 3, 2018. https://www.wired.com/story/jpay-securus-prison-email-charging-millions/.

LIS Virginia Law. Bill Text: VA SB622, 2020 Regular Session, Chaptered, sec. 53.1-60. https://legiscan.com/VA/text/SB622/2020.

Lockwood, Susan Klinker, John M. Nally, and Taiping Ho. "Race, Education, Employment, and Recidivism among Offenders in the United States: An Exploration of Complex Issues in the Indianapolis Metropolitan Area." *International Journal of Criminal Justice Sciences* 11, no. 1 (2016): 57–74. http://www.ijcjs.com/pdfs/lockwoodetalijcjs2016vol11issue1.pdf.

Looney, Adam, and Nicholas Turner. *Work and Opportunity Before and After Incarceration.* Washington, DC: Brookings Institution, 2018. https://www.brookings.edu/wp-content/uploads/2018/03/es_20180314_looneyincarceration_final.pdf.

Lynch, Mona. "Legal Change and Sentencing Norms in Federal Court: An Examination of the Impact of the Booker, Gall, and Kimbrough Decisions." Paper presented at the American Society of Criminology Annual Meeting, Washington, DC, November 16–19, 2011.

MacKenzie, Doris. *What Works in Corrections: Reducing the Criminal Activities of Offenders and Delinquents.* New York: Cambridge University Press, 2006.

Mai, Chris, and Ram Subramanian. *The Price of Prisons: Examining State Spending Trends, 2010–2015.* New York: Vera Institute of Justice, 2017. https://www.vera.org/publications/price-of-prisons-2015-state-spending-trends.

Marshall Project. *A State-by-State Look at Coronavirus in Prisons.* Updated May 22, 2020. https://www.themarshallproject.org/2020/05/01/a-state-by-state-look-at-coronavirus-in-prisons.

Martinson, Robert. "What Works—Questions and Answers about Prison Reform." *Public Interest* 35 (Spring 1974): 22–54. https://www.nationalaffairs.com/public_interest/detail/what-works-questions-and-answers-about-prison-reform.

McGarry, Peggy, Alison Shames, Allon Yaroni, Karen Tamis, Ram Subramanian, Lauren-Brooke Eisen, Leon Digard, Ruth Delaney, and Sara Sullivan. *The Potential of Community Corrections to Improve Safety and Reduce Incarceration.* New York: Vera Institute of Justice, July 2013. https://www.vera.org/publications/the-potential-of-community-corrections-to-improve-safety-and-reduce-incarceration-configure.

McKillop, Matt, and Alex Boucher. *Aging Prison Populations Drive up Costs.* Philadelphia: Pew Charitable Trusts, 2018. https://www.pewtrusts.org/en/research-and-analysis/articles/2018/02/20/aging-prison-populations-drive-up-costs.

McLaughlin, Michael, Carrie Pettus-Davis, Derek Brown, Chris Veeh, and Tanya Renn. "The Economic Burden of Incarceration in the U.S." Working Paper #CI072016. St. Louis: Concordance Institute for Advancing Social Justice, George Warren Brown School of Social Work, Washington University, 2016. https://joinnia.com/wp-content/uploads/2017/02/The-Economic-Burden-of-Incarceration-in-the-US-2016.pdf.

McShane, Marilyn D. *Prisons in America.* New York: LFB Scholarly Publishing, 2008.

Messemer, Jonathan E. "The Historical Practice of Correctional Education in the United States: A Review of the Literature." *International Journal of Humanities and Social Science* 1, no. 17 (2011): 91–100. http://www.ijhssnet.com/view.php?u=http://www.ijhssnet.com/journals/Vol_1_No_17_Special_Issue_November_2011/9.pdf.

Morenoff, Jeffrey D., and David J. Harding. "Incarceration, Prisoner Reentry, and Communities." *Annual Review of Sociology* 40 (2014): 411–29. https://doi.org/10.1146/annurev-soc-071811-145511.

Mukamal, Debbie, and Rebecca Silbert. *Don't Stop Now.* Corrections to College California, March 2018. https://correctionstocollegeca.org/assets/general/dont-stop-now-report.pdf.

Mukamal, Debbie, Rebecca Silbert, and Rebecca M. Taylor. *Degrees of Freedom: Expanding College Opportunities for Currently and Formerly Incarcerated Californians.* Berkeley, CA: Opportunity Institute Renewing Communities Initiative, February 2015. https://www.law.berkeley.edu/files/DegreesofFreedom2015_FullReport.pdf.

Murray, Joseph, and David P. Farrington. "The Effects of Parental Imprisonment on Children." In *Crime and Justice: A Review of Research*, vol. 37, edited by Michael Tonry, 133–206. Chicago: University of Chicago Press, 2008.

Nagin, Daniel S. "Deterrence in the Twenty-first Century." *Crime and Justice* 42, no. 1 (2013): 199–263. https://doi.org/10.1086/670398.

Nagin, Daniel S., Francis T. Cullen, and Cheryl L. Jonson. "Imprisonment and Reoffending." *Crime and Justice* 38, no. 1 (2009): 115–200. https://doi.org/10.1086/599202.

Nally, John M., Susan Lockwood, Taiping Ho, and Katie Knutson. "Post-Release Recidivism and Employment among Different Types of Released Offenders: A 5-Year Follow-Up Study in the United States." *International Journal of Criminal Justice Sciences* 9, no. 1 (2014): 16–34. http://sascv.org/ijcjs/pdfs/nallyetalijcjs2014vol9issue1.pdf.

National Commission on Correctional Health Care. *Women's Health Care in Correctional Settings.* Position statement. Reaffirmed with revision May 3, 2020. https://www.ncchc.org/womens-health-care.

National Institute of Justice. *Five Things about Deterrence.* June 5, 2016. https://nij.gov/five-things/pages/deterrence.aspx#addenda.

National Prison Rape Elimination Commission. *National Prison Rape Elimination Report* (June 2009). https://www.ncjrs.gov/pdffiles1/226680.pdf.

Nietzel, Michael T. "Congress Should Pass the REAL Act and Make Prisoners Eligible for Pell Grants Again." *Forbes*, April 15, 2019. https://www.forbes.com/sites/michaeltnietzel/2019/04/15/congress-should-pass-the-real-act-and-make-prisoners-eligible-for-pell-grants-again/#55be52212f0c.

Perkins, Douglas D., Joseph Hughey, and Paul W. Speer. "Community Psychology Perspectives on Social Capital Theory and Community Development Practice." *Journal of the Community Development Society* 33, no. 1 (2002): 33–52. https://doi.org/10.1080/15575330209490141.

Pew Center on the States. *State of Recidivism: The Revolving Door of America's Prisons.* Washington, DC: Pew Charitable Trusts, April 2011. https://www.pewtrusts.org/en/research-and-analysis/reports/0001/01/01/state-of-recidivism.

Pfeiffer, Robert S. *Poverty in the United States: Why It's a Blight on the American Psyche.* Pennsauken, NJ: Bookbaby, 2018.

Prison Policy Initiative. *Responses to the COVID-19 Pandemic*, updated May 27, 2020. https://www.prisonpolicy.org/virus/virusresponse.html.

Prison University Project. "Accreditation." Accessed May 19, 2020. https://prisonuniversity-project.org/about-us/accreditation/.

———. "Education." Accessed May 19, 2020. https://prisonuniversityproject.org/what-we-do/education/.

Rabury, Bernadette, and Daniel Kopf. *Prisons of Poverty: Uncovering the Pre-Incarceration Incomes of the Imprisoned.* Northampton, MA: Prison Policy Initiative, July 9, 2015. https://www.prisonpolicy.org/reports/income.html.

RAND Corporation. *How We're Funded.* Accessed May 19, 2020. https://www.rand.org/about/clients_grantors.html.

Reingle Gonzalez, Jennifer M., and Nadine M. Connell. "Mental Health of Prisoners: Identifying Barriers to Mental Health Treatment and Medication Continuity." *American Journal of Public Health* 104, no. 12 (2014): 2328–33. https://doi.org/10.2105/AJPH.2014.302043.

Rhodes, William, Christina Dyous, Ryan Kling, Dana Hunt, and Jeremy Luallen. *Recidivism of Offenders on Federal Community Supervision.* Cambridge, MA: ABT Associates, 2013. https://www.ncjrs.gov/pdffiles1/bjs/grants/241018.pdf.

Roberts, Dorothy E. "The Social and Moral Cost of Mass Incarceration in African American Communities." Faculty Scholarship Paper 583. Philadelphia: University of Pennsylvania Law School, 2004. https://scholarship.law.upenn.edu/cgi/viewcontent.cgi?article=1582&context=faculty_scholarship.

Rose, Dina R., and Todd R. Clear. "Incarceration, Reentry and Social Capital: Social Networks in the Balance." In *Prisoners Once Removed: The Impact of Incarceration and Reentry on Children, Families, and Communities*, edited by Jeremy Travis and Michelle Waul, 313–42. Washington, DC: Urban Institute Press, 2003.

Ruhland, Ebony. "The Impact of Fees and Fines for Individuals on Probation and Parole." *Robina Institute of Criminal Law and Criminal Justice Blog. University of Minnesota*, Robina Institute of Criminal Law and Justice, May 23, 2016. https://robinainstitute.umn.edu/news-views/impact-fees-and-fines-individuals-probation-and-parole.

Ruhland, Ebony, Edward Rhine, Jason Robey, and Kelly Lyn Mitchell. *The Continuing Leverage of Releasing Authorities: Findings from a National Survey.* Minneapolis: University of Minnesota, Robina Institute of Criminal Law and Criminal Justice, 2016. https://robinainstitute.umn.edu/publications/continuing-leverage-releasing-authorities-findings-national-survey.

Sams, Dylan. "AU Extends Prison Education Programs to 3 States, D.C." *Times-Gazette,* February 23, 2018. https://www.times-gazette.com/special/20180228/au-extends-prison-education-programs-to-3-states-dc.

Sarkadi, Anna, Robert Kristiansson, Frank Oberklaid, and Sven Bremberg. "Fathers' Involvement and Children's Developmental Outcomes: A Systematic Review of Longitudinal Studies." *Acta Paediatrica* 97 (2008): 153–58. https://doi.org/10.1111/j.1651-2227.2007.00572.x.

Sawyer, Wendy. *The Gender Divide: Tracking Women's State Prison Growth.* Northampton, MA: Prison Policy Initiative, January 9, 2018. https://www.prisonpolicy.org/reports/women_overtime.html.

———. "How Much Do Incarcerated People Earn in Each State?" *Prison Policy Initiative Blog.* Northampton, MA: *Prison Policy Initiative*, April 10, 2017. https://www.prisonpolicy.org/blog/2017/04/10/wages.

———. *Youth Confinement: The Whole Pie.* Northampton, MA: Prison Policy Initiative, February 27, 2018. https://www.prisonpolicy.org/reports/youth2018.html.

Sawyer, Wendy, and Peter Wagner. *Mass Incarceration: The Whole Pie 2020.* Northampton, MA: Prison Policy Initiative, March 24, 2020. https://www.prisonpolicy.org/reports/pie2020.html.

———. *Youth Confinement: The Whole Pie 2019.* Northampton, MA: Prison Policy Initiative, December 19, 2019. https://www.prisonpolicy.org/reports/youth2019.html#facilities.

Schrantz, Dennis, Stephen DeBor, and Marc Mauer. *Decarceration Strategies: How 5 States Achieved Substantial Prison Population Reductions.* Washington, DC: Sentencing Project, September 5, 2018. https://www.sentencingproject.org/publications/decarceration-strategies-5-states-achieved-substantial-prison-population-reductions/.

Sentencing Project. *Fact Sheet: Trends in U.S. Corrections.* Washington, DC: Sentencing Project, 2018. https://sentencingproject.org/wp-content/uploads/2016/01/Trends-in-US-Corrections.pdf.

———. *Private Prisons in the United States.* Washington, DC: Sentencing Project, October, 24, 2019. https://www.sentencingproject.org/wp-content/uploads/2017/08/Private-Prisons-in-the-United-States.pdf.

Skorton, David, and Glenn Altschuler. "College behind Bars: How Educating Prisoners Pays Off." *Forbes,* March 25, 2013. https://www.forbes.com/sites/collegeprose/2013/03/25/college-behind-bars-how-educating-prisoners-pays-off/#4359e3727077.

Smith, Ashley A. "Momentum for Prison Education." *Inside Higher Ed,* November 6, 2018. https://www.insidehighered.com/news/2018/11/06/colleges-push-more-resources-support-prison-education-programs.

Smoyer, Amy B., Trace A. Kershaw, and Kim M. Blankenship. "Confining Legitimacy: The Impact of Prison Experiences on Perceptions of Criminal Justice Legitimacy." *Journal of Forensic Social Work* 5, nos. 1–3 (2015): 258–70. https://doi.org/10.1080%2F19369 28X.2015.1092905.

Tennessee Higher Education Initiative. "Turney Center Industrial Complex." Accessed May 20, 2020. thei.org/tcix.

Tennessee Office of the Governor. "Gov. Bill Lee Announces Strategies to Improve Criminal Justice System." February 28, 2019. https://www.tn.gov/governor/news/2019/2/28/gov--bill-lee-announces-strategies-to-improve-criminal-justice-system.html.

Toreld, Eva Marie, Kristin Opaas Haugli, and Anna Lydia Svalastog. "Maintaining Normality When Serving a Prison Sentence in the Digital Society." *Croatian Medical Journal* 59 (2018): 335–39. https://doi.org/10.3325/cmj.2018.59.335.

Travis, Jeremy. *But They All Come Back: Facing the Challenges of Prisoner Reentry.* Washington, DC: Urban Institute Press, 2005.

Travis, Jeremy, Bruce Western, and F. Stevens Redburn, eds. *The Growth of Incarceration in the United States: Exploring Causes and Consequences.* Washington, DC: National Academies Press, 2014. https://johnjay.jjay.cuny.edu/nrc/NAS_report_on_incarceration.pdf.

Troilo, Maddy. *Locking up Youth with Adults: An Update.* Northampton, MA: Prison Policy Initiative, February 27, 2018. https://www.prisonpolicy.org/blog/2018/02/27/youth/.

Tzanakis, Michael. "Social Capital in Bourdieu's, Coleman's and Putnam's Theory: Empirical Evidence and Emergent Measurement Issues." *Educate* 13, no. 2 (2013): 2–23. http://www.educatejournal.org/index.php/educate/issue/view/42.

Ubah, Charles B. A. "Abolition of Pell Grants for Higher Education of Prisoners." *Journal of Offender Rehabilitation* 39, no. 2 (2014): 73–85. https://doi.org/10.1300/J076v39n02_05.

Uggen, Christopher. "Ex-Offenders and the Conformist Alternative: A Job Quality Model of Work and Crime." *Social Problems* 46, no. 1 (1999): 127–51. https://doi.org/10.2307/3097165.

Uggen, Christopher, Ryan Larson, and Sarah Shannon. *6 Million Lost Voters: State-Level Estimates of Felony Disenfranchisement.* Washington, DC: Sentencing Project, October 6, 2016. https://www.sentencingproject.org/publications/6-million-lost-voters-state-level-estimates-felony-disenfranchisement-2016/.

Uggen, Christopher, and Robert Stewart. "Piling on: Collateral Consequences and Community Supervision." *Minnesota Law Review* 99 (2014): 1871–1910.

U.S. Bureau of Labor Statistics. *Occupational Outlook Handbook.* Last modified April 10, 2020. https://www.bls.gov/ooh/.

U.S. Council of Economic Advisers. *Fines, Fees, and Bail: Payments in the Criminal Justice System that Disproportionately Impact the Poor.* Issue Brief. Washington, DC: U.S. Executive Office of the President, Council of Economic Advisers, December 2015. https://obamawhitehouse.archives.gov/sites/default/files/page/files/1215_cea_fine_fee_bail_issue_brief.pdf.

U.S. Department of Education, National Center for Education Statistics. *Literacy behind Bars: Results from the 2003 National Assessment of Adult Literacy Prison Survey,* by Elizabeth Greenberg, Eric Dunleavy, and Mark Kutner. NCES 2007–473. Washington, DC, May 2007. http://nces.ed.gov/pubs2007/2007473.pdf.

U.S. Department of Education, Policy and Program Studies Service. *State and Local Expenditures on Corrections and Education.* July 2016. https://www2.ed.gov/rschstat/eval/other/expenditures-corrections-education/brief.pdf.

U.S. Department of Justice. *Prisoners and Prisoner Re-entry.* Accessed May 25, 2020. https://www.justice.gov/archive/fbci/progmenu_reentry.html.

U.S. Department of Justice, Archives. *Prison Reform: Reducing Recidivism by Strengthening the Federal Bureau of Prisons.* Washington DC: GPO, last modified March 6, 2017. https://www.justice.gov/archives/prison-reform.

U.S. Department of Justice, Bureau of Justice Statistics. *Census of State and Federal Correctional Facilities, 2005*, by James J. Stephan. Special Report NCJ 222182. Washington, DC, October 2008. https://www.bjs.gov/content/pub/pdf/csfcf05.pdf.

———. *Correctional Populations in the United States*, by Danielle Kaeble and Mary Cowhig. Bulletin NCJ 251211. Washington, DC, April 2018. https://www.bjs.gov/content/pub/pdf/cpus16.pdf.

———. *Drugs and Crime Facts.* Washington, DC. Accessed February 23, 2020. https://www.bjs.gov/content/dcf/enforce.cfm.

———. *Drug Use and Dependence, State and Federal Prisoners, 2004*, by Christopher J. Mumola and Jennifer C. Karberg. Special Report NCJ 213530. Washington, DC, October 2006. https://www.bjs.gov/content/pub/pdf/dudsfp04.pdf.

———. *Drug Use, Dependence, and Abuse among State Prisoners and Jail Inmates, 2007–2009*, by Jennifer Bronson, Jessica Stroop, Stephanie Zimmer, and Marcus Berzofsky. Special Report NCJ 250546. Washington, DC, June 2017. https://www.bjs.gov/content/pub/pdf/dudaspji0709.pdf.

———. *Jail Inmates in 2017*, by Zhen Zeng. Bulletin NCJ 251774. Washington, DC, April 2019. https://www.bjs.gov/content/pub/pdf/ji17.pdf.

———. *Mental Health Problems of Prison and Jail Inmates*, by Doris J. James and Lauren E. Glaze. Special Report NCJ 213600. Washington, DC, modified December 14, 2006. https://www.bjs.gov/content/pub/pdf/mhppji.pdf.

———. *Prisoners in 2010*, by Paul Guerino, Paige M. Harrison, and William J. Sabol. Bulletin NCJ 236096. Washington, DC, modified February 9, 2012. https://www.bjs.gov/content/pub/pdf/p10.pdf.

———. *Prisoners in 2016*, by E. Ann Carson. Bulletin NCJ 251149. Washington, DC, August 7, 2018. Accessed February 23, 2020, https://www.bjs.gov/content/pub/pdf/p16.pdf.

———. *Probation and Parole in the United States, 2016*, by Danielle Kaeble. Bulletin NCJ 251148. Washington, DC, April 2018. https://www.bjs.gov/content/pub/pdf/ppus16.pdf.

———. *Recidivism of Prisoners Released in 30 States in 2005: Patterns from 2005 to 2010*, by Matthew R. Durose, Alexia D. Cooper, and Howard N. Snyder. Special Report NCJ244205. Washington, DC, April 2014. https://www.bjs.gov/content/pub/pdf/rprts05p0510.pdf.

———. *Sexual Victimization Reported by Adult Correctional Authorities, 2009–11*, by Allen J. Beck and Ramona R. Rantala. Special Report NCJ243904. Washington, DC, January 2014. https://www.prearesourcecenter.org/sites/default/files/library/sexualvictimizationreported-bycorrectionalauthorities2009-2011.pdf.

———. *Sourcebook of Criminal Justice Statistics 2002*, by Kathleen Maguire, Ann L. Pastore, and Johnna Christian. Washington, DC, 2004. https://www.hsdl.org/?abstract&did=711164.

U.S. Department of Justice, National Institute of Corrections. *Correctional Health Care: Addressing the Needs of Elderly, Chronically Ill, and Terminally Ill Inmates*, by Jaye B. Anno, Camelia Graham, James E. Lawrence, and Ronald Shansky. Accession number 018735. Washington, DC, 2004. https://nicic.gov/correctional-health-care-addressing-needs-elderly-chronically-ill-and-terminally-ill-inmates.

U.S. Internal Revenue Service. "Projections of Federal Tax Return Filings: Calendar Years 2011–2018," by Brett Collins. *Statistics of Income Bulletin.* Washington, DC, Winter 2012. https://www.irs.gov/pub/irs-soi/12rswinbulreturnfilings.pdf.

van den Bergh, Brenda, Alex Gatherer, Andres Fraser, and Lars Moller. "Imprisonment and Women's Health: Concerns about Gender Sensitivity, Human Rights and Public Health." *Bulletin of the World Health Organization* 89 (2011): 689–94. https://doi.org/10.2471/BLT.10.082842.

Vieraitis, Lynne M., Tomislav V. Kovandzic, and Thomas B. Marvell. "The Criminogenic Effects of Imprisonment: Evidence from State Panel Data, 1974–2002." *Criminology & Public Policy* 6, no. 3: 589–622. https://doi.org/10.1111/j.1745-9133.2007.00456.x.

Vuong, Linh, Christopher Hartney, Barry Krisberg, and Susan Marchionna. *The Extravagance of Imprisonment Revisited*. Berkeley: University of California Faculty Publications, 2010. https://www.nccdglobal.org/sites/default/files/publication_pdf/specialreport-extravagance.pdf.

Wagner, Peter, and Bernadette Rabury. *Following the Money of Mass Incarceration*. Northampton, MA: Prison Policy Initiative, January 25, 2017. https://www.prisonpolicy.org/reports/money.html.

Western, Bruce. "The Impact of Incarceration on Wage Mobility and Inequality." *American Sociological Review* 67, no. 4 (August 2002): 526–46. https://www.jstor.org/stable/3088944.

Wexler, Ellen. "Prisoners to Get 'Second Chance Pell.'" *Inside Higher Ed*, June 24, 2016. https://www.insidehighered.com/news/2016/06/24/us-expands-pell-grant-program-12000-prison.

Wildeman, Christopher. "Parent Imprisonment, the Prison Boom, and the Concentration of Childhood Disadvantage." *Demography* 46, no. 2 (May 2009): 265–80. https://doi.org/10.1353/dem.0.0052.

Wiley, Hannah. "Trump Administration Looks to Texas as It Pushes a Criminal Justice Reform Bill." *Texas Tribune*, December 3, 2018. https://www.texastribune.org/2018/12/03/first-step-act-prison-reform-texas-criminal-justice/.

Wilson, David B., Catherine A. Gallagher, and Doris L. MacKenzie. "Meta-Analysis of Corrections-Based Education, Vocation, and Work Programs for Adult Offenders." *Journal of Research in Crime and Delinquency* 37, no. 4 (November 2000): 347–68. https://doi.org/10.1177/0022427800037004001.

Wilson, Meagan, Rayane Alamuddin, and Danielle Cooper. *Unbarring Access: A Landscape Review of Postsecondary Education in Prison and Its Pedagogical Supports*. Ithaka S+R Organization research report, May 30, 2019. https://doi.org/10.18665/sr.311499.

Winton, Richard. "As Inmate Deaths and Infections Rise, Chino, Avenal Prisons Will Test All Employees for Coronavirus." *Los Angeles Times*, May 26, 2020. https://www.latimes.com/california/story/2020-05-26/with-nine-inmates-at-chino-prison-dead-after-getting-covid-19-it-and-avenal-prison-require-all-staff-testing.

Wolff, Nancy, and Jing Shi. "Childhood and Adult Trauma Experiences of Incarcerated Persons and Their Relationship to Adult Behavioral Health Problems and Treatment." *International Journal of Environmental Research and Public Health* 9, no. 5 (May 2012): 1908–26. https://doi.org/10.3390/ijerph9051908.

———. "Contextualization of Physical and Sexual Assault in Male Prisons: Incidents and Their Aftermath." *Journal of Correctional Health Care* 15, no. 1 (January 2009): 58–82. https://doi.org/10.1177/1078345808326622.

World Prison Brief. *Data: Europe*. London: World Prison Brief, 2020. Accessed February 23, 2020. https://www.prisonstudies.org/world-prison-brief-data.

Yohanna, Daniel. "Deinstitutionalization of People with Mental Illness: Causes and Consequences." *Virtual Mentor, American Medical Association Journal of Ethics* 15, no. 1 (October 2013): 886–91. https://doi.org/10.1001/virtualmentor.2013.15.10.mhst1-1310.

Zoukis, Christopher. *College for Convicts: The Case for Higher Education in American Prisons*. Jefferson, NC: McFarland, 2014.

Index

About the Authors

Dr. Roger C. Byrd, EdD, is professor of criminal justice and political science and director of prison programs at Brewton-Parker College. Roger is civically active through his board memberships with Ronald McDonald House Charities of Central Georgia, the Civic Affairs Foundation, and as a senior fellow with the Philemon Fellowship. Prior to his career in education, Roger served twenty-two years in the Georgia House of Representatives. Roger currently resides in Dublin, Georgia, with his wife, April, and their daughter, Olivia.

Dr. Harvey McCloud, PhD, is an editorial and research consultant with longtime interests in the US corrections system, especially the relation of correctional education to post-release success. A member of the Correctional Education Association, Dr. McCloud taught at the University of Kansas and Washburn University and has expertise in the areas of self-determination theory and social capital. He currently resides in Boise, Idaho, with his wife, Teresa.